THE TEACH YOURSELF BOOKS

URDU

Uniform with this volume
and in the same series

Teach Yourself Afrikaans
Teach Yourself Arabic
Teach Yoursel Colloquia` Arabic
Teach Yourself Bengali
Teach Yourself Comparative Linguistics
Teach Yourself Chinese
Teach Yourself Czech
Teach Yourself Danish
Teach Yourself: A Short Dictionary of Languages
Teach Yourself Dutch
Teach Yourself English for Swahili-speaking People
Teach Yourself English Grammar
Teach Yourself Good Eng ish
Teach Yourself Old English
Teach Yourself Esperanto
Teach Yourself Finnish
Teach Yoursel French
Teach Yourself Everyday French
Teach Yourself French Grammar
Teach Yourself: French Revision
Teach Yourself German
Teach Yourself A First German
Teach Yourself German Grammar
Teach Yourself More German
The Teach Yourself German Reader
Teach Yourself Greek
Teach Yourself New Testament Greek
Teach Yourself Modern Greek
Teach Yourself Hausa
Teach Yourself Hebrew
Teach Yourself Icelandic
Teach Yourself Indonesian
Teach Yourself Irish
Teach Yourself Italian
Teach Yourself Japanese
Teach Yourself Latin
Teach Yourself: Latin Revision
Teach Yourself Latvian
Teach Yourself to Learn a Language
Teach Yourself Malay
Teach Yourself Maltese
Teach Yourself Norwegian
Teach Yourself Modern Persian
Teach Yourself Polish
Teach Yourself Portuguese
Teach Yourself Russian
Teach Yourself Russian Through Reading
Teach Yourself Samoan
Teach Yourself Serbo-Croat
Teach Yourself Spanish
Teach Yourself Everyday Spanish
Teach Yourself Swahili
Teach Yourself Swedish
Teach Yourself Turkish
Teach Yourself Welsh
Teach Yourself Yoruba

TEACH YOURSELF

URDU

By the late
T. GRAHAME BAILEY, M.A., B.D., D.Litt.
sometime Nizam's Reader in Urdu in the University of London
at the School of Oriental and African Studies

Edited by
J. R. FIRTH, O.B.E., M.A.
Professor of General Linguistics in the University of London

and the late
A. H. HARLEY, M.A.
Nizam's Reader in Urdu in the University of London

THE ENGLISH UNIVERSITIES PRESS LTD
ST. PAUL'S HOUSE   WARWICK LANE
LONDON EC4

First printed 1950
under the title " Teach Yourself Hindustani ".
Now revised and adjusted as " Teach Yourself
Urdu ", 1956
This impression 1967

This volume is published in the U.S.A. by
David McKay Company Inc., 750 Third Avenue,
New York, N.Y. 10017

Printed in Great Britain for the English Universities Press, Ltd.,
by Richard Clay (The Chaucer Press), Ltd., Bungay, Suffolk

CONTENTS

PREFACE

THIS book is based on material left by the late Dr. Grahame Bailey, the well-known Indianist, who died in 1942. Among his posthumous papers there were at least two versions of what he intended should become a grammar and language course of Urdu.

With the assistance of Mr. A. H. Harley and others, I have collected what seem to have been his last intentions, and, with certain changes and additions mentioned below, present the result as an introduction to one of the principal languages of the world to-day by one of the most distinguished European scholars of Urdu.

The romanic orthography employed is the outcome of my own work on an All-India alphabet,* and was substituted for the transcription which Dr. Grahame Bailey used throughout. We have introduced the Persi-Arabic or Urdu script from Lesson 18 to the end, since students normally expect to begin reading in the language. The transition lessons are adequate and should enable any serious student to read the lessons which follow, and thereafter simple Urdu in the Persi-Arabic script.

I am responsible for the Introduction to the spelling and pronunciation, which should promote ease and speed of learning, make for early fluency, and pave the way for the transition to the Urdu script.

The romanic orthography, both phonetically and linguistically, as every speaker of Urdu will at once recognize, serves as a grammatical spelling which Indians and Pakistanis themselves could use, parallel as it is with the script.

The alphabetical order of the Urdu–English Glossary departs to some extent from the Roman order, as indeed it must, but will soon be understood.

I should like to acknowledge the generous assistance of Mr. Munib-ur-Rahman, Miss E. M. Evans and other colleagues, the skilled work of my secretary, Mrs. Newman, and the technical help and patience of the printers and publishers.

School of Oriental and African Studies.   J. R. FIRTH

* Also applied in A. H. Harley's *Colloquial Hindustani* (Kegan Paul) and in Miss H. M. Lambert's *Marathi Language Course* (Oxford University Press, Bombay).

INTRODUCTION

The Spelling and Pronunciation

THE romanic spelling used in this book is similar to that previously employed in *Colloquial Hindustani*,* but improved in the direction of making it more representative from the Indian point of view. It is more " phonetic " than the spelling of Italian or Spanish, but the reader must not expect to learn how to pronounce Urdu from this or any other book without the help of a teacher or of a Pakistani or Indian speaker. The spelling does, however, indicate all the minimum essential differences that have to be systematically maintained in speech; not one of the distinctions can be ignored, and they all correlate with the essentials of Indian systems of writing, Devanagari and Persi-Arabic.

In attempting pronunciation remember especially that what may be described as " the demobilization " of non-Indian sounds in your own speech is just as important as establishing those characteristic of Urdu. The practice drills which follow are based on this advice, for you are only allowed six " near-English " vowel sounds out of *the twenty-one* a Southern English speaker normally uses, and out of twenty English consonant sounds you may use only *ten* towards the minimum of *thirty-one* (not including the semi-vowels **y** and **v**) essential to Urdu. After the first drill, which uses only the *six* near-English vowels and the *ten* near-English consonants, all the rest, gradually added in subsequent drills, are foreign, and they are presented in ascending order of difficulty for English-speaking learners in suitably small doses.

You are advised to work steadily through the eight

* *Colloquial Hindustani*, by A. H. Harley, with an Introduction by J. R. Firth (Kegan Paul, London, 1944).

practice lessons in pronunciation with a teacher, preferably an Indian or Pakistani speaker, before beginning the grammatical lessons proper. At least an hour should be given to each practice, and two hours would not be excessive.

If you are fortunate enough to have an Indian or Pakistani listener, pronounce a single word once only, and ask him to tell you the meaning in English. If he can recognize that you are saying aṭa not ata, gəe and not gae or gəi, nəw not nao, you are making progress. Similarly you should be able to recognize his word after hearing it once, and to give him the number or translation of the word in the exercise. Ask your Indian teacher to dictate the words one at a time, and to repeat them as often as you may find necessary, so that you can establish a relation between the spelling and pronunciation. Correct your exercise from the text.

The phonetic backbone of the language is the consonant system given opposite in Table I. Though Urdu is on the whole an easy language to learn, the pronunciation of the consonants is difficult for all foreigners, and not only for Englishmen.

The most important set of consonant distinctions for European foreigners to learn are those between the retroflex series ṭ, ṭh, ḍ, ḍh (including the very difficult ṛ) and the dental series t, th, d, dh. These are precisely the ones which Englishmen habitually ignore. They usually fuss over what are called " the difficult Arabic sounds " x, ɣ and q, for which millions of Indian speakers substitute kh, g and k without dire consequences, though in good northern Urdu, courtesy requires x, ɣ, q. They occur much less frequently than the typical Indian sounds ṭ, ṭh, ḍ, ḍh, ṛ and t, th, d, dh, and are not so very difficult to acquire. Again the differences between the aspirated and unaspirated series (the first and fourth *horizontal* " columns " in Table I) *must* be maintained. English speakers will have considerable difficulty at first in satisfying an Indian listener that they can pronounce the *unaspirated* series k, c, ṭ, t, p.

TABLE I

Consonants

		Velar Back of tongue and soft palate	Palatal Front of tongue and front part of hard palate. Tip down	Retroflex Edge or rim of tongue behind or on teeth ridge	Dental Tip of tongue touches upper teeth	Bi-labial and labio-dental
PLOSIVES	Voiceless — Unasp.	k	c	t	t	p
	Voiceless — Asp.	kh	ch	th	th	ph
	Voiced — Unasp.	g	j	ḍ	d	b
	Voiced — Asp.	gh	jh	ḍh	dh	bh
NASALS		—	—	—	n	m
FRICA-TIVES	Voiceless	x (kh)	ʃ	—	*Alveolar* s	f
	Voiced	ɣ (g)	(ʒ)	—	z	—
Flapped and tapped sounds		—	—	ɽ aspirated ṛh	r	—
Uvular plosive (Arabic)		q (k)	—	—	—	—
Aspirate, semi-vowels and liquid		h	y	—	l	v

The principal difficulties for the great majority of foreign learners are:—

- (i) The two so-called "t" and "d" sounds, ṭ, t; ḍ, d.
- (ii) The five unaspirated voiceless plosives, especially c and t.
- (iii) The five aspirated voiced plosives, ġh, jh, ḍh, dh, bh.
- (iv) Double consonants.
- (v) The retroflex flapped ṛ.
- (vi) The two simple un-diphthongized vowels e and o.
- (vii) The so-called diphthongs əy and əw.

TABLE II

Vowels

Normal	ə 1	a 2	y 3	i 4	w 5	u 6	e 7	əy 8	o 9	əw 10
Nasalized	əŋ	aŋ		iŋ		uŋ	eŋ	əyŋ	oŋ	əwŋ
h-coloured or aspirated	əh	ah		(ih)		uh	eh		oh	

PRACTICE I

A. *Vowels:* ə, a ; y, i ; w, u.
Consonants: gə, bə, nə, mə, ʃə, sə, zə, fə, hə, yə.

The first six vowels fall into three pairs which present very little difficulty to the English-speaking learner. y and i are similar to the English short and long vowels in *bid* and *bead* and w and u to those in *full* and *fool* or *hood* and *food*. The important difference between the members of each pair is difference of vowel quality, not difference of length.

ə.

Between the obscure, weak or neutral vowel in the first syllable of *arise* and the vowel of *but*. The Urdu word **səb** is more like the first syllable of *subject* (verb) than of *subject* (noun), but in Urdu the vowel ə occurs in all positions and not as in English only in unstressed position.

a.

Similar to the *a* in *father*. **kam** (work) sounds like the Yorkshire or Lancashire pronunciation of *calm*.

y.

Not very different from the *y* in *system* or *mystery* or the *i* in *bid*, *sit*.

i.

Like the vowel in *seem* or *cease* or the second vowel in *immediately*, without trace of diphthongization.

w.

Like the vowels of *put*, *foot*.

u.

Not very different from the Received English pronunciation of the vowel in *too*, *root*, *moodily*, without trace of diphthongization.

The consonant sound ʃ is like the English *sh* in *ship*, but usually without lip-rounding. Since the sequence *s* plus *h* occurs in Urdu and since *h* is associated with aspiration, this special letter ʃ is an advantage.

1. əb, *now*
2. səb, *all*
3. gəz, *yard (measure)*
4. səbəb, *cause*
5. ʃam, *evening*
6. gaf, *letter " g "*
7. ana, *to come*
8. saman, *luggage*
9. yn, *these*
10. ys, *this*

11. hysab, *account* (*n.*)
12. ynsan, *human being*
13. si, *like* (*adj.f.sg.*)
14. sin, *scene*
15. ʃiʃə, *glass*
16. zəhin, *quick of memory*
17. wn, *those*
18. ws, *that*
19. bwna, *wove* (*m.sg.*)
20. mwbani, *founder* (*n.*)
21. un, *wool*
22. nun, *letter* " *n* "
23. mayus, *pessimistic, hopeless*
24. nəmunə, *sample* (*n.*)

B.i. *Vowels Nasalized :* əŋ, aŋ, iŋ, uŋ.

The mark of nasalization for vowels is ŋ immediately following the vowel. Thus aŋ and oŋ stand for ã and õ, being rather like the French syllables *an* and *on*. The ŋ symbol is *not* a consonant and must *not* be pronounced like the " ng " in *hang*. It indicates that the preceding vowel is nasalized and nothing more.

ii. *Semi-vowels :* yə, və.

y.

A very short " consonantal " form of the vowel y, but not so close or tense as the " y " of English, and never fricative. Indians do not properly pronounce the " y " sound after the " b " which distinguishes *beauty* from *booty*. The Urdu loan word ḍyuṭi is in fact very different from the English pronunciation of *duty*.

v.

Similarly the Indian v is much more of a vowel than a consonant. It has all the back or " oo " quality of " w ", but is without lip-rounding. The middle only of the lower lip barely touches the middle of the upper teeth. Contact is often with the *inside* of the lower lip. There is rarely any contact with or closing of the sides of the lower lip. The Indian v is in a sense the reverse of the English " v ".

1. haŋ, *yes*
2. bəyan, *description*
3. saŋs, *breath*
4. yəhaŋ, *here*
5. vəhaŋ, *there*
6. baŋs, *bamboo*
7. baŋg, *crying out*
8. nəhiŋ, *not*

9. yəhiŋ, *in this very place*
10. gəiŋ, *went (f.pl.)*
11. siŋ, *horn*
12. hiŋ, *asafœtida*

13. huŋ, *am*
14. huŋga, *will be*
15. guŋga, *dumb (m.sg.)*
16. miaŋ, *Sir*

Note: **əŋ** without a following **k** or **ġ** is rare, but it does occur in **həŋsna,** *to laugh.*

iii. *Vowel Junctions:*

1. nəi, *new (f.sg.)*
2. gəi, *went (f.sg.)*
3. gəiŋ, *went (f.pl.)*
4. miaŋ, *sir*
5. sais, *groom (n.)*
6. bənai, *made (f.sg.)*
7. ainə, *mirror*

8. na-ynsafi, *injustice*
9. hua, *happened (m.sg.)*
10. sui, *needle*
11. auŋ, *may come*
12. gaoŋ, *village*
13. swnauŋga, *shall tell*

C. *Differentiation:*

1. səf, *row, line*
2. həm, *we*
3. səbəb, *cause*
4. yn, *these*
5. afys, *office*
6. məmnun, *thankful*
7. saman, *luggage*
8. zəhin, *quick of memory*
9. nun, *letter " n "*
10. nəi, *new (f.sg.)*
11. həŋs, *laugh*
12. həns, *swan*

saf, *clean*
ʃam, *evening*
əsbab, *causes, luggage*
sin, *scene*
əfim, *opium*
mwnasyb, *proper*
yəhaŋ, *here*
nəhiŋ, *not*
huŋ, *am*
nəhiŋ, *not*
saŋs, *breath*
həŋs, *laugh*

PRACTICE 2

A. *Consonants:* **ḍə, də.**

ḍ.

The main thing in the production of this and the other retroflex sounds is not *where* you touch the teeth ridge or just behind it, but *how* you touch it. The point of articulation is about where English speakers make the *d* of *dry* or *droop*, but the contact is made not with the upper edge of the tip of the tongue in the English manner, but with the very edge or rim of the tip, which is curled back slightly, almost as when you try to prevent an elusive pill from rolling off the tip of your tongue. As one would expect, English *d* is replaced by ɖ in loan-words such as: ɖyu, soɖa, ɖrama, propəgənɖa, ɖaynyng hal.

d.

Unlike ɖ, d is pronounced with a flat tongue spread out, the tip touching the cutting edge of the front teeth and the edges touching the inside of the upper teeth *all round*. Some English people use a dental *d* of this type in *width*, *breadth*, on account of the following *th*-sound. Compare the English *d* in *dry*, which is nearer to ɖ, with the *d* in *breadth*, which is nearer to the dental **d**. Dental **d** is usual in French and other Romance languages.

n followed by ɖ and d takes on the articulation of the following consonant. **n** is *retroflex* in ənɖa but *dental* in **bənd**.

1. ɖubna, *to sink*
2. ɖub, *dip* (*n.*)
3. ɖayən, *witch*
4. ɖaŋɖi, *dandy* (*n.*)
5. ɖiŋg, *boasting*
6. ɖaŋɖ, *stick* (*n.*)
7. mənɖi, *market-place*
8. ɖənɖi, *stick* (*f.sg.*)
9. ɖənɖa, *stick* (*m.sg.*)
10. ənɖa, *egg*
11. saŋɖ, *bull*
12. haŋɖi, *cooking-pot*
13. dəs, *ten*
14. dam, *price*
15. dyn, *day*
16. din, *religion*
17. dəfa, *turn* (*n.*)
18. mədəd, *help*
19. ʃayəd, *perhaps*
20. əndaz, *manner*
21. damad, *son-in-law*
22. wmdə, *nice*
23. diŋ, *gave* (*f.pl.*)
24. dəbna, *to be suppressed*

B. *Consonants Doubled:*

The doubling of consonant sounds is not very common in English. We must, however, do so in such words as *unnecessary, unknown*, in which there are doubled " *n* " sounds. In the following practice list the two consonants together are to be held, the first one of the pair closing the first syllable, and the second opening the next syllable.

1. bəggi, *carriage*
2. ḍybba, *box (m.sg.)*
3. bwnna, *to weave*
4. bənna, *to pretend*
5. zymmə, *responsibility*
6. həmmam, *hammam*
7. əssi, *eighty*
8. hyssə, *share (n.)*
9. mwəzzyn, *muezzin*
10. ʃəffaf, *clear*
11. mwəyyən, *fixed*
12. həḍḍi, *bone*
13. gəḍḍi, *bundle*
14. əḍḍa, *central place*
15. gwḍḍa, *doll (m.sg.)*
16. zyddi, *stubborn*
17. nəddi, *river*
18. mwddəi, *plaintiff*

C. *Differentiation:*

1. ḍəs, *sting (v.)*   dəs, *ten*
2. bəs, *only*   bad, *after*
3. din, *religion*   dyn, *day*
4. din, *religion*   diŋ, *gave (f.pl.)*
5. saṇḍ, *bull*   bənd, *shut*
6. əndaz, *manner*   ənḍa, *egg*
7. swnna, *to hear*   bənna, *to pretend*
8. dwmbə, *ram*   ḍubna, *to sink*
9. bwna, *wove (m.sg.)*   bwnna, *to weave*
10. zəmin, *earth*   zymmə, *responsibility*
11. saman, *luggage*   həmmam, *hammam*
12. hysab, *account (n.)*   hyssə, *share*

PRACTICE 3

A. *Vowels:* **e, o, eŋ, oŋ.**

e.

A pure or simple vowel like Italian and other continental values of *e*. A vowel quality between the Scottish and North of England vowels in such words as *made, grey, ace*; not at all like the Southern English vowels in those words. In Southern English some people approach it in the slight diphthong represented by the *a* in *cessation*.

o.

Another pure vowel of continental, Scottish or Northern English type. Some people use a short *o* of this type in such words as *November* or *phonetics*. Keep the tongue and lip positions steady and the lower jaw steady when practising **e** and **o** long—no chin movement, no lip diphthong.

eŋ, oŋ.

Nasalizations of the above vowels. There is no final nasal consonant sound of any sort.

1. de, *give!* (*sg.*)
2. se, *from*
3. mez, *table*
4. dena, *to give*
5. do, *give!* (*pl.*)
6. so, *correlative conjunction*
7. bona, *to sow*
8. dedo, *give*
9. deŋ, *give* (*1st p. pl.*)
10. dedeŋ, *give* (*pl.*)
11. hoŋ, *be*
12. donoŋ, *both*
13. hoŋge, *will be* (*pl.*)
14. gaoŋ, *village*

B. The five voiced plosives exemplifying the five points of articulation for plosives:

gə, jə, ḍə, də, bə.

Note that **j** is pronounced with the tip of the tongue down, behind the lower teeth. **j** is rather like a "dy" sound pronounced with the tip of the tongue down. English *j* is not a good beginning for this sound, it has too much affrication or friction on release and is nearer to Urdu **jh.**

əng, ənj, əṇḍ, ənd, əmb.

The above syllables close with a nasal homorganic with the stop or plosive immediately following. Both nasal and stop share the same point of articulation.

1. gəz, *yard* (*measure*)
2. age, *in front*
3. gəe, *went* (*m.pl.*)
4. nənga, *naked*
5. jo, *that which*
6. jəhaz, *ship*
7. janna, *to know*
8. ənjən, *engine*
9. ḍəs, *sting* (*vb.*)
10. ḍayən, *witch*

11. ḍubna, *to sink*
12. ḍənḍa, *stick*
13. des, *country*
14. wdas, *sad*
15. damad, *son-in-law*
16. gənda, *dirty*
17. bəja, *o'clock*
18. bəjna, *to sound*
19. bab, *door*
20. bədmaʃ, *rogue*
21. bəmbei, *Bombay*

C. *Consonants:* rə, lə.

r.

May be fricative or tapped. There is a special difficulty for English speakers when a final r is preceded by i, u or e. ʃer, der and dur are not at all like Southern English *share, dare* or *doer*. The title *Amir* in Urdu is quite unlike the sound of *a mere* in English. In Urdu you must hang on to the pure undiphthongized vowel i, e, o or u, to the very instant the r is made. There must be no neutral or glide vowel between the i, e, o or u and the final r, which is always to be clearly pronounced.

l.

Always clear like the *l* at the beginning of such words as *lee, leaf*, as pronounced in Southern English. Never as in *feel*, or *field*. The so-called " thick " *l* of Glasgow or certain American dialects does not sound well in Urdu.

1. roz, *day*
2. rəhe, *were (m.pl.)*
3. rəddi, *waste-paper*
4. ḍər, *fear*
5. gyr, *fall (vb.)*
6. ʃer, *lion*
7. zərur, *certainly*
8. wrdu, *Urdu*
9. lena, *to take*
10. ləgega, *will affect (m.sg.)*
11. logoŋ, *people*
12. mel, *re-union*
13. gwl, *flower*
14. gol, *round*
15. bolna, *to speak*
16. ḍalna, *to put in*
17. fərraʃ, *servant*
18. rozmərrə, *daily routine*
19. bylli, *cat*
20. wllu, *owl*
21. der, *delay*
22. dur, *distant*
23. əmir, *Amir*

D. *Differentiation:*

1. gəz, *yard (measure)*	des, *country*
2. dəs, *ten*	mez, *table*
3. bəja, *o'clock*	raja, *rajah*
4. gwl, *flower*	gol, *round*
5. bwnna, *to weave*	bolna, *to speak*
6. ser, *seer (weight)*	ʃer, *lion*
7. huŋ, *am*	hoŋ, *be*
8. huŋga, *I will be*	hoŋge, *they will be*
9. myli, *met (f.sg.)*	bylli, *cat*
10. dedeŋ, *give (pl.)*	donoŋ, *both*
11. fərraʃ, *servant*	zəra, *small quantity*
12. wrdu, *Urdu*	məzdur, *labourer*

PRACTICE 4

A. *Vowels:* əy, əw ; əyŋ, əwŋ.

əy.

There are two types of pronunciation of this vowel, one diphthongal and the other a simple half-open front vowel like the Southern English vowel in *ham*. In fact, the common word **həy** (is) sounds rather like southern *had* or northern *head* stopping short just before the " d ". This is the pronunciation recommended. The diphthongal pronunciation may perhaps be approximately arrived at by taking the two vowels of *amiss* or *amid*, and coalescing them, " ə " and " y ". This diphthongal pronunciation is difficult for English speakers who habitually perpetrate the English word *high* for the Urdu word **həy**. It is of high grammatical importance that the following Urdu sounds be kept distinct : **ai, ae, əi, əe, əy.**

əyŋ.

The nasalization of **əy**. No nasal consonant of the English " ng " type must be heard.

əyŋ must be kept distinct from **aiŋ, aeŋ** and **əiŋ**

əw.

Foreigners habitually mispronounce this sound when a diphthong is attempted. It must *never* be pronounced to rhyme with the English words *how, now*, neither should it resemble the vowel in the Southern English pronunciation of *gnawed*. Attempt to isolate the vowel in Southern English *nod* without lip-rounding. If you stop short before the " d " of *nod*, you may get something like **nəw**, the Urdu word for *nine*. If you say the English *now*, it will suggest Urdu **nao** or **nav** (boat).

əwŋ.

The nasalization of **əw**. No nasal consonant must be heard. Care must be given to the distinct pronunciation of **əw, ao, əv ; əwŋ, aoŋ** and **auŋ**, which are grammatically differentiated.

1. həy, *is*
2. məy, *liquor*
3. səyr, *visit to a place*
4. məyl, *dirt*
5. jəw, *barley*
6. səw, *hundred*
7. əwr, *and*
8. fəwj, *army*
9. həyŋ, *are*
10. məyŋ, *I*
11. hue həyŋ, *have been* (*m.pl.*)
12. rəhe həyŋ, *are*
13. ləwŋg, *clove*
14. ḍəwŋga, *canoe*
15. jəysa, *so*
16. əysa, *so*

B. *Consonants:* **khə, chə, ṭhə, thə, phə.**

These strongly aspirated consonants are sometimes compared with the rapid succession of final plosives with a following " h "-sound in such sequences as *blockhouse, blockhead, bulkhead, hothouse* (**ṭh**), *tophat*. Such aids are only helpful if some violence is done to English pronunciation and stressing in such a word as *bulkhead*, for instance, dividing it thus: *bul-'khead*, with the incidence of stress in the " k ".

ph is not really like the junction of *p* and *h* in *tophat*. It is one effort, a " p " sound with a good pressure of " chest air " behind the stop so that when the lips are released there is a sudden escape of breath. These consonants must be sharply distinguished from the unaspirated correlates which are much more difficult for English speakers (see Practice 5).

1. kha, *eat*
2. khwl, *open (vb.)*
3. rəkhni, *put (f.sg.)*
4. rəkh do, *put!*
5. cha, *cover (vb.)*
6. chəy, *six*
7. chuna, *to touch*
8. muɳch, *moustache*
9. ʈhənḍ, *coldness*
10. ʈhəyrna, *to wait*
11. wʈhna, *to rise*
12. saʈh, *sixty*
13. rəha tha, *was (m.sg.)*
14. rəhi thi, *was (f.sg.)*
15. rəhe the, *were (m.pl.)*
16. sath, *with*
17. phəl, *fruit*
18. phul, *flower*
19. phulna, *to flower*
20. əphərna, *to swell up*
21. vəhi, *that one*
22. vala, *eminent*
23. vəhaɳ, *there*

C. *Phrases:*

1. məyɳ kha rəha tha. *I (m.) was eating.*
2. məyɳ kha rəhi thi. *I (f.) was eating.*
3. həm kha rəhe the. *We were eating.*
4. vəhi lahəwr gəya həy. *He has gone to Lahore.*
5. yəhi bəmbei gəi həy. *She has gone to Bombay.*
6. həm dylli jaeɳge. *We will go to Delhi.*

D. *Differentiation:*

1. mel, *re-union*   məyl, *dirt*
2. məyɳ, *I*   meɳ, *in*
3. so, *conjunction*   səw, *hundred*
4. səwda, *goods*   soḍa, *soda (water)*
5. log, *people*   ləwɳg, *clove*
6. sath, *with*   saʈh, *sixty*
7. thəyli, *purse*   ʈhəyrna, *to wait*
8. səval, *question*   səvar, *rider*
9. vəhaɳ, *there*   yəhaɳ, *here*
10. jəj, *judge*   muɳch, *moustache*
11. phyr, *then*   phul, *flower*
12. əjəb, *wonderful*   azad, *free*

13. gae, *cow*   gəi, *she went*
14. gəe, *they went*   ai, *she came*
15. nəw, *nine*   nao, *boat*

PRACTICE 5

A. *Consonants:*

kə, cə, ṭə, tə, pə.
ənk, ənc, ənṭ, ənt, əmp.

This series of unaspirated consonants is much more difficult for English speakers to establish in their habitual pronunciation of Urdu than the aspirated or voiced correlates. The five points of articulation are similar to those of ġ, j, ḍ, d and b (see Practice 3). The place for the retroflex contact of ṭ is about where most Englishmen make the " t " of *true*. Some English people use a dental articulation similar to that of the Urdu dental t in the word *at* in such phrases as *at the theatre, at three, at thirty*, spoken quickly, or in *eighth*.

The English consonants " p " and " k " in such words as *pack, kick* and *keep*, occurring in stressed position at the end of a sentence, are *all* aspirated, both initially and finally in those words. Indians mispronounce such words in speaking English, and even for the pronunciation of final " k " and " p ", sound much better if they think of them as nearer to their own kh and ph, than to k and p. It will be realized at once, therefore, that such Urdu words as piṭ, kaṭ, ṭuṭ, tək, cwp, kuc are, on the other hand, extremely difficult for English speakers to pronounce. An almost uncomfortable restraint of " chest air " is necessary in learning to pronounce these sounds. Northern Englishmen find them less difficult than southerners.

The most difficult of this series is c, which is rather like the " ty " combinations in the English word *tumultuous*, but pronounced with the tip of the tongue down, i.e. behind the lower teeth. The " ch " in *church* will do for the *aspirated* ch of Urdu, but is a bad beginning for the unaspirated c.

Urdu **k, c, ṭ, t, p** are released with a minimum of breath. There must be no audible outward puff of breath from the lungs. To understand this, practise **p** and **k** while holding your breath. You may produce a sort of " popping " explosion of " p ". That is the basis. Eliminate the audible " pop " and you have an unaspirated **p**. The opposite action of leaving your throat open for freely flowing breath is what you do in English and more so for aspirated **kh** and **ph** in Urdu.

The syllables **ənk, ənc, ənṭ, ənt** and **əmp** illustrate each one of the unaspirated stops immediately preceded by the nasal consonant homorganic with it—that is, pronounced in the same place, at the same point of articulation. The four nasals represented by **n** are different, each one being as closely associated with the following plosive as **m** is with **p** (compare Practice 3, B).

1. kam, *work*
2. kəl, *to-morrow*
3. kərna, *to do*
4. ḍənk, *sting*
5. ca, *tea*
6. car, *four*
7. cəca, *paternal uncle*
8. ync, *inch*
9. ṭuṭ, *break*
10. ṭoṭa, *loss*
11. ṭykəṭ, *ticket*
12. iṇṭ, *brick*
13. tab, *strength*
14. tez, *fast*
15. aṭa, *flour*
16. savənt, *brave*
17. pani, *water*
18. ap, *self*
19. upər, *upon*
20. ləymp, *lamp*

B. *Consonant Junctions:*

The distinction between single and double consonants must be maintained. The double **k** in **pəkka** is rather like the long " k "-sound in *bookcase,* and the junction of **ṭ** with **ṭh** in **pəṭṭha** is suggested by the long " t "-sound in *hot tea.* The junction of the retroflex **ṭ** and **ṭh** with the dental **t** is common in such participial forms as **bəyṭhta, wṭhta, kaṭta.** The verbal forms **bəyṭhta tha, kaṭta tha,** are difficult sequences and good exercise.

1. pəkka, *ripe*
2. məkkhən, *butter*
3. tak-na, *to stare*
   tak-ta, *staring*
   tak-a, *stared*
4. lykh-na, *to write*
   lykh-ta, *writing*
   lykh-a, *wrote*
5. kəcca, *raw*
6. əccha, *good*
7. bəc-na, *to avoid*
   bəc-ta, *avoiding*
   bəc-a, *avoided*
8. puch-na, *to ask*
   puch-ta, *asking*
   puch-a, *asked*
9. təʈʈi, *hedge*
10. cyʈʈhi, *letter*
11. pəʈ-na, *to be thatched, etc.*
    pəʈ-ta
    pəʈ-a
12. wʈh-na, *to rise*
    wʈh-ta, *rising*
    wʈh-a, *rose*
13. pətta, *leaf*
14. pətthər, *stone*
15. ytna, *this much*
16. cəppu, *oars*
17. tap-na, *to warm oneself, etc.*
    tap-ta
    tap-a
18. bəyʈhna, *to sit*
    bəyʈh-ta, *sitting*
    bəyʈh-a, *sat*
19. wtna, *that much*

C. *Phrases* :

1. əcchi bat həy.   That's good.
2. admi ata tha.   The man came or was coming.
3. əwrət ati thi.   The woman came or was coming.
4. bat twm ko yad həy?   Do you remember it ?
5. kys ke pas həy?   Who has got it ?
6. bəccə dekhta tha.   The child was looking.
7. bəccə cyʈʈhi lykhta tha.   The child was writing a letter.
8. kwch kam kəro.   Do some work !
9. ws ka ek beʈa tha.   He had one son.
10. cwp rəho, twm kya kya bəkte ho.   Be quiet, what nonsense you talk !

D. *Differentiation:*

1. savənt, *brave*   kənʈh, *throat*
2. khata, *eating (vb.)*   caʈa, *licked*
3. kuc, *departure*   kwch, *some*
4. khwl, *open (vb.)*   kəl, *to-morrow*
5. pir, *Monday*   phyr, *then*

6. piţh, *back*	phəţ, *burst* (*vb.*)
7. pwl, *bridge*	phul, *flower*
8. ap, *you*	cwp, *quiet*
9. phaţək, *gate*	pətta, *leaf*
10. kəptan, *captain*	abdar, *water-carrier*
11. wtarna, *to bring down*	wţhana, *to raise*
12. vərzyʃ, *exercise*	bərdaʃt, *patience*
13. sath, *with*	sat, *seven*
14. aţh, *eight*	kaţ, *cut*

PRACTICE 6

A. *Vowels:* **ah, eh, oh, uh, əh.**

The ten basic vowel sounds of Urdu given in Practice 1 are pronounced with a " bright " or " clear " voice quality using a minimum of breath. We have seen in Practices 1 and 3 that eight of these vowels are commonly nasalized. There are four further vowels having similar basic formation but pronounced either with a following voiced " h " sound like the " h " in *behind* or alternatively with a breathy or " h "-coloured voice quality at the end, rather like the " sighing out " of *ah !* The exclamatory syllables *ah !* and *oh !* in English can be pronounced either with " bright " voice using a minimum of breath, or breathily quite in the Indian manner.

N.B.—In the syllables **ah, eh, oh** and **uh,** the basic formation of the vowels is similar to that of the correlated simple vowels. Special attention must, however, be given to the breathy vowel **əh** immediately followed by a consonant, in such words as **rəhna, rəhta ; kəhna, kəhta.** In all such cases the vowel quality is similar to that given in Practice 4 for the non-diphthongal pronunciation of **əy.** That is to say, the above four words sound as if they might be written **rəyhna, rəyhta ; kəyhna, kəyhta.** But that would be grammatically inconvenient and would make such verbs irregular, besides being unnecessary. In the past tense forms **rəha, kəha,** no opening or " fronting " of the vowel takes place, since the syllabic sequence is **rə-ha, kə-ha.**

The " h "-colouring of **ə** always produces a quality rather like the Southern English vowel in *man* when immediately followed by another consonant. Certain words like **pəhyla, pəhyle,** have two phonetic possibilities. The first is straightforward, suggested by **pə-hy-le.** In the second case there is reduction to two syllables which may be regarded either as coalescence **pəyhle** or as elision **pəhle.** This pronunciation suggests the possibility of **əyh** as an alternative pronunciation. It will not, however, be taken as a basis for spelling.

Similar coalescence takes place in the common word **bəhwt,** which, if immediately followed by a word beginning with a consonant, is a two-syllable word **bə-hwt** as in **bəhwt gərm.** But in normal rapid colloquial, especially when immediately followed by a word beginning with a vowel, it is pronounced as one syllable, e.g. **bəwht əccha.** This common alternative pronunciation provides an instance of a breathy vowel **əwh,** but it will not be regarded as the basis of spelling.

There is an interesting parallel in the case of **yeh** and **voh,** both of which are spelled according to the sound, recognizing the effect of " h "-colouring on the vowels **y** and **w.** **yeh,** or more commonly **ye,** is really **yyh,** and **voh,** or **vo,** is **vwh.** In final position the " h " of the Indian traditional spelling of certain numerals, for example, is disregarded, and the resulting open vowel **ə** considered sufficient; e.g. **ģyara, bara, tera,** and similarly in many other words. This changed spelling affects the grammatical treatment especially of gender. See p. 20 and footnote.

1. cah, *affection*
2. cahna, *to like*
3. mahtab, *moon*
4. yeh, *this*
5. behtər, *better*
6. mehman, *guest*
7. mehr, *kindness*

8. zəhr, *poison*
9. məhrəm, *confidant*
10. səhna, *to bear*
    səhta, *bearing*
11. rəhna, *to remain*
    rəhta, *remaining*
12. voh, *that*

13. mohkəm, *strengthened*
14. koh, *mountain*
15. mohr, *seal*
16. bəhwt, *very much*
17. nuh, *Noah*
18. pəhyle, *first (adv.)*
19. mehtər, *sweeper*
20. kəhna, *to say*
    kəhta, *saying*
21. mehrbani, *please*

B. *Consonants:* g̱hə, jhə, ḍhə, dhə, bhə.

These are the voiced correlates of **kh, ch, ṭh, th** and **ph** (see Table I), and are produced in a similar way only with the forcible expulsion of voiced breath. When they occur between vowels as in **ydhər** and **wdhər**, they are not difficult to pronounce. For such positions the usual method of learning is by running together the middle consonants of *log-house, road-house* (for **ḍh**) and *cab-horse* for **bh**. But the English syllable division and incidence of stress is entirely unsuitable. To approximate to the Indian **bh**, for instance, you must divide the syllables in a very un-English way, e.g. *ca-bhorse*. A variant method is to begin saying *hab-hab-hab* and then speed up the repetition, change over from *hab-hab* to *ha-bha* and continue repeating *bha-bha*, etc. Another device is to regard the **b** part of **bh** as a closed lip position from which you proceed to pronounce *ha*, which you have all ready inside under pressure, so to speak. The *ha* part begins with a voiced **h**.

1. ghər, *house*
2. ghi, *clarified butter*
3. gholna, *to mix*
4. uŋgh, *drowsiness*
5. jhəṭ, *quick*
6. jhuṭ, *lie (n.)*
7. jhənḍa, *flag*
8. bujh, *comprehension*
9. ḍher, *heap*
10. ḍhiṭ, *obstinate*
11. ḍhaŋp, *cover (vb.)*
12. ḍhuŋḍna, *to find out*
13. dhup, *sunshine*
14. dhoka, *fraud*
15. dhobi, *washerman*
16. dudh, *milk*
17. bhaṭ, *minstrel*
18. bhari, *heavy*
19. bhitər, *inside*
20. labh, *profit*

C. *Phrases:*

1. məyŋ ghər ghər gəya.   *I went from house to house.*
2. məyŋ ghər pər tha.   *I was at home.*
3. do pəhr ke bad.   *After twelve noon.*

4. bəhwt saman rəh gəya.   *A great deal of luggage was left.*
5. ʈhik do pəhr həy.   *It is exactly twelve noon.*
6. mwjhe wrdu nəhiŋ ati.   *I don't know Urdu.*
7. həmeŋ sui dhaga cahie.   *We want needle and thread.*
8. məyŋ kwch kərna cahta huŋ.   *I want to do something.*

D. *Differentiation:*

1. ko, *to, on, by*   koh, *mountain*
2. ca, *tea*   cah, *affection*
3. kor, *blind*   mohr, *seal*
4. car, *four*   zəhr, *poison*
5. ɖher, *heap*   ɖər, *fear*
6. ʈopi, *cap*   dhobi, *washerman*
7. behtər, *better*   bəyʈha, *sitting (m.)*
8. kapi, *copy (n.)*   khati, *eating (f.)*
9. fəwj, *army*   bojh, *burden*
10. ghər, *house*   gəhra, *deep*
11. beva, *widow*   bheja, *sent*
12. kana, *one-eyed*   khana, *to eat*
13. bəhai, *set adrift (f.sg.)*   bhai, *brother*
14. bəhanə, *pretence*   bhana, *to be pleased*
15. bəhao, *flow*   bhao, *price*
16. bəhi, *account book*   bhi, *also*

PRACTICE 7

A. *Vowels:* **whŋ, ehŋ, əhŋ.**

Three vowel qualities combine aspiration and nasalization. The vowels are produced with breathy nasality. As in the case of **əh** (see p. xxviii) so also with **əhŋ**, the quality is open and fronted rather like **əyhŋ** ; e.g. **məhŋga** sounds as though it might be written **məyhŋga**. In words like **pəhwŋcna** (pə-hwŋc-na) there is often coalescence resulting in a pronunciation which sounds like **pəwhŋcna**, i.e.

two syllables **pəwhŋc-na**, in which the first is nasalized aspirated **əw** (**əwhŋ**). But since this pronunciation is an alternative provided for in the spelling, there is no need for *two* spellings (cf. **bəhwt**, p. xxix).

1. mwhŋ, *face*
2. ehŋ, *oh!*
3. mehŋ, *rain*

4. məhŋga, *expensive* (*m.sg.*)
5. pəhwŋcna, *to reach*

B. *Consonants:* **əʈə, əʈ ; əʈhə, əʈh.**

It will be noticed from the above syllables that the retroflex flapped **ʈ** does not occur initially. It is in fact a medial and final form of **ḍ**. If it were not for loan words like **soḍa** and **pəyḍ**, a special letter would not be necessary. However, both Muslims and Europeans have the impression that it is a sort of " r "-sound. And indeed some English speakers pronounce *better* and *butter* as though the middle " t " were an " r ". One may hear something like " lerra go ! " for " let her go ! " That is in fact what Indians do. They turn the medial and final **ḍ** into a very rapidly flapped sound which suggests a sort of " r " sound to foreigners. But it is quite distinct from **r**, and bears no resemblance either to Southern English or West Country " r " or to Scottish " r ". It is perhaps the most difficult sound for a foreigner to acquire.

The body of the tongue is drawn backwards with the blade curled back as for **ḍ** or **ʈ** (see pp. xvii, xxv). Having your teeth apart, try to point towards the back of your mouth with the tip of the tongue, but do not touch anywhere. From that position the blade is rapidly flapped forward and down, and when the sound is made a very rapid flick of the under edge of the tip of the tongue catches the gums as it flaps past, finishing up behind the lower teeth. Since the blade of the tongue must be retroflexed for this sound, the quality of the immediately preceding vowel must obviously be affected, so that you can always hear it coming. It may help you to perceive it and make it if you pay some attention to vowels immediately preceding **ʈ**. It also occurs aspirated, **ʈh.**

1. bəɽa, *big (m.sg.)*
2. ghəɽi, *clock*
3. gaɽi, *cart*
4. ghəɽa, *earthen vessel for water*
5. bhiɽ, *crowd*
6. moɽ, *turning (road)*
7. thəppəɽ, *slap, blow*
8. taɽ, *palm tree*
9. bəɽhana, *to increase*
10. siɽhi, *ladder*
11. ʈeɽha, *crooked*
12. buɽha, *old (m.sg.)*
13. ənpəɽh, *illiterate*
14. ɖeɽh, *one and a half*
15. bəɽh, *increase (vb.)*
16. gəɽh, *citadel*
17. toɽna, *to break*
18. ləɽki, *girl*
19. pəgɽi, *turban*
20. cəmɽa, *leather*
21. pəɽhna, *to read*
22. bəɽhna, *to increase*
23. papəɽ, *wafer*
24. pəyɖ, *pad*
25. soɖa, *soda water*

C. *Phrases:*

1. yeh kəmra jhaɽ do. — *Clean this room!*
2. yeh cəmɽa rəkh do. — *Put this leather away!*
3. voh pəɽh rəha həy. — *He is reading.*
4. voh pəɽha kərta həy. — *He's always reading.*
5. yeh ghoɽa tez dəwɽ səkta həy. — *This horse can run fast.*
6. voh khəɽi rəhi. — *She remained standing.*
7. dərvazə kholo əwr khyɽki bənd kəro. — *Open the door and shut the window.*
8. jəb məyŋ vəhaŋ pəhwŋca voh pəɽhna ʃwru kər cwke the. — *When I got there, they had started reading.*

D. *Differentiation:*

1. kəmra, *room* — cəmɽa, *leather*
2. bwɖɖha, *old man* — buɽha, *old (m.sg.)*
3. phyr, *then* — bhiɽ, *crowd*
4. wʈhna, *to rise* — wɽna, *to fly*
5. bwra, *bad* — bəɽa, *big*
6. gəɽha, *ditch* — ghəɽa, *earthen vessel*
7. gora, *fair-skinned* — ghoɽa, *horse*
8. lərza, *trembled* — ləɽka, *boy*
9. kəh do, *say* — ke, *of*

    10. do, *give*   dho, *wash*
    11. dhəjji, *rag*   əcchi, *good (f.)*
    12. pəhwŋcna, *to reach*   poŋchna, *to wipe*

PRACTICE 8

A. *Consonants:* **xə, ɣə, qə.**

These consonants occur only in loan words of Arabic origin, most of which reached Urdu through Persian. Though they are really foreign to the typical Indian consonant system as shown in Table I, they are used by more than fifty million Pakistanis and Indians, and are essential for a good pronunciation of northern Urdu.

x.

This is sometimes described as the " ch "-sound of *loch*, or the " ach "-sound of German. It is similar to these, but further back and more " scrapy ".

ɣ.

Though this is pronounced slightly further back than **x**, it may be treated as the voiced counterpart of **x**. It is similar to the fricative or " rubbing " pronunciation of the " g " in *Wagen* by some Germans, or to the intervocalic " g " of Spanish. It is further back than the " back r " of German *waren* or French *aurons*, but it must *not* be rolled or trilled.

q.

A good nonsense word in which to practise this sound is **aqa**, with a back kind of " a " sound. Keep the mouth fairly wide open, that is, with the lower jaw well down, and make the furthest back " k " sound possible. The back of the tongue has to close the arches or fauces at the back of the mouth, including contact with the uvula. To make this easier, it is necessary to squeeze the sides of the throat nearer together to narrow the opening which has to be stopped by the back of the tongue.

1. xət, *letter*
2. xwʃ, *happy*
3. xydmət, *service*
4. xubsurət, *beautiful*
5. əxbar, *newspaper*
6. tarix, *date*
7. səxi, *charitable*
8. dərxast, *application*
9. ɣalyb, *triumphant*
10. ɣərib, *poor*
11. ɣwssə, *anger*
12. ɣalybən, *perhaps*
13. baɣ, *garden*
14. daroɣə, *police inspector*
15. məɣryb, *west*
16. xwdɣərəz, *selfish*
17. qwli, *coolie*
18. qysmət, *luck*
19. qərib, *near*
20. qələm, *pen*
21. fəqir, *beggar*
22. yəqin, *certainty*
23. nwqsan, *loss*
24. fərq, *difference*

B. *Phrases:*

1. qwli bəɽa səxt kam kərte həyŋ
   Coolies do very heavy work.

2. mahigir qyssə kəh rəha tha.
   The fisherman was telling a story.

3. voh xət pəɽh rəha həy.
   He is reading a letter.

4. yeh ek ɣərib əwrət həy.
   She is a poor woman.

5. voh ɣalybən kamyab hoga.
   Perhaps he will be successful.

6. yeh zəruri kaɣəzoŋ meŋ nətthi kər do.
   Clip it together with the important papers.

7. yeh xət meri prayvət fayl meŋ ləga do.
   File this letter in my private file.

C. *Differentiation:*

1. khari, *brackish*   xar, *thorn*
2. xal, *mole*   khal, *skin*
3. khana, *food*   xanə, *house*
4. ghol, *mix (vb.)*   ɣol, *crowd*
5. ɣwrrə, *pride*   ghoɽa, *horse*
6. gali, *abuse*   ɣalyb, *triumphant*

B

7. koli, *embrace*   qwli, *coolie*
8. qamət, *stature*   kəmənd, *noose*
9. kwmhar, *potter*   qəmis, *shirt*
10. qərz, *loan*   yərəz, *purpose*
11. xwlus, *sincerity*   qwsur, *fault*
12. hwqqə, *hookah*   pəkka, *ripe*

THE ACCENT

Englishmen cannot fail to notice the effect of Indian languages on the English spoken by most Indians, especially in the matter of accent. The effect of the strong stress accent of the Englishman on his Urdu, coupled with his usual pronunciation howlers, is incredible distortion of the language.

Urdu ordinarily moves evenly within a narrower range of intonation than English and without strong stresses. The prominence of Urdu syllables in the sentence seems to be partly due to a slight increase of force coupled with a change in the direction of intonation which may be up or down, but which is usually down followed by a rise, somewhat like Welsh.

A rough idea of the intonation of a simple phrase may be indicated by the following arrangement of syllables :

voh ˌja rə ha
həy.

He go " stayed " (*m.*) is.
i.e. *He is going.*

Notice the relative pitches of the prominent syllable **ja-**, and one of the weakest syllables **-ha.** It is almost the antithesis of an English pattern with a stress on the first syllable of *going.* To assist students to observe the intonation patterns for themselves, the following short graphic representation is given as an individual example of one good style.

A GRAPHIC REPRESENTATION OF URDU INTONATION
(One mark per syllable)

Name	yeay	fe	qaf	kaf	gaf	lam	mim	nun	vao	he	ye y, etc.
	y	f	q	k	g	l	m	n	v	h	y, etc.
Detached form											
Final											
Medial											
Initial											

Name	zal	re	te	ze	3e	sin	jin	svad	zvad	toe	zoe	ayn
	z	r	r	z	3	s	s	s	z	t	z	—
Detached form												
Final												
Medial												
Initial												

Name	elyf e, etc.	be	pe	te	te	se	jim	ce	he	xe	dal	dal
	e, etc.	b	p	t	t	s	j	c	h	x	d	d
Detached form												
Final												
Medial												
Initial												

The following are alternative forms for **sin** and **ʃin**:

Cursive Forms

Name	Detached form	Final	Medial	Initial
sin	س	س	ـسـ	ـسـ
ʃin	ش	ش	ـشـ	ـشـ

"te" and "toe", "se", "sin" and "svad", "ze", "zoe" and "zvad" are not differentiated in pronunciation. "ze", "zoe", "zvad" and "ʒe" are often pronounced like "jim". The five unnecessary letters are partly responsible for the foreigner's failure to distinguish "te" and "ṭe", which is a cardinal error.

Vowels are as follows : *(reading from right to left)* :

mul	mwl	mil	myl	mal	məl
مُول	مُل	مِیل	بِل	مال	مَل

məwlvi	mol	məyl	mel
مولوی	مول	مَیل	میل

'əyn

The letter **'əyn** in the Urdu script is not realized as a consonant in any form of the spoken language. Syllables in which **'əyn** occurs in Urdu spelling are pronounced with the vowels **a, ə** or **e**, according to derivation and structure, and are so represented in the romanic spelling. See footnote on p. 152, and various examples on pp. 4–6, 12, 14, 155, 259, 274, 276, 298, 302, 309. It will be noticed that some words have more than one romanic form, e.g., **dəfə** and **dəfa**, **mwamylə** and **mamlə**, **mwaf** and **maf**.

GRAMMAR

NOUNS

It will be sufficient at first if the beginner learns one case in addition to the nominative—viz. the oblique or postpositional, which is used with all postpositions. The vocative can be learnt a little later.

Nouns have two declensions and three cases. The cases are : (*a*) nominative, (*b*) oblique, postpositional or locative, and (*c*) vocative. See Notes on Cases, p. 8.

FIRST DECLENSION

This contains a few masculine nouns ending in **-a**, all masculine nouns not ending in **-a**, and all feminine nouns whatever their ending. All these nouns are indeclinable in their singular. In the plural they are declined alike, except in the nominative, which is formed in three ways, as follows :—

(i) Masculine nouns	nominative plural	no change
(ii) Feminine nouns ending in **-i**	nominative plural	add **-aŋ** (or **-eŋ** in conversation)
(iii) Other feminine nouns	nominative plural	add **-eŋ**

Examples :—

(i) Masculine nouns ending in **-a** or **-ə**.

	Singular	Plural
Nominative :	raja	raja
Oblique :	raja	rajaoŋ
Vocative :	raja	rajao

1

	Singular	*Plural*
Nominative :	dhobi, washerman	dhobi
Oblique :	dhobi	dhobioŋ
(Vocative :	dhobi	dhobio)

So :—

    ghər, house : ghər, ghəroŋ (ghəro)

    bycchu, scorpion : bycchu, bycchuoŋ (bycchuo)

(ii) Feminine nouns ending in **-i.**

Nominative :	bətti, lamp	bəttiaŋ (or bəttieŋ in conversation)
Oblique :	bətti	bəttioŋ
(Vocative :	bətti	bəttio)

Note that **dhobi** and **bətti**, though both ending in **-i,** differ in the nominative plural because one is masculine, and the other feminine.

In speaking, but not in writing, feminine nouns in **-i** very often make their plural in **-eŋ,** as **ləɽki, ləɽkieŋ.**

Feminine nouns in **-ia** make their plural as if the singular ended in **-i** :—

    cyɽia, sparrow, little bird; plural : cyɽiaŋ, cyɽioŋ

    (voc. : cyɽio)

(iii) Other feminine nouns.

	Singular	*Plural*
Nominative :	mez, table	mezeŋ
Oblique :	mez	mezoŋ
Vocative :	mez	mezo

So :- -

    mala, *f.,* necklace : malaeŋ, malaoŋ (malao)

    jhaɽu, *f.,* broom : jhaɽueŋ, jhaɽuoŋ (jhaɽuo)

Note once more that all nouns of this declension are *identical in declension* except in the nominative plural.

Urdu speakers dislike declining nouns ending in **-ao, -aoŋ, -ae** or **-aeŋ,** sometimes even those ending in **-o,** and adopt various devices to avoid doing so.

gaoŋ, *m.*, village; **paoŋ**, *m.*, foot; **daoŋ**, *m.*, trick primarily in wrestling, are kept unchanged.

bhao, *m.*, rate, price, is confined to the singular; **ghao**, *m.*, wound, makes plural oblique **ghaoŋ**, but is often replaced by **zəxm**, *m.*, plural oblique **zəxmoŋ**.

For **nao**, *f.*, boat, the plural forms **naveŋ**, **navoŋ**, may be heard occasionally under Hindi influence, but in Urdu **nao** is used even in the plural nominative. More often **kyʃti**, also meaning boat, is substituted for it.

For **gae**, cow, the forms **gaeŋ** or **gayeŋ** and **gayoŋ** would be correct according to rule, but as far as possible they are avoided. Sometimes they say **gae bəyl**, cows and bulls, etc., to avoid saying **gaeŋ**.

rae, *f.*, opinion, is always kept singular.

foʈo, *m.* (= English photo), photograph, is either kept unchanged or altered to **foʈu**, which may easily be declined; oblique plural, **foʈuoŋ**.

sʈuɖio is not declined.

Under the First Declension, masculine nouns, come the following :—

A. Some nouns ending in **-a** or **-ə**.

(*a*) Words denoting relatives of a generation older than one's own.

əbba, father	məwsa, mother's sister's husband
bapdada, *m.pl.* ancestors	
cəca, father's younger brother	nana, mother's father
dada, father's father	pərdada, dada's father
kaka, father's elder brother	aja, dada's father
lala, father, etc. (Hindu word)	pərnana, nana's father
	phwppa, phupa, phupha, father's sister's husband
mama (mamuŋ), mother's brother	taya, father's elder brother

Exception : **swsra**, father-in-law; oblique, **swsre**.

To these must be added **aka**, elder brother; **bhəiya**, respectful word for brother; **ləɽaka**, *m.* or *fem.*, person of combative disposition.

(*b*)

xwda, God	baba, bava, old or holy man
mwlla, Muslim priest	raja, rajə, king
məwlana, learned Muham-	rana, kind of rajah
madan	hymalia, the Himalayas
dərya, river	xəlifa, xəlifə,* vice-regent,
gyrja, church (building,	title given to barber, tailor
service)	

Examples :—

cəca :	plural,	cəca, cəcaoŋ (cəcao)
dərya :	,,	dərya, dəryaoŋ (dəryao)
xəlifa :	,,	xəlifa, xəlifaoŋ (xəlifao)

bapdada, ancestors, usually does not decline at all, but occasionally it is like **dada**, making **bapdadaoŋ**, etc.

B. **xansamaŋ**, cook, steward, has all singular and nominative plural **xansamaŋ**; oblique plural, **xansamaoŋ** (vocative plural, **xansamao**).

C. Nouns ending in **-go**, **-jo**, such as **ɣəzəlgo**, writer of ghazals (lyrics); **əybjo**, over-critical; **jəngjo**, bellicose, insert **y** before **oŋ** or **o** of the plural oblique or vocative, as **ɣəzəlgoyoŋ**.

iii (*a*) Feminine nouns ending in **-ə** change **-ə** to **-a** and add **eŋ** in the nominative plural :—

> **faxtə**, dove, plural **faxtaeŋ**; **xalə**, mother's sister, **xalaeŋ**; **dəfə**, a time, a section in a book, **dəfaeŋ**.

---

* *xəlifa* is a word of Arabic origin and is feminine in form, but is masculine in use.

Arabic feminines ending in -ə, not often found in the plural, are declined in the same way. Such are :—

> **valdə**, mother; **fatyhə**, first *sura* in the Quran (sometimes masculine); **məlkə**, queen.

(*b*) The suffix **-sahybə**, lady, never used alone, takes the Persian plural -sahyban. In actual use the word is almost always **sahəb**. Thus the poet *Anis* speaks of **valydə sahəb**, a mother.

(*c*) Feminine nouns in **-a** ('ə, i.e. *əyn*, see p. 6) usually change **-a** to **-eŋ** in the plural :—

> vəza, fashion, etc., vəzeŋ.

SECOND DECLENSION

Almost all masculine nouns ending in **-a** or **-ə**. There are no feminine nouns in this declension.

	Singular	*Plural*
Nominative :	bəkra, goat	bəkre
Oblique :	bəkre	bəkroŋ
(Vocative :	bəkre	bəkro)

The ending **-əh** in Urdu script of some Arabic and Persian words is pronounced **-ə**. The spelling **-əh** is not usual in Roman, for the **h** is silent. As the short vowels written **ə**, **y**, **w** in Roman are rarely written at all in Urdu, **bəndəh** is in Urdu written simply ' bndh '. The oblique singular, vocative singular, and even the nominative plural are in Urdu script sometimes written exactly like the nominative singular, but never pronounced the same, for they change the ending **-əh** to **-e**.

Something similar holds of the words in the next section, those which end in **-a** (**-ə'**, i.e. *'əyn*, see *supra*, p. xxxix), such as **məwqa**. The oblique singular, vocative singular and nominative plural of **məwqa** are **məwqe**. When the short vowel of the second syllable in Urdu script is omitted, there is no difference in writing between the nominative singular and these cases. In Roman, however, they are written **məwqe**, and the nominative singular **məwqa**.

[See also **məzbəh**, p. 7.]

Nouns in **-a** often have a feminine form in **-i**; as **bəkra**, he-goat; **bəkri**, she-goat. Those in **-ə** sometimes have a similar form, as **bəccə**, male young one; **bəcci**, female; **bəndə**, servant (of God), your servant (ceremonious); feminine : **bəndi**; another form, **bandi**, means maid-servant.

Most masculine nouns in **-a** with final *'əyn* in Urdu script (i.e. **ə'**) belong to this declension. The commonest are :—

məwqa, opportunity	məwza, town
nəfa, profit	mwrəbba, square
zyla, small section of the country, part of a *'təhsil'*	bwrqa, dress covering woman from head to foot
mətba, printing press	mysra, line of verse

The last syllable of these is pronounced **-a**, as **məwqa**, **zyla**, etc., and they are declined accordingly. The *'əyn* must be inserted in writing the Urdu script. In Urdu script the nominative and oblique singular are the same, the short vowel of the second syllable not being written, but in Roman the oblique is **məwqe**.

məwqa, məwqe : məwqoŋ (məwqo)

mwtalea, reading, study, is often pronounced and declined as if it were **mwtala**. Otherwise it is as follows :—

mwtalea, mwtale

Actually the plural does not occur :—

vaqia, event, occurrence, has vaqe, vaqeoŋ (vaqeo)

A noun ending in **-aŋ** is declined like one in **-a**, except that the final vowel is nasal, thus :—

kuaŋ, a well; kueŋ, kuoŋ (kuoŋ)

Similar are **dhuaŋ**, smoke; **ruaŋ**, small hair on body.

məzbəh (pronounced **məzba**), place of sacrifice. As spoken this word is declined like **bəkra**—viz., **məzba**, **məzbe, məzboŋ, məzbo**. In Urdu script the nominative and oblique singular are alike.

rwpia, rwpəya, rupee; rwpəe, rwpəoŋ
kyrayə, rent, fare; kyrae, kyrayoŋ

When nouns of this declension are compounded with the Persian endings **-ban**, **-dar**, **-baz**, or **-var**, or, in the case of proper names, have the word **ʃah**, **xan**, or **lal** added to them, they are put into the oblique singular, as :—

ʈhekedar, contractor	ʈhəʈʈebaz, jester
gəlleban, shepherd	sylsylevar, in order
ryʃtedar, relative	

We also get **nygehban** (as well as **nygəhban**), although **nygah** is feminine and belongs to the first declension.

Proper names :—

buʈe ʃah, swbe xan, pyare lal

Some Persian and Arabic nouns ending in **-a** belong to the first declension (see pp. 4, 5). The following common ones, however, belong to the second. They are masculine.

təmaʃa, an entertainment	majra, remarkable event, wonder
məsala, ingredients	nəʃa, intoxication
dava, claim	mwsəlla, prayer-mat
mwjra, payment on account, salutation, dance	

mane, *m.pl.*, meaning or meanings. It is plural even when it means one meaning :—

ys ke ek mane yeh həyŋ	this is one meaning of it
do mane	two meanings
yn manoŋ meŋ	with this meaning, with these meanings

NOTES ON CASES

Accusative

The idea of the accusative is expressed in Urdu by either (*a*) the nominative, or (*b*) the oblique case with **ko** (to or for), or with some other postposition. **ko** is used when the noun or pronoun is thought of as definite. It is always necessary with names of persons, with first and second personal pronouns, and also with third personal pronouns when they refer to animate beings. With inanimate or unimportant things **ko** often has the effect of English " the ", as :—

bylli dekhi, saw a cat*   bylli ko dekha, saw the cat

Oblique or Postpositional

This is used with all postpositions.

Locative or Instrumental

This case has the same form as the oblique or post-positional, and therefore has not been given in the declensions above. It is used without postpositions; if a postposition occurs, the case is called not locative or instrumental, but oblique or postpositional. The locative or instrumental case is used :—

(*a*) to express *at* or *in* or *to* a place,
(*b*) in time phrases,
(*c*) as an instrumental case to show means or cause or instrument.

* See p. 52.

Very often the oblique or postpositional case with a postposition may be substituted for it.

Examples of Locative or Instrumental Case :—

voh syalkoṭ rəhta həy	he lives in Sialkot
voh gwjranvale gəya	he went to Gujranwala
mere ghər aya	he came to my house
dyn rat	night and day, continuously
ek bəje	at one o'clock
məngəl ke dyn	on Tuesday

Along with these should be given examples of an old locative, or perhaps oblique, case in **-oŋ** :—

twm dudhoŋ nəhao	bathe in milk, i.e., may you prosper !
həzaroŋ mən pani pəṛa	rain fell to the amount of thousands of maunds of water
səykṛoŋ admi khəṛe the	hundreds of men were standing (men to the number of hundreds)
məyŋ bhukhoŋ mər rəha huŋ	I am dying of hunger

Nouns referring to a single person are often made plural out of respect. They are always plural when connected with **twm** or **ap**, you, either expressed or understood. But the form of the noun remains singular except in the nominative of second declension nouns. The form for the oblique and the vocative remains singular.

twm bəcce ho	you are a child, *or* you are children
ap ke sahəbzade vəhaŋ the	your son was there, *or* your sons were there
ap ke sahəbzade ne kəha	your son said. This could not be **sahəbzadoŋ**, for that would mean "sons"
ap ki sahəbzadi kəhti həyŋ	your daughter says
ap ki sahəbzadiaŋ kəhti həyŋ	your daughters say

əy ləɽke, kya kər rəhe ho	boy, what are you doing?
əy ləɽko	boys !

Words denoting pairs of things, such as scissors, spectacles, are in most cases singular in Urdu.

qəynci, *f.*, scissors	əynək, *f.*, spectacles

Also all words for trousers, as : **paejamə**, *m.*, and **pətlun**, *f.* Exceptions to the rule are **dəstanə**, *m.*, glove; **dəstane**, gloves; **həthkəɽi**, *f.*, handcuff; **həthkəɽiaŋ**, handcuffs; also words for socks.

GENDER

Urdu has two genders, masculine and feminine. Though for many nouns it is impossible to give any rule that will help in determining their gender, for many others useful rules can be given.

Preliminary Rule which must be Regarded as Over-riding all other Rules :

All nouns which mean males are masculine and those meaning females are feminine. To this there is no real exception. The following peculiarities should be noted :—

  qəbilə, *m.*, family, and **ghər**, *m.*, house, family, are sometimes incorrectly used for "wife". They are always masculine.

  əsami, *f.*, vacancy, tenant. (When meaning "tenant" is sometimes masculine.)

  səvari, *f.*, riding; also means passenger in train, ship, carriage, etc.

  sərkar, *f.*, government. When it means "his honour" or "your honour" (to a man) it is masculine, but for "her honour" or "your honour" (woman) is feminine.

  polis, pwlis, *f.*, the police as a body.

  rəiyət, *f.*, plural : **ryaya**, subject, tenant.

  məvəyʃi, *f.*, cattle.

Few words denoting animals have both masculine and

feminine forms in ordinary use. Most have only one. Thus we have :—

Masculine :—

pəryndə, bird
wllu, owl
kəwva, crow
wqab, eagle

cita, cheetah
dəryndə, ravenous beast
həyvan, beast
bheɽia, wolf (feminine very rare)
teŋdva, panther, leopard (feminine rare)
bhalu, bear

Feminine :—

cyɽia, little bird
cil, kite
məyna, starling
mwnia, amadavat
bəʈer, quail
faxtə, dove

lomɽi, fox
məchli, fish
məkkhi, fly
gyləhri, squirrel
koel, '*koel*' (kind of cuckoo)

Note :—

cuha, *m.*, rat, has feminine **cuhia, cuhi**, which means mouse, not rat.

MASCULINE NOUNS

1. Nearly all nouns ending in **-a** or **-ə** are masculine.

Exceptions :—

Arabic nouns : most Arabic abstract nouns in **-a** are feminine, as :—

xəta, fault
bəla, calamity
kimia, chemistry

dwa, prayer
ʃyfa, ʃəfa, healing

and six more mentioned lower down under Arabic infinitives.

Also some which are not abstract :—

dwnya, world
həva, air

dəva (also dəvai), medicine
ɣyza, food

2. Practically every Arabic noun ending in -ə, i.e., -ə with
" silent **h** " (see p. 5), is masculine ; e.g. **mwamlə**, trans-
action, etc.

Exceptions :—

təwbə, *f.,* repentance
dəfə, *f.,* a time, as in " three times ", section of a book
mərtəbə, *f.,* a time, as in " three times ".

A few Persian words common in Urdu are feminine.
Only the following are worth noting :—

səza, *f.,* punishment	dəya, *f.,* deceit
pərva, *f.,* caring	kərəvansəra, inn

A few Sanskrit words common in Urdu are feminine.
Only the following are worth noting :—

ghəṭa, black cloud	mala, necklace
puja, worship	səbha, assembly
jəṭa, matted hair	sitla, smallpox
dəya, mercy, pity	kyrpa, mercy, kindness

A few common nouns in **-a** are feminine :—

Birds

məyna, *f.,* starling	mwnia, *f.,* female of small
cyṛia, *f.,* sparrow, little bird	bird
	ʃama, *f.,* pied robin

Geographical Names

gənga, *f.,* the Ganges	jəmna, *f.,* the Jumna
əjodhia, *f.,* name of a town	lənka, *f.,* Ceylon

Others are :—

gwṛia, *f.,* doll	pwṛia, *f.,* folded paper for
pəchva, *f.,* west wind	powder
əngia, *f.,* bodice	pwrva, *f.,* east wind
	janghia, *f.,* drawers

Of nouns in **-ə**, as distinguished from **-a**, hardly any are
feminine apart from those which denote females. We have

already noted **təwbə**, *f.*, repentance; **dəfə**, *f.*, a time or section of a book; and **mərtəbə**, a time.

Words denoting females are :—

xalə, *f.*, aunt
faxtə, *f.*, female dove
zəccə, *f.*, woman who has recently borne a child
madə, *f.*, a female
bərrə, *m.*, lamb, can be feminine if **madə**, female, is added.

-ə is a feminine ending in some Arabic nouns used in Urdu, as **məlkə**, queen, **valdə**, mother (see pp. 4, 5).

3. Nouns in **-ao** :—

bənao, *m.*, making, etc.   bhao, *m.*, price

Almost all are abstract.

Exception :—

nao, *f.*, boat

4. Nouns in **-pən** :—

bəcpən, *m.*, childhood

All are abstract.   No exceptions.

5. Arabic infinitives of the forms IV to VIII, and X are almost all masculine.   The following are the details.   The exceptions given are all that need be learnt except by advanced students.   Urdu has about 950 nouns of these forms, of which about 620 are masculine and 330 feminine.

All ending in **-i** are feminine.
All ending in **-ət** are feminine.
All ending in **-ə** (but not **-a**) are masculine.

Form IV **yqtal**; about 130 words, excluding those in **-ət** and **-ə**.

They are masculine, with four common exceptions :—

yslah, *f.*, correction   iza, *f.*, pain
ymdad, *f.*, help   ynʃa, *f.*, literary composition

Form V **təqəttwl** (in this form the second radical letter of the Arabic is doubled); about 173 words, plus fourteen ending in **-i** which are feminine. They are masculine, except three rather common ones :—

> təvəjjwh, *f.*, attention   təvəqqw, *f.*, hope
> təmənna, *f.*, desire

Form VI **təqatwl**; sixty-six words, excluding twelve in **-i** and three in **-ə**. The sixty-six are all masculine except one :—

> > tənaswb, *m.*, proportion
> > təvazw, *f.*, politeness

Form VII **ynqytal**; thirty-five words, all masculine.

Form VIII **yqtytal**; 130 words, all masculine, with ten exceptions, of which seven are common, viz. :—

> ybtyda, *f.*, beginning   yltyja, *f.*, petition
> yntyha, *f.*, end   yttyla, *f.*, announcement
> ehtyaj, *f.*, need   ehtyat, *f.*, care
> ystylah, *f.*, conventional
>   usage in literature

Form X **ystyqtal**; sixty-eight words, all masculine with four exceptions, two of them common, viz. :—

> ystedad, *f.*, capacity, ability   ystyda, *f.*, request

Words of the type **mwfaylət**, **mwfaylə**; these all end in either **-ə** and are masculine, or in **-ət** and are feminine.

> mwhasrə, *m.*, besieging   mwhafyzət, *f.*, protection

mamlə, *m.*, affair, etc., omits the first and third vowels of the Arabic word, and thus has two syllables instead of four.

FEMININE NOUNS

1. Nouns ending in **-i**. The only exceptions to be noted are :—

> (*a*) The every-day words **pani**, *m.*, water; **ji**, *m.*, heart, etc.; **ġhi**, *m.*, a kind of oily butter; **moti**, *m.*, pearl; **dəhi**, *m.*, curds.

(b) Names of months : **jənvəri**, January; **jwlai**, July; **fərvəri**, February; **məy**, May.

Some people make these feminine, others again give the feminine gender to English months ending in **-i**, but the masculine gender to Persian months with the same ending.

(c) **mazi**, *m.* and *f.*, past tense (sometimes feminine) : **mwtəəddi**, *m.*, transitive

Nouns of the second declension—i.e., nouns in **-a** or **-ə**, which denote animate beings—usually change **-a** to **-i** to denote the female. See under *Second Declension*, page 5.

2. Abstract nouns ending in **-ət**, as :—

yzzət, *f.*, honour   hyfazət, *f.*, protection

See also under Arabic infinitives.

3. Abstract nouns ending in **-yʃ**. Most of these are Persian. No exceptions.

danyʃ, *f.*, wisdom   malyʃ, *f.*, rubbing

4. Abstract nouns ending in **-hət** and **-vət**. No exceptions.

ghəbrahət, *f.*, distress,   bənavət, *f.*, making
perturbation

5. Most nouns ending in **-ah**. For **-ġah**, see next paragraph. Two common exceptions :—

gwnah, *m.*, sin   nykah, *m.*, marriage ceremony

Between thirty and forty nouns end in **-ġah**, place; all are feminine except :—

qybləgah, *m.*, ceremonious word for father
xərgah, *m.*, royal tent or palace

təmaʃagah, place of amusement, and **bəndərgah**, harbour, are both masculine and feminine.

6. Arabic infinitives of the form **təqtil** (form II) are all feminine except one :—

təsxir, *f.*, conquest   taviz, *m.*, amulet

There are approximately 230 of these nouns. In addition there are forty nouns belonging to this form which end in either **-ət** (all feminine) or **-ə** (all masculine). See also page 13.

7. Words in **-əh** or **-eh**, with the **h** pronounced at least in deliberate speech, are nearly all feminine, as :—

> jəgəh jəgeh, *f.*, place
> vəjəh vəjeh, *f.*, reason, cause
> swləh swleh, *f.*, peace

Letters of the Alphabet

There are thirty-five letters in the alphabet (see Table *supra*), of which twenty-one are feminine, viz. :—

Seventeen ending in **-e** (including **toe** and **zoe**).
Three ending in **-l** (**dal**, **d̤al**, **zal**).
One ending in **-o** (**vao**).

The remaining fourteen are masculine.

ADJECTIVES

Adjectives, except most of those which end in **-a**, and some which end in **-ə** (see p. 17), are indeclinable.

Almost all adjectives ending in **-a**, and some ending in **-ə**, are declined as follows :—

They end in **-a** or **-ə** before or when connected with masculine nouns in the nominative singular, or in what we may call the objective or accusative case *without* **ko**.

They end in **-e** for any other part of the singular and for the whole plural of masculine nouns.

They end in **-i** with any feminine noun.

uŋca məkan, a high house	uŋce məkan, high houses
uŋce məkan meŋ, in a high house	uŋce məkanoŋ pər, upon high houses

ləmbi gaɽi, a long carriage   ləmbi gaɽiaŋ, long carriages
ləmbi gaɽi meŋ, in a long   ləmbi gaɽioŋ se, from long
  carriage   carriages

Persian and Arabic adjectives in **-a** rarely change.
Adjectives in **-ə** do not often change. These are
generally Persian or Arabic.

    meri maŋ əbhi zyndə həy   my mother is still alive

The following is a fairly full list of those which change :—

fwlanə, a certain	mandə (in **thəkamandə**),
gəndə, dirty, foul	tired
xasə, pretty good, etc.	becarə, bycarə, unfortun-
kəminə, mean, base	ate, poor
sadə, plain, simple	-zadə, born of, i.e., son
divanə, mad	

The adjectival ending **-zadə**, as in **reiszadə**, gentleman's
son, is changed to **-zadi** to mean daughter. **beğanə**, foreign,
not one's own, and **tazə**, fresh, generally change.

  jwda, separate, very rarely changes; **zəra**, a little, etc.,
adverb or adjective, sometimes changed in former days,
but now practically never changes.

ADJECTIVES AS NOUNS

 All adjectives can be used as nouns, and when so used are
declined as nouns. It follows that an adjective which does
not change for the feminine cannot have a feminine form
when used as a noun. Thus we can have **bycari**, meaning
poor woman, but we cannot have a feminine form for
bwzwrğ, elderly, etc., or **zyndə**, living.

bycari ka koi ghər nəhiŋ	the poor woman has no house
həmare bwzwrgoŋ ne kəha	our elders or ancestors have said
dəwlətməndoŋ meŋ	among the rich
yəriboŋ ki roṭi	poor people's food

bwzwrg, yərib and **dəwlətmənd** have no feminine form.

ka, of, added to nouns and pronouns, forms an adjective. Being an adjective ending in **-a**, it agrees with the following noun:—

bhaika beṭa	brother's son
ghər ki khyṛkiaŋ	the house's windows
bənie ki dukanka dərvazə	the shopkeeper's shop's door
bəṛe admioŋka məkan	great men's house (house suitable for great men)
sukhi ləkṛika ḍher	a heap of dry wood

ADJECTIVES AS ADVERBS

Adjectives are often used as adverbs; when so used they agree with their nouns or pronouns like adjectives. To understand the rule for agreement, note the following cases:—

voh əccha gati həy	she sings well
əccha lykhti həy	she writes well

In these two sentences **gati**, sing, and **lykhti**, write, have a transitive sense, and **əccha** is a kind of object, meaning " a good thing ".

bəṛa, big, great, is sometimes, but not often, used as an adverb meaning " very ". For " very ", **bəhwt** is commoner. The four-volume Urdu dictionary, **nur wl lwyat**, under **bəṛa** or **bəṛe** gives the following instances of the meaning " very " :—

bəṛi bhari yəlti	a very great error
bəṛa zyddi	very obstinate
bəṛa zalym	very tyrannical
bəṛe nek	very good or pious
bəṛe pak	very holy
etc.	

In these **bəṛa** is declined like an adjective.

Repetition of adjectives—see under Repetition of Words, pp. 130–33.

COMPARISON OF ADJECTIVES

In Urdu there are no real forms for the comparative and superlative. Comparison is expressed by the postposition **se**, than, with the ordinary form of the adjective.

kwtte-se choṭa,   dog-than small,   smaller than a dog
səb-se choṭa,   all-than small,   smallest of all

Sometimes **zyadə**, more ; **əwr bhi**, more still ; **kəhiŋ**, much more ; or the words **mwqabylə**, **nysbət**, comparison, are used.

bylli zyadə (əwr bhi) syani həy — the cat is cleverer (still cleverer)

bəkre-se bəkri zyadə kali həy — the she-goat is blacker than the he-goat

Here we could say : əwr bhi kali, still blacker.

mali ki nysbət sais hoʃyar həy — in comparison with the gardener, the groom is intelligent, i.e., he is more intelligent

mali se kəhiŋ hoʃyar — much more intelligent than the gardener

hyndwstan ke mwqabyle meŋ ynglystan bəhwt choṭa həy — in comparison with India, England is very small

A few Persian comparatives in **-tər**, and superlatives in **-tərin**, are used in Urdu, but they can hardly be said to contain much idea of comparison. Thus :—

donoŋ meŋ yeh behtər həy — in the two, i.e., of the two, this is better

Here for **behtər** we could say : əccha, good.

Similarly, **bəhwt behtər** means "very good", "all right". **kəmtərin**, your insignificant servant, is used in signing letters, but not for purposes of comparison. Literally it means "least".

We do, however, sometimes find **yeh behtərin təriqə**

həy, this is the best method; and a few similar expressions.

Arabic comparatives, too, have lost their comparative meaning.

əfzəl, excellent ala, exalted

NUMERALS

CARDINAL NUMBERS

1 ek	29 wnəttis	57 sətavən
2 do	30 tis	58 əṭṭhavən
3 tin	31 ykəttis	59 wnsəṭh
4 car	32 bəttis	60 saṭh
5 paŋc	33 tetis, teŋtis	61 yksəṭh
6 che, chəy	34 cəwŋtis	62 basəṭh
7 sat	35 pəyŋtis	63 tresəṭh
8 aṭh	36 chəttis	64 cəwsəṭh,
9 nəw	37 səyŋtis	cəwŋsəṭh
10 dəs	38 əṛtis	65 pəyŋsəṭh
11 gyarə *	39 wntalis	66 cheasəṭh
12 barə	40 calis	67 sərsəṭh
13 terə	41 yktalis	68 əṛsəṭh
14 cəwdə	42 bealis	69 wnhəttər
15 pəndrə	43 tetalis, teŋtalis	70 səttər
16 solə	44 cəwalis	71 ykhəttər
17 sətrə	45 pəyŋtalis	72 bəhəttər
18 əṭṭharə	46 chealis	73 tyhəttər
19 wnnis	47 səyŋtalis	74 cəwhəttər
20 bis	48 əṛtalis	75 pəchəttər
21 ykkis	49 wncas	76 chyhəttər
22 bais	50 pəcas	77 səthəttər
23 teis	51 ykyavən	78 əṭhəttər
24 cəwbis	52 bavən	79 wnasi
25 pəccis	53 trepən	80 əssi
26 chəbbis	54 cəwvən	81 ykasi
27 səttais	55 pəcpən	82 beasi
28 əṭṭhais	56 chəppən	83 tyrasi

* Final ə (for əh) has an open quality somewhat like that of a.

84 cəwrasi	92 banve	99 nynnanve
85 pycasi	93 tyranve	100 səw
86 chyasi	94 cəwranve	101 ek səw ek
87 sətasi	95 pycanve	156 ek səw chəppən
88 əṭhasi	96 chyanve	125 səva səw
89 nəwasi	97 səttanve	250 ḍhai səw
90 nəvve	98 əṭṭhanve	375 pəwne car səw
91 ykanve		

1000 (ek) həzar; 100,000 (ek) lakh; 10,000,000 (ek) kəroṛ
  or kəṭoṛ

For **səva**, **ḍhai** and **pəwne** in the above numbers, 125,
250 and 375, see below.

854,697,253 is **pycasi kəroṛ, chealis lakh, səttanve
həzar, do səw trepən.**

ORDINAL NUMBERS

1st pəhyla (fem.	3rd tisra (fem.	5th pəŋcvaŋ
pəhyli)	tisri)	6th chəṭa, chəṭha
2nd dusra	4th cəwtha	

After the first six **-vaŋ** is added to the cardinal.

12th barəvaŋ	16th soləvaŋ
42nd bealisvaŋ	100th səwvaŋ

Ordinals are declined like adjectives in **-a** such as **bəṛa**;
those ending in **-vaŋ** have the final vowel nasalised.

tisri bar, the third time   wnnisviŋ dəfə, the nine-
                                          teenth time

ek, one, is added to some numerals to express the idea
of approximately, as : **bis ek**, about 20; **car ek**, about 4;
səw ek, about 100. **do ek**, however, means "a few".

After the first few numerals only the tens (20, 30, 40,
etc.), 100, 1000, and a few others are used with **ek** in this
way.

ek adh means "a very few, one here and there".

do car and **do car dəs panc** mean "a few" :—

  do car dəs panc admi jəma   a few people collected
  hue

I. Fractional Numbers

pəwn, meaning "three-quarters", is used with weights and measures, for the time 12.45 a.m. or p.m., and with **kəroṛ** (**kəṛoṛ**), ten million. It is always singular.

pəwn mil	three-quarters of a mile
pəwn ser	three-quarters of a ser (ser = 2 lbs.)
pəwn bəje	at 12.45 a.m. or p.m.
pəwn bəja həy	it is 12.45 o'clock

pəwne (but not **pəwn**), minus a quarter, is used with all numerals from 2 to 99.

pəwne car, $3\frac{3}{4}$ pəwne solə ane, $15\frac{3}{4}$ annas
pəwne pycasi, $84\frac{3}{4}$

səva, plus a quarter, is used with weights and measures, with all numerals except the numeral one, and for the time 1.15 a.m. or p.m. It takes the noun in the singular.

səva mən, a maund and a quarter (maund = about 78 lbs.)
səva bəje, at 1.15   seva calis, $40\frac{1}{4}$

Note that when used with **səw**, **həzar**, **lakh**, **kəroṛ**, it adds a quarter of the whole amount.

səva həzar, 1250   səva kəroṛ, 12,500,000

ḍeṛh, one and a half, is used with weights and measures, for the time 1.30, and with the numbers **səw**, **həzar**, **lakh**, **kəroṛ**, to which it adds half the total amount.

ḍeṛh rwpia, a rupee and a   ḍeṛh səw, 150
  half   ḍeṛh lakh, 150,000
ḍeṛh bəje, at 1.30

ḍhai, two and a half, is used in the same way as **ḍeṛh**, and with the same words, but normally takes a plural noun, whereas **ḍeṛh** takes the singular.

ḍhai gəz, $2\frac{1}{2}$ yards   ḍhai pəyse, $2\frac{1}{2}$ pice
ḍhai həzar, 2,500   ḍhai bəje, at 2.30

saṛhe, plus a half, is used with all numbers from 3 to 99;

it is not used without a number. It is not used with **səw, həzar, lakh** or **kəroṛ**.

saṛhe car fwṭ, 4½ ft.   saṛhe sat səw, 750
saṛhe tin bəje, 3.30 o'clock   saṛhe tin lakh, 350,000

səykṛa, hundred, is used in two ways :—

(a) for per cent., and is then undeclined; as per hundred :—

am tin rwpəe səykṛa bykte   mangoes were selling at Rs. 3
the   per hundred

(b) **səykṛoŋ**, hundreds :—

səykṛoŋ admi jəma ho gəe   hundreds of men collected
səykṛoŋ ghəṛe pani pəṛ gəya   hundreds of gharas of water
                             fell on him, i.e., he was
                             greatly humiliated

sədi, f., a Persian word, means "hundred" and is used as follows :—

(a) per cent., per hundred, in the expression : **fi sədi.**

ws ne fi sədi nəvve ko naraz   he annoyed ninety out of
kər dia   every hundred, or ninety
                              per cent. of them

(b) to mean "century", as : **bisviŋ sədi,** the 20th century.

A number of Persian and Arabic numerals are used in high-flown Urdu; it is not necessary to give them here.

The only common collective numeral noun is **koṛi**, f., a score.

II. Fractional Parts

There are words for a half, a third, and a quarter, but after that the ordinal number is used with **hyssə**, m., part.

adha, adh, half   pao, chəwthai, a quarter
nysf, half   pəŋcvaŋ hyssə, a fifth part
tyhai, a third part   chəṭa hyssə, a sixth part

bisvaŋ hyssə, a twentieth part

do tyhai, two-thirds

tin cəwthai, three-quarters

Examples:—

pao kos, a quarter of a kos

do tyhai sytare, two-thirds of the stars

tin cəwthai səməndər, three-quarters of the sea

tyhai rat, a third of the night

adhe sytare, half the stars

adh ser, half a ser

In all these cases the noun at the end will decide the number and gender of the verb or adjective following :—

tin cəwthai səməndər kala tha

three-quarters of the sea was black

Apart from actual arithmetical terminology, fractions more complicated than these can be expressed as follows :—

paŋc meŋ se tin hysse

three parts out of five; three-fifths

nynnanve meŋ se pycasi hysse

eighty-five parts out of ninety-nine

III. " Times "

" Times ", as in so many times, or as the size of any-thing, is expressed by **gwna**; *feminine*, **gwni.**

dwgwna, duna, dogwna

tygwna, tin gwna

cəwgwna, car gwna

twice the size of, etc.

three times the size of, etc.

four times the size of, etc.

After that the ordinary cardinal numbers are used, as :—

pəcas gwna

səw gwna

yeh bəṛi kytab ws choṭi se aṭh gwni bhari həy

fifty times the size of

100 times the size of, or as much as

this big book is eight times as heavy as that little one

do cənd (indeclinable) is the Persian for **dogwna**, and is fairly common in Urdu.

IV. " Time " or " Times "

" Time " or " times ", in statements of frequency, is expressed by **dəfə**, *f.*; **bar,** *f.*; and **mərtəbə**, *f.* The noun is always singular.

pəhyli mərtəbə (or dəfə)	the first time
do mərtəbə (or dəfə)	twice
ek dəfə	once, once upon a time
tin bar	three times
kytni dəfə	how often ?
əb ki dəfə	(now's the time), this time

dəfə is the commonest of these words.

V. Single, Double, Threefold and Fourfold

Single, double, threefold, fourfold, for garments, cloth, strands in a rope or in twine, also of words or sentences said singly or repeated, are expressed by :—

ykəhra ; *f.*, ykəhri,	single
dohra ; *f.*, dohri	double
tehra ; *f.*, tehri	threefold
cəwhra ; *f.*, cəwhri	fourfold

Higher numbers are not ordinarily used.

The word **səvari**, a riding, is used with one of these words for a conveyance, such as **ḍoli**, a dooly, or **palki**, *f.*, a palanquin, carrying one, two, three or four passengers at the time spoken of. Thus **dohri səvari** means a conveyance with two passengers.

VI. Indefinite Numerical Adjectives

See page 31.

kəi, kəi-ek, a good many, some	kəy, how many ?
bəhwt, many	thoṛe (plural of thoṛa), a few, few
baz, some	kwch, some (*indecl.*)
səb, all	sare (plural of sara), all
kwl, the whole of, in totality	hər, every
əksər, most, the majority	əwr, others

kwch with singular noun is like English " some " with a singular noun. With plural nouns (usually denoting human beings), it means " some, a few ".

Note: **kəi admi**, a good many people; **kəy admi**, how many people?

VII. Expressions like: all four, all ten, both of them, all ten of them

Expressions like: all four, all ten, both of them, all ten of them, are rendered in two ways :—

(a) By adding **-oŋ** to the number. This occurs only with a few of the smaller numbers, as :—

tinoŋ, all three   dəsoŋ, all ten

do takes the form **donoŋ**.

(b) By saying the number twice over, the first time in the genitive.

səw ke səw	the whole hundred
pəcas ke pəcas	the whole fifty
pəndrə ke pəndrə	all the fifteen
aṭh ke aṭh	the eight of them

See special note, p. 88.

PRONOUNS

The vocative, which of course occurs only in second person pronouns, is the same as the nominative. Pronouns have no special forms for the feminine.

twm kya kəhti ho	what are you (fem.) saying?
ap kəhaŋ gəi thiŋ	where had you (fem.) gone?

həm, we, is sometimes treated as masculine even though referring to women. The rules are as follows :—

(a) When **həm** is used by a woman speaking of herself alone, it is masculine plural :—

həm əbhi ləwʈ ae həyŋ   I have just returned

(b) If **həm** refers to several women, and a plural feminine noun is inserted, the verb is feminine :—

həm donoŋ ləɽkiaŋ khel   both of us girls were playing
rəhi thiŋ

(c) When there is no noun, **həm** may be either masculine or feminine. Azad, the great Urdu stylist, makes some women say :—

jəb tək həmari bat nə kəh   until you say what we want,
dega, nə pylaeŋgi   we shall not give you
                            water

In this sentence **pylaeŋge** would also have been correct. In all these it makes no difference whether the word **həm** is actually expressed or not. The use of **həm** for " I " is common among old Delhi families in talking to servants and subordinates, but it should not be copied by foreigners. The student should always say **məyŋ** for " I ".

With the postposition **ne**, by, some pronouns have a form differing from the ordinary oblique. For the use of **ne** see p. 49. The postposition **ka** is not normally used with pronouns of the first and second persons (see a few lines down), a possessive adjective is used instead.

Nominative :	məyŋ, I	həm, we
Possessive Adjective :	mera	həmara
Ordinary Oblique :	mwjh	həm
Oblique with **ne** :	məyŋ	həm

Nominative :	tu, thou	twm, you
Possessive Adjective :	tera	twmhara
Ordinary Oblique :	twjh	twm
Oblique with **ne** :	tu	twm

For **mwjh ko**, **həm ko**, **twjh ko**, **twm ko**, we may always say **mwjhe**, **həmeŋ**, **twjhe**, **twmheŋ**, without **ko**. Europeans should make a habit of using these short forms constantly.

ka can be employed with **mwjh**, **həm**, **twjh**, **twm**, if a

c

noun, or adjective used as a noun, comes between the
pronoun and **ka** :—

| həm Pənjabioŋ ka dəstur | a custom of us Panjabis |
| mwjh bədqysmət ka hal | the condition of me, un-fortunate one |

mera, həmara, tera, twmhara, are adjectives in **-a**
declined like **unca** and **ləmba**; see p. 16. They agree in
gender and number with the thing possessed.

| meri lə<u>r</u>ki, my girl | twmhare nəwkər, your ser-vants |

tu, thou, is employed in prayer, in poetry, and in conversation with little children.

twm, you, meaning either one person or more than one,
is used in addressing boys and girls, servants, small shop-
keepers, ordinary villagers, and other people of similar
position.   For people of higher rank than these **ap** is used.

ap is a respectful word for you (one or more persons).
It takes its verb in the third person plural and is indeclinable.   In ceremonious Urdu it often means he, she, they,
the verb always being third plural.

> ap kəwn həyŋ?   who are you? who are they?

If I meet a friend with a stranger and say **ap kəwn həyŋ ?**
the only possible meaning is, " Who is he, your friend? "
But normally it would mean, " Who are you?   I do not
recognize you."

> ap kəb jaeŋgi   when will you (feminine) go?

An adjective related to **twm** or **ap**, or agreeing with
a noun related to **twm** or **ap**, is plural, even when only
one person is addressed or spoken of.   Consequently adjectives in **-a** or **-ə** which change will in such cases end in **-e**
when masculine and **-i** when feminine.   Other adjectives
do not change.

| ap bə<u>r</u>e bhəlamanəs həyŋ | you are a very worthy man |
| twm cho<u>t</u>e ho | you are small |

Both these sentences may refer to either one person or to several persons.

yeh, voh

Nominative :	yeh, this; he, she, it (all near)	yeh, these, they (near)
Ordinary Oblique :	ys	yn
Oblique with **ne** :	ys	ynhon
Nominative :	voh, that, he, she, it (not near)	voh, those, they (not near)
Ordinary Oblique :	ws	wn
Oblique with **ne** :	ws	wnhoŋ

When **yeh** and **voh**, referring to inanimate things, occur as direct objects, they are often omitted; indeed, most pronouns are omitted far more frequently than in English.

məyŋ ne dekha	I saw it
phyr kya kəha?	then what did you say? (or he, or she, they say)
zəmin dekhi? nəhiŋ dekhi	have you seen the land? No, I have not

kəwn, jo

	Singular	*Plural*
Nominative :	kəwn, who?	kəwn
Ordinary Oblique :	kys	kyn
Oblique with **ne** :	kys	kynhoŋ
Nominative :	jo, who, which	jo
Ordinary Oblique :	jys	jyn
Oblique with **ne** :	jys	jynhoŋ

As well as **məyŋ**, **həm**, **tu**, **twm**, the singular and plural of **yeh**, **voh**, **kəwn** and **jo** have short forms for use with **ko**.

Sing. Nom.	*Obl. with ko.*	*Pl. Nom.*	*Obl. with ko.*
yeh	yse, ys ko	yeh	ynheŋ, yn ko
voh	wse, ws ko	voh	wnheŋ, wn ko
kəwn	kyse, kys ko	kəwn	kynheŋ, kyn ko
jo	jyse, jys ko	jo	jynheŋ, jyn ko

koi

Nominative : **koi**, some one, any one. No plural in common use. Oblique : **kysi**.

The difference between **kys**, the oblique of **kəwn**, who, and **kysi**, the oblique of **koi**, some one, any one, should be noticed :—

       kysi ka, someone's   kys ka, whose?

koi is also an indeclinable adverb meaning approximately, as :—

məharaja ne koi car mən-dyroŋ ka kam ʃwru kəraya	The Maharaja got work begun in about four temples

As with nouns, the nominative form of pronouns is often used for the objective, but this never happens with First and Second Personal Pronouns.

kya

kya, what? is used only in the singular. The oblique is **kahe**.

kahe ka, of what?	kahe ko, for what, why?
kahe meŋ ḍala, what did you put it in?	kahe pər rəkkha, what did you put it on?

kwch

kwch, something, anything, is not declined and cannot be used with a postposition. As an adjective with a plural noun it means a few :—

kwch ləɽke	some boys
kwch zəmindaroŋ ka bəɽa nwqsan hua	some farmers suffered great loss (lit. some farmers' great loss became)

so

so is used only as a correlative to **jo** and cannot be followed by a postposition.

    jo boega so kaṭega   what he sows he will reap

əwr

əwr, other, others :—

    əwroŋ ne kia   others did it
    əwroŋ se maŋgo   ask it of others

All pronouns, except **məyŋ**, **həm**, **tu**, **twm**, can be used as adjectives qualifying nouns.

A list of Indefinite Adjectives of Number was given on p. 25; the following can in conversation, but not in literature, be also pronouns :—

Nominative	*Conversational Oblique*
kəi ek, some, a good many	—
kəi, a good many	kəioŋ
bəhwt, many	bəhwtoŋ
baz, some	baz, bazoŋ
əksər, most people	əksəroŋ (rare even in speech)
səb, all	səb, səbhoŋ

The following compound pronouns should be noted :—

Nominative	*Oblique.*
jo koi, whoever (very rare in nominative)	jys kysi (common in speech)
jo kwch, whatever	—
əwr kəwn, who else ?	əwr kysi
əwr kwch, something else	—
kwch əwr, some more	—
səb kwch, everything	—
əwr kya, what else ?	əwr kahe
əwr koi ⎱ someone else, any-	əwr kysi
koi əwr ⎰ one else	kysi əwr

The idea of no one, nothing, is expressed by adding a negative to **koi** and **kwch**.

koi nəhiŋ, no one   kwch nəhiŋ, nothing

koi koi means a few, one here and there; it is singular.

kwch kwch means some, a little; with a plural noun, a few, some.

koi nə koi, some one or other; this can be an adjective.
kwch nə kwch, something or other.

koi nə koi jəgəh   some place or other
kysi nə kysi jəgəh   in some place or other

Beginners should notice the difference between **kysi** and **kys** :

kysi comes from koi : kysi ka, some one's
kys comes from kəwn : kys ka, whose?

ap (reflexive), and xwd

We have seen the respectful use of **ap**. There is another use. **ap** is often reflexive, meaning self or selves, as in myself, yourselves.

məyŋ ap, I myself	həm ap, we ourselves
tu ap, thou thyself	twm ap, you yourselves
voh ap, he himself, she her-self, it itself, they them-selves	
ləɽka ap, the boy himself	ləɽkiaŋ ap, the girls them-selves

The form **ap ap** is not used. In this case the word **xwd** is used, **ap xwd**.

xwd means the same as **ap** (reflexive), but it is never followed by a postposition. It is always connected with the subject of the sentence, and when the subject is followed by **ne**, **xwd** follows **ne** :—

məyŋ ne xwd kəha, *or* məyŋ   I said it myself
    ne ap kəha

ap (with postpositions)

With **ko** the usual form is **əpne ap ko**; less common, **əpne ko**.

With **meŋ**; **apəs meŋ**, among ourselves, yourselves, themselves.

With other postpositions; **əpne**, as **əpne se choṭa**, smaller than himself, herself, ourselves, themselves, etc.

əpna

The word **əpna** is used for my, our, your, their, his, her, when referring to the subject of the sentence. This occurs when the possessor is the subject. It is like the Latin *suus*, but applied to all persons, both numbers and both genders.

voh əpni kytab pəṛh rəha həy	he is reading his book
voh ws ki kytab pəṛh rəha həy	he is reading another person's book
həm əpni kytabeŋ pəṛhte həyŋ	we read our books

The above rule is not always strictly adhered to, thus we may have :—

məyŋ ne wse əpni bivi ko marte dekha	I saw him beating his wife
wn meŋ se kysi ko əpni beyzzəti nə kərane do	do not let any one of them permit himself to be insulted

[beyzzəti kərna, insult;
beyzzəti kərana, cause dishonour to be done, i.e., let one-self be insulted]

In these sentences **ws ki** is changed to **əpni** because of its position. Ambiguity is possible, but the context usually prevents this.

Other examples :—

ws ke ləhje se voh ɣəyr zəban malum hota həy	from his pronunciation he appears to be a foreigner

| wse əpne bəccoŋ se bat kərne do | let him speak to his children |
| twm əpne bəccoŋ se wse bat kərne do | let him speak to your children |

The position of **wse** helps to decide the meaning here.

ws ki hərkətoŋ se bədmaʃ maluɱ hota həy	by his deeds he seems to be a scoundrel
voh əpni ʃəhadət se bədmaʃ sabyt hua	(just think !) it was through his own evidence that he was proved a scoundrel
yeh kys ki pleʈeŋ həyŋ ?	(to a servant :) whose are these plates ?
əpni həyŋ	they are ours (i.e., my master's)
əpni jan səb ko əziz həy	every one loves his own life
əpnoŋ ki mədəd hər vəqt kərni cahie	one should always help one's own people

əpna is often added to a possessive pronoun or noun for the sake of emphasis :—

| yeh meri əpni kytab həy | this is my own book |
| voh sahəb ka əpna ghoɽa həy | that is the gentleman's own horse |

sa

The word **sa** is added to nouns, pronouns and sometimes verbs. The following are its meanings.

1. Like.

| ʃer sa admi | a man like a tiger |
| ʃer si surət | a man looking like a tiger |

This might also be :—

| ʃer ki si surət | appearance rather like a tiger |
| bərf se badəl | snow-like clouds |

Phrases like **ʃer sa janvər**, a tiger-like animal, are not used if the first noun ends in **-a** or **-ə** ; thus they do not say

kwtta sa janvər; but if the order is changed and the second noun comes first the phrase is correct, as :—

voh ghoɽa tha kwtta sa	that horse was dog-like (of the size of a dog)

In these cases **sa** agrees in gender and number with the second noun, i.e., the noun with which comparison is made.

Instead of **sa** immediately after the noun (i.e., without **ka** intervening), **jəysa** is much commoner, as :—

kwtte jəysa	dog-like

The noun preceding **jəysa** is in the oblique case.

2. So to speak, as it were :—

ek nala sa bəhta tha	a stream, so to speak, was flowing
ek nədi si bəhti thi	a river, as it were, was flowing
voh mər si gəi	she almost died (she, as it were, died). This means she was shocked or dismayed

sa agrees in number and gender with the subject.

3. When it is used with adjectives, it is hard to say what meaning, if any, it has. This explains why it is sometimes said to be intensive, having the sense of " very ", and sometimes to have the opposite sense, like English -ish. In most cases it is a mere habit of speech like the " very " in the common English phrase " he's not very well ". Actually it is never really intensive.

ytna sa, so much	bəhwt se, many
ytni si (*f.*)	
kala sa cehrə, a face, so to speak, black ; a blackish face, or simply : a black face	

When it follows the first and second personal pronouns, the pronouns are in the ordinary oblique case :—

mwjh sa, like me   twjh sa, like thee

sa is not used with **yeh**, **voh**, **jo**, **kya** and **kwch**. Added to **kəwn** it slightly changes the meaning :—

kəwn

voh kəwn ləṛki həy?	what girl is that? (I know nothing about her)
voh kəwn si ləṛki həy?	which girl is that? (out of the girls who, I know, are in the class)

kəwn is used as a pronominal adjective with nouns denoting human beings.

jəwn

Added to **jəwn**, an obsolete form of **jo**, it has a similar meaning :—

jəwn sa caho, le jao	take away whichever you like
jəwn si ghəṛi pəsənd həy, xərid lo	whichever watch you like (lit. is agreeable), buy

koi

koi sa is " any you like ".

PRONOMINAL ADJECTIVES

əysa, like this, this kind of	jəysa (relative), like which, which kind of
kəysa, what kind of, like what?	vəysa, like that (chiefly correlative to **jəysa**)
jəysi bat swnta həy, kərta həy	he talks as he hears others talk [lit. what-kind-of thing he hears, that-kind he does (i.e., speaks)]

ytna, so much or many	jytna, as much or many (relative)
kytna, how much or many?	wtna, so much or many (usually correlative to **jytna**)

The following table of common adjectives, pronouns and adverbs should be studied :—

Near :
    yeh, this   əysa, this kind of   ytna, so much or many

Remote :
    voh, that   vəysa, that   ,,   wtna, so much or many

Interrogative :
    kəwn, who?   kəysa, what ,, ? kytna, how much or many?

Relative :
    jo, who   jəysa, which ,, jytna, as much or many

Near :	əb, now	yəhaŋ, here
Remote :	təb, then	vəhaŋ, there
Interrogative :	kəb, when?	kəhaŋ, where?
Relative :	jəb, when	jəhaŋ, where

təb, then, generally used in reasoning; not often of time except as correlative to **jəb**.

Others have been given under Indefinite Adjectives of number, see pp. 25–6 and 31.   Add :—

    yəyr, other, foreign   fwlana, a certain
    kya, what   əwr, other, different, more

əwr

When **əwr** is unstressed, it means " and "; when stressed, " other, more, different ", etc.

bylli əwr kwtta	a cat and a dog
yeh bylli əwr həy	this is a different cat
tin əwr	three more

əwroŋ ki rae	the opinion of others
əwr bhi	still more
kwch əwr do	give some more
voh to əwr mamlə tha	that was another affair or business

ɣəyr

| ɣəyr qəwmeŋ | foreign nations or races |
| ɣəyr admi | a stranger |

kya

kya is used only with the nominative form of a noun.

yeh kya bevwqufi həy !   what folly is this !

THE VERB

For the occasional use of **həm**, we, as masculine, even when referring to women, see p. 27, under Pronouns.

is, was

məyŋ huŋ, I am	həm həyŋ, we are
tu həy, thou art	twm ho, you are
	ap həyŋ, you are
voh həy, he, she, it is	voh həyŋ, they are

Feminine the same.

Negative :—

məyŋ . . . nəhiŋ, *or* məyŋ nəhiŋ huŋ, I am not
tu . . . nəhiŋ, *or* tu nəhiŋ həy, thou art not
voh . . . nəhiŋ, *or* voh nəhiŋ həy, he, she, it is not
həm . . . nəhiŋ, *or* həm nəhiŋ həyŋ, we are not
twm . . . nəhiŋ, *or* twm nəhiŋ ho, you are not
ap . . . nəhiŋ, *or* ap nəhiŋ həyŋ, you are not
voh . . . nəhiŋ, *or* voh nəhiŋ həyŋ, they are not

The omission of **huŋ, həy**, etc., is explained by the fact that **nəhiŋ** itself means is, am, are not ; as well as no, not.

THE VERB

Example :—

tu cor həy, you are a thief

məyŋ tha, I was
tu tha, thou wert

voh tha, he, it was

məyŋ cor nəhiŋ, I am not a thief

həm the, we were
twm the, you were
ap the, you were
voh the, they were

Feminine :—

məyŋ thi
tu thi

voh thi

həm thiŋ (sometimes **the**)
twm thiŋ
ap thiŋ
voh thiŋ

Negative :—

nə or **nəhiŋ** is inserted and may not be omitted.
məyŋ nə tha or **məyŋ nəhiŋ tha**   I was not

The auxiliary verbs **huŋ**, **həy**, etc., and **tha**, **thi**, etc., are quite distinct from the verb **hona**, to be or become. See note on **tha** and **hua** on p. 109.

REGULAR VERB

The conjugation of transitive and intransitive verbs differs in tenses formed from the past participle. See p. 49.

INTRANSITIVE VERB

bəcna, escape, i.e., avoid a calamity.   Root **bəc.**

Infinitive, gerund or verbal noun, gerundive (future participle) :—

bəcna, to escape, escaping, etc.

Agent : bəcnevala, one who escapes *or* is about to escape.

Participles :—

Present : bəcta   escaping
          bəcta hua   escaping (more emphasis on state)
          bəcte bəcte hi   while escaping, etc., etc.

Past :   bəca   escaped
              bəca hua   escaped (more emphasis on
                                      state)

Conjunctive :—

    bəckər, bəcke, having escaped, escaping, though
escaping, etc.

Notes on bəcna

bəcna, when gerund or verbal noun, belongs to the second
declension, but is declined only in the singular.

        bəcna   an escaping
        bəcne ka   of escaping
        bəcne se   by escaping, etc.

bəcna, when gerundive (sometimes future participle), is
an adjective, and in agreement with nouns. It may become
bəcne, **bəcni**. This use is especially common with transitive
verbs; then it is passive, like the Latin gerundive.

Every infinitive may be either a gerund or a gerundive.

Agent **bəcnevala** is a second declension noun, and an
adjective.

    bəcnevala, bəcnevale, bəcnevaloŋ. Fem. : bəcnevali,
bəcnevalioŋ, etc.

The participles **bəcta** and **bəca** are adjectives in **-a** and
decline :—

    bəcta, bəcte, bəcti, bəcta hua, bəcte hue, bəcti hui.
    bəca, bəce, bəci, bəca hua, bəce hue, bəci hui.

IMPERATIVE

Singular	*Plural*
Present :—	
(tu) bəc, escape thou	(twm) bəco, escape (you)
	(ap) bəcie, escape (you)

Timeless or future :—

tu bəcna, escape thou   twm bəcna, escape (you)
[some time]

ap bəcna
ap bəciega } [some time]

The form **bəcna** is often used in a friendly way for the present, as :—

dekhna, sahəb ji, dekhna !   take care, sahib, take care !

With **ap** the third plural of the present subjunctive is common for the imperative, as :—

ap bəceŋ   you escape !

The form in **-ie** is used in two other ways: (*a*) as present subjunctive, and (*b*) as impersonal passive.

əgər ap zəra si bat pər əysa   if you find fault with him so
phətkarie   for a trifle
əccha dekhie   well, we shall see (lit. it will
                  be seen)

Another form not so common is **bəcio**, a present imperative with **tu**.

bəciega, a ceremonious form, is future imperative, or simple future, as :—

bəciega   be pleased to escape
ap kəb jaiega   when will you go ?

It does not change for the feminine.

The feminine for the whole imperative is the same as the masculine.

Negative :—

nə bəc, mət bəc ;   nə bəco, mət bəco ;
nə bəcie, nə bəciega ;   nə bəcio

Sometimes for the sake of emphasis the negative is put after the verb, as :—

bəco nə, bəco mət

In this case the stress is laid on **nə** and **mət**. Occasionally

nəhiŋ is used in this way, as : ro nəhiŋ, do not cry; mət is rather brusque, and should be used sparingly. It cannot occur with respectful forms.

PRESENT INDICATIVE

I escape or am escaping

The present participle with **huŋ, həy**, etc.

məyŋ bəcta huŋ, I escape, or am escaping

tu bəcta həy, thou escapest, or art escaping

voh bəcta həy, he escapes, or is escaping

həm bəcte həyŋ, we escape, or are escaping

twm bəcte ho, you escape, or are escaping

ap bəcte həyŋ, you escape, or are escaping

voh bəcte həyŋ, they escape, or are escaping

Feminine : **bəcti** throughout : **məyŋ bəcti huŋ**, etc. In the first plural the masculine is sometimes used for the feminine, **həm bəcti həyŋ** or **bəcte həyŋ**. See pp. 27–8 and 38.

Negative: **məyŋ nəhiŋ bəcta** or **məyŋ nəhiŋ bəcta huŋ**, etc. The former is commoner.

PRESENT CONTINUOUS

I am escaping at this moment

Change **bəcta** to **bəc rəha. rəha** comes from **rəhna**, remain.

məyŋ bəc rəha huŋ, I am escaping

tu bəc rəha həy, thou art escaping

voh bəc rəha həy, he is escaping

həm bəc rəhe həyŋ, we are escaping

twm bəc rəhe ho, you are escaping

ap bəc rəhe həyn, you are escaping

voh bəc rəhe həyŋ, they are escaping

Feminine : **rəhi** instead of **rəha**, **rəhe**.   In the first plural the masculine form is sometimes used.   See pp. 27 and **38**.

məyŋ bəc rəhi huŋ   I am escaping

Negative is rare.   It would occur only in phrases of special emphasis, as :—

məyŋ bəc to nəhiŋ rəha huŋ   I am not *escaping*

IMPERFECT OR PAST CONTINUOUS

I was escaping

First form :   present participle with **tha**.

məyŋ bəcta tha, I was escaping	həm bəcte the, we were escaping
tu bəcta tha, thou wert escaping	twm bəcte the, you were escaping
	ap bəcte the, you were escaping
voh bəcta tha, he was escaping	voh bəcte the, they were escaping

Feminine : **bəcti thi** in singular; **bəcti thiŋ** in plural. The first plural may sometimes be **bəcte the**.   See pp. 27 and 38.

Negative :   add **nə** or **nəhiŋ** :—

məyŋ nə bəcta tha *or* məyŋ   I was not escaping
nəhiŋ bəcta tha

Second form :   I was escaping at that moment.
                   Change **bəcta** to **bəc rəha**.

məyŋ bəc rəha tha, I was escaping	həm bəc rəhe the, we were escaping
tu bəc rəha tha, thou wert escaping	twm bəc rəhe the, you were escaping
	ap bəc rəhe the, you were escaping
voh bəc rəha tha, he was escaping	voh bəc rəhe the, they were escaping

Feminine : **bəc rəhi thi**; plural, **bəc rəhi thiŋ**, etc.
First plural may be : **bəc rəhe the.** See pp. 27 and 38.

Negative very rare. See note on negative of present continuous on p. 43. Add **nə** or **nəhiŋ**.

məyŋ bəc to nəhiŋ rəha tha   I was not *escaping*

FUTURE

I shall or will escape

məyŋ bəcuŋga	həm bəceŋge
tu bəcega	twm bəcoge
	ap bəceŋge
voh bəcega	voh bəceŋge

Feminine changes **-ga** to **-gi**, and **-ge** to **-gi.**

məyŋ bəcuŋgi	ap bəceŋgi

First plural may be the same as the masculine. See pp. 27 and 38.

Negative : add **nə** or **nəhiŋ**.

məyŋ nə bəcuŋga *or* **nəhiŋ bəcuŋga**   I shall or will not escape

CONTINUOUS FUTURE OR PRESENT PRESUMPTIVE

I shall be escaping, no doubt he is escaping, etc.

First Form :—

məyŋ bəcta huŋga	həm bəcte hoŋge
tu bəcta hoga	twm bəcte hoŋge
	ap bəcte hoŋge
voh bəcta hoga	voh bəcte hoŋge

This tense generally expresses doubt. He will be escaping, i.e., no doubt he is escaping, I suppose he is escaping.

For **huŋga** see under **hona**, to be or become, p. 56.

Feminine : **məyŋ bəcti huŋgi**, **voh bəcti hogi**, etc. For the first plural, the masculine is sometimes used. See pp. 27 and 38.

Negative : insert **nə** or **nəhiŋ** before **bəcta**, etc. **voh nə bəcta hoga**, etc.

THE VERB

THE VERB

THE VERB 45

Second Form :—

Second form lays stress on escaping at the moment; e.g. :—

məyŋ bəc rəha huŋga	I shall be escaping at the moment, etc.
voh bəc rəha hoga	he will be, or no doubt he is, escaping at the moment

Etc.

Feminine : **məyŋ bəc rəhi huŋgi**, etc.
Negative (very rare) : **məyŋ nə bəc rəha huŋga** or **məyŋ nəhiŋ bəc rəha huŋga**.

PAST INDICATIVE

I escaped

məyŋ bəca, I escaped	həm bəce, we escaped
tu bəca, thou escapedst	twm bəce, you escaped
	ap bəce, you escaped
voh bəca, he escaped	voh bəce, they escaped

Feminine : singular, **bəci** ; plural, **bəciŋ**. First plural may be **bəce**, see pp. 27 and 38.

Negative : insert **nə** before **bəca** ; **məyŋ nə bəca**, I did not escape. Sometimes we find **nəhiŋ** before **bəca**, but **nəhiŋ** belongs properly to the next tense, the Present Perfect.

PRESENT PERFECT

I have escaped

məyŋ bəca huŋ, I have escaped	həm bəce həyŋ
tu bəca həy	twm bəce ho
	ap bəce həyŋ
voh bəca həy	voh bəce həyŋ

Feminine : **bəci** for **bəca**, **bəce**. The first plural is sometimes **bəce**. See pp. 27 and 38.

Negative : insert **nəhiŋ** before **bəca**, etc. The auxiliary verbs **huŋ, həy, həyŋ**, etc. are omitted more often than not.

voh nəhiŋ bəca, etc.	he has not escaped
voh nəhiŋ bəca həy	(less common)

PLUPERFECT

I had escaped

Also means : I escaped.

məyŋ bəca tha	həm bəce the
tu bəca tha	twm bəce the
	ap bəce the
voh bəca tha	voh bəce the

Feminine : **bəci thi**; plural, **bəci thiŋ**. First plural is sometimes **bəce the**. See pp. 27 and 38.

Negative : **məyŋ nə bəca tha, ap nə bəce the**, etc.

FUTURE PERFECT OR PAST PRESUMPTIVE

I shall have escaped, no doubt I escaped, etc.

məyŋ bəca huŋga	həm bəce hoŋge
tu bəca hoga	twm bəce hoge
	ap bəce hoŋge
voh bəca hoga	voh bəce hoŋge

Feminine : **məyŋ bəci huŋgi**; **həm bəci hoŋgi**, etc. First plural is sometimes as masculine. See pp. 27 and 38.

Negative : **məyŋ nə bəca huŋga**, etc.

PRESENT SUBJUNCTIVE OR CONDITIONAL

I may escape, (if) I escape or should escape ; shall I escape ? etc.

məyŋ bəcuŋ	həm bəceŋ
tu bəce	twm bəco
	ap bəceŋ
voh bəce	voh bəceŋ

Feminine : the same.

Negative : **məyŋ nə bəcuŋ. nəhiŋ** is not used.

CONTINUOUS PRESENT SUBJUNCTIVE OR CONDITIONAL

I may be escaping, etc.

First Form :—

məyŋ bəcta huŋ *or* houŋ	həm bəcte hoŋ
tu bəcta ho	twm bəcte ho
	ap bəcte hoŋ
voh bəcta ho	voh bəcte hoŋ

Feminine : **bəcti** instead of **bəcta, bəcte**. First plural may be the same as the masculine. See pp. 27 and 38.

Negative : **məyŋ nə bəcta huŋ. nəhiŋ** is not used.

Second Form :—

məyŋ bəc rəha huŋ *or* houŋ,	I may be escaping at the
həm bəc rəhe hoŋ	moment, etc.

Feminine : **məyŋ bəc rəhi huŋ**, etc. First plural may be the same as the masculine. See pp. 27 and 38.

Negative : **məyŋ nə bəc rəha huŋ**, etc. **nəhiŋ** is not used.

Note.—There are two words **huŋ**, (*a*) I am, (*b*) I may be. Therefore, **məyŋ bəcta huŋ**, or **bəc rəha huŋ**, may be either : I am escaping *or* I may be escaping. The context will always make the meaning clear.

PAST CONDITIONAL OR SUBJUNCTIVE

(if) I were to escape or **had escaped ; I might** or **would** or **should escape** or **have escaped**

This takes the same form as the present participle :—

məyŋ bəcta	həm bəcte
tu bəcta	twm bəcte
	ap bəcte
voh bəcta	voh bəcte

Feminine : **bəcti**; plural, **bəctiŋ**. In first plural the masculine form is sometimes used, see pp. 27 and 38.

Negative : **məyŋ nə bəcta**, etc. **nəhiŋ** is not used.
Note difference between **nə** and **nəhiŋ** :—

| voh nə ata | he would not have come (Past Con.) |
| voh nəhiŋ ata | he does not come, he will not come (Pres. Ind.) |

PRESENT PERFECT SUBJUNCTIVE OR CONDITIONAL

məyŋ bəca huŋ *or* **houŋ**, etc.   I may have escaped, if I have escaped, etc.

Feminine : **məyŋ bəci huŋ**, etc.
Negative : **məyŋ nə bəca huŋ**, etc. **nəhiŋ** is not used.

PLUPERFECT CONDITIONAL OR SUBJUNCTIVE

Practically the same meaning as the Past Conditional, but more distinctly pluperfect in meaning.

məyŋ bəca hota   (if) I had escaped previously, I should have escaped, etc.

Feminine : **məyŋ bəci hoti**, etc.
Negative : **məyŋ nə bəca hota**. **nəhiŋ** may not be used.

PAST CONDITIONAL CONTINUOUS OR PAST SUBJUNCTIVE CONTINUOUS

I may have been escaping, (if) I had been escaping, etc.

First Form :—

məyŋ bəcti hoti, etc.
Feminine : **bəcti hoti**, etc.
Negative : **məyŋ nə bəcta hota**, etc. **nəhiŋ** may not be used.

Second Form :—

məyŋ bəc rəha hota, etc.
Feminine : **məyŋ bəc rəhi hoti**, etc.
Negative : **məyŋ nə bəc rəha hota**, etc. **nəhiŋ** may not be used.

TRANSITIVE VERBS

The conjugation of transitive and intransitive verbs is the same except in tenses formed from the past participle. The words " transitive " and " intransitive " are here used with the meaning given them by the Concise Oxford Dictionary for words *used* transitively and intransitively. A few verbs can be used in both ways.

It must be remembered that the following rule is general, not universal, and that several verbs which we should call transitive follow the conjugation of intransitive verbs, and vice versa.

The rule in an easily remembered form is as follows :—

RULE : Verbs usually transitive take **ne** in tenses formed from the past participle, and those usually intransitive do not.

Fuller details in special note, p. 106.

It is not correct to say that any verb that can be intransitive may, when intransitive, be conjugated all through without **ne** ; e.g., the verbs " see " and " hear " can be intransitive, but the Urdu verbs **dekhna** and **swnna** must always take **ne** in tenses made from the past participle. There are, however, a few verbs which take or dispense with **ne** according as they are used transitively or intransitively.

TRANSITIVE VERBS—TENSES FORMED FROM THE PAST PARTICIPLE

The construction of these tenses is based upon an old passive. Instead of saying " I wrote a letter ", Urdu has " By me a letter was written ". In a sentence like this " written " agrees with " letter ", not with the logical subject. There is a variety of this construction explained on p. 53 in which the verb is impersonal. This old passive which is now looked upon as an active is quite different from the modern passive in Urdu.

In the following tenses it will be seen that the pronouns **məyŋ**, **tu**, and the plural of **voh**, do not take the same form with **ne** as with other postpositions. If, however, a noun in apposition with these pronouns comes between them and **ne**, the ordinary oblique form is used. The same applies to the plural of the pronouns **yeh, kəwn, jo**, which also, as mentioned on p. 29, have separate forms for **ne**.

mwjh bəd nəsib ne lykha	I unfortunate one, wrote
wn bəd qysmətoŋ ne nə lykha	those unfortunate ones did not write

In the case of **voh** (and so for other pronouns which can be adjectives as well as pronouns) there is a change from " they unfortunate ones " to " those unfortunate ones ", and the pronouns become adjectives.

PAST INDICATIVE

lykhna, to write, I wrote

məyŋ ne lykha	by me—written *or* was written	I wrote
tu ne lykha	by thee—written *or* was written	thou didst write
ws ne lykha	by him, her, it—written *or* was written	he, she, it wrote
həm ne lykha	by us—written *or* was written	we wrote
twm ne lykha	by you—written *or* was written	you wrote
ap ne lykha	by you—written *or* was written	you wrote
wnhoŋ ne lykha	by them—written *or* was written	they wrote

It will be noticed the verb is always the same, no matter who the agent is, whether masculine or feminine, singular or plural. The verb is always masculine singular when there is no object. For object see pp. 52–3.

Negative : **məyŋ ne nə lykha**, I did not write, etc.

The past indicative is sometimes used for the present perfect.

PRESENT PERFECT

I have written

məyŋ ne lykha həy	by me—written is	I have written
tu ne lykha həy		thou has written
ws ne lykha həy		he has written
həm ne lykha həy		we have written
twm ne lykha həy		you have written
ap ne lykha həy		you have written
wnhoŋ ne lykha həy		they have written

Negative : **məyŋ ne nəhiŋ lykha**, or, less common, **məyŋ ne nəhiŋ lykha həy**, I have not written, etc.

When there is no object the verb is masculine singular. For object see pp. 52 and 53.

PLUPERFECT

I had written

məyŋ ne lykha tha   by me—written was   I had written

And so on for the other persons.

This tense is often used for the past, I wrote.

Negative : **məyŋ ne nə lykha tha**, I had not written, etc.

When there is no object the verb is masculine singular. For object see pp. 52 and 53.

FUTURE PERFECT OR PRESENT PERFECT PRESUMPTIVE

shall have written, I suppose I have written.

məyŋ ne lykha hoġa, I shall have written.

And so on for the other persons.

Negative : **məyŋ ne nə lykha hoġa**, I shall not have written.

If no object is expressed, the verb is masculine singular. For object see below.

PRESENT PERFECT SUBJUNCTIVE OR CONDITIONAL

məyŋ ne lykha ho   (if) I have *or* may have written

Negative : **məyŋ ne nə lykha ho**.

If no object is expressed, the verb is masculine singular. For object see below.

PLUPERFECT SUBJUNCTIVE OR CONDITIONAL

məyŋ ne lykha hota　　　　　(if) I had written; I would have written, etc.

Negative : **məyŋ ne nə lykha hota**, etc.

If no object is expressed, the verb is masculine singular. For object see below.

THE OBJECT

When the object of the action is mentioned, the sentence runs in one of two ways :—

1. When the speaker wishes to express the object of the action, i.e., the logical object, without **ko**, then that object is made the grammatical nominative.

məyŋ ne cyṭṭhi　　by me—letter written,　　I wrote a letter
　lykhi　　　　　　　　or was written

In this **lykhi** agrees with **cyṭṭhi**, which is the grammatical nominative though the logical object. It does not matter who wrote the letter, the verb is the same whoever the writer may be.

wnhoŋ ne cyṭṭhi　by them—letter written　　they wrote a
　lykhi　　　　　　　　　　　　　　　　　　letter

The remaining tenses correspond :—

məyŋ ne cyṭṭhi lykhi həy	I have written a letter	
məyŋ ne cyṭṭhi lykhi thi	I had written a letter	
məyŋ ne cyṭṭhi lykhi hogi	doubtless I have written a letter	
məyŋ ne cyṭṭhi lykhi ho	(if) if I have written a letter	
məyŋ ne cyṭṭhi lykhi hoti	(if) if I had previously written a letter, etc.	

2. When the speaker wants to use **ko**, which means " as for ", " with reference to ", etc., governing the logical object, the construction is impersonal.

məyŋ ne əwrət ko dekha	as for the woman, by me it was seen; I saw the woman
ws ne kytaboŋ ko pəɽha	as for the books, by him it was read; he read the books

In these sentences " it was seen ", " it was read " are purely impersonal, corresponding to the English " it is believed ", " it is said ", " it is thought ".

PASSIVE

For special section on the passive, see pp. 105–6.

Less use is made of the passive than in English; in particular when the agent is mentioned it is generally better to change the construction so that the verb may be in the past indicative, active voice. (See above.)

Infinitive :	dekha jana	to be seen, being seen, etc.
Agent :	dekha janevala	(rare)

Participles :

Present :	dekha jata	(found only in finite tenses)
Past :	dekha gəya	(found only in finite tenses)

It should be remembered that the ordinary past participle **dekha, dekha hua**, seen (feminine : **dekhi, dekhi hui**), is also passive, just as the corresponding participle is in English. The past participle of a transitive verb is always passive.

Conjunctive :   not used

Imperative :   practically never found

Present Indicative :   məyŋ dekha jata huŋ   } I am being
                     məyŋ dekha ja rəha huŋ }   seen

Feminine : **dekhi jati huŋ, dekhi ja rəhi huŋ.** First plural may be as masculine. See pp. 27 and 38.

Negative : **məyŋ nəhiŋ dekha jata (huŋ),** or **məyŋ dekha nəhiŋ jata (huŋ).**

Imperfect :   məyŋ dekha jata tha   }   I was being
            məyŋ dekha ja rəha tha }   seen

Feminine : **məyŋ dekhi jati thi, dekhi ja rəhi thi.** First plural may be as masculine. See pp. 27 and 38.

Negative : **məyŋ nəhiŋ** (or **nə**), **dekha jata tha,** or **nə, nəhiŋ,** may come after **dekha.**

Future :   məyŋ dekha jauŋga   I shall be seen

Feminine : **məyŋ dekhi jauŋgi.** First plural may be as masculine.

Negative : **məyŋ nə** (or **nəhiŋ**) **dekha jauŋga,** or **nə, nəhiŋ** after **dekha.**

Past :   məyŋ dekha gəya   I was seen

Feminine : **məyŋ dekhi ĝəi.** First plural may be as masculine.

Negative : **məyŋ nə dekha ĝəya** or **dekha nə ĝəya.**

Present Perfect : məyŋ dekha gəya huŋ   I have been seen

Feminine : **məyŋ dekhi ĝəi huŋ.** First plural may be as masculine.

Negative : **məyŋ nə dekha ĝəya huŋ,** or **dekha nə ĝəya huŋ.**

Pluperfect :   məyŋ dekha gəya tha   I had been seen

Feminine : **məyŋ dekhi ĝəi thi.** First plural may be as masculine.

Negative: **məyŋ nə dekha ĝəya tha,** or **nə** after **dekha.**

Present Subjunctive or Conditional :—

məyŋ dekha jauŋ   I may be seen, etc.
həm dekhe jaeŋ

Feminine : **məyŋ dekhi jauŋ, həm dekhi jaeŋ** (or as masculine).

Negative : **məyŋ dekha nə jauŋ**, or **nə dekha jaun.**

Past Conditional or Subjunctive :—

məyŋ dekha jata   I might be seen, might have
                            been seen
həm dekhe jate, etc.

Feminine : **məyŋ dekhi jati, həm dekhi jatiŋ** (or as masc.).

Negative : **məyŋ nə dekha jata**, or **dekha nə jata.**

The other tenses can be formed on the same model. The above will be enough to show the method.

IRREGULARITIES IN VERBS

These are few and trifling.

1. The following verbs insert **j** in the ceremonious imperative : **dena**, give; **lena**, take; **pina**, drink; **kərna**, do; **hona**, be, become.

     dijie, dijiega; lijie, lijiega; kijie, kijiega; pijie, pijiega

In older Urdu **hona** used to make **hujie, hujiega**, but these are not now found.

On **dena**, **lena**, **hona**, and **kərna**, see further in nos. 3–5 on p. 56.

2. Verbs whose roots end in **-a** or **-o** insert **y** in the masculine singular of the past participle.

ana, come : aya	bənana, make : bənaya
sona, sleep : soya	rona, weep : roya

aya, soya, roya, have two syllables; **bənaya** has three.

3. **dena**, give, and **lena**, take, drop the **e** before a vowel, except in the past participle, where they change it to **i**, which is dropped in the feminine. The ceremonious imperative, as has been seen, changes **e** to **i**, and inserts **j**.

Imperative, ceremonious :—

	2nd pl. :	do		lo
	dijie	dijiega	lijie	lijiega

Future :

	dunga	denge	lunga	lenge
	dega	doge	lega	loge
		ap denge		ap lenge
	dega	voh denge	lega	voh lenge

Past :

Past :	dia		lia
Feminine :	di		li
Plural :	die		lie
Feminine :	din		lin

Presen: Subjunctive :—

	dun	den	lun	len
	de	do	le	lo
		ap den		ap len
	de	voh den	le	voh len

4. **hona**, be, become, changes **o** to **u** in the past participle, and contracts in the future and present subjunctive.
In ordinary speech the ceremonious imperative is regular :—

	hoie	hoiega	

Future :

	hunga	honge
	hoga	hoge
		ap honge
	hoga	voh honge

Past :

Past :	hua	hue
Feminine :	hui	huin

Present Subjunctive :—

	huŋ (sometimes houŋ)	hoŋ
	ho	ho
		ap hoŋ
	ho	voh hoŋ

Note on **hua**, p. 109.

5. **kərna**, do, has irregularities in the ceremonious imperative and the past.

Imperative :	kijie	kijiega
Past :	kia	kie
Feminine :	ki	kiŋ

6. **jana**, go, has :—

Past :	gəya	gəe
Feminine :	gəi	gəiŋ

7. **mərna**, die, is regular, but has also a past, **mua**.

On the whole Urdu verbs are extremely regular, more so, perhaps, than in any other inflected language.

Note : **sena**, hatch eggs, has past, **sea**; plural, **see** (two syllables) ; feminine : **sei, seiŋ** ; habitual, **sea kərna**.

khena, row a boat, has no masculine past; the feminine past is **khei**, plural, **kheiŋ**.   It has no habitual form.

CAUSAL VERBS

Causal verbs are a striking feature of Urdu.   We must distinguish carefully between (*a*) their meaning, and (*b*) the method of their formation.

Meaning of Causal Verbs :

(i) The causal of an intransitive verb is simply the transitive verb corresponding to it.   Thus :—

cəlna, move, etc.   cəlana, cause to move, make some
                                   one move

ḍəwṛna, run   ḍəwṛana, cause to run, make some
                               one run

(ii) Transitive verbs. There is no causal of the active
voice of a transitive verb. The so-called causal is the
causal of its passive. It means " to cause the action of the
transitive verb to be performed ", not " to make some one
perform it ".

wṭhana, lift   wṭhvana, cause something to be
                               lifted

The object of **wṭhvana** is the thing to be lifted, not the
person who is going to lift it.

ws ko wṭhvao means " get it or him lifted up ". It does
not mean " make so and so lift it up ".

So **bənana**, make; **bənvana**, cause something to be
made. It does not mean " get some one to make some
thing ". The object of **bənvana** is the thing made, not the
carpenter who makes it.

It will be seen from the above that verbs can have two
causals, and further down it will appear that some actually
have three.

Examples of Two Causals

ləṛki jagi   the girl awoke
maŋ ne ləṛki ko jəgaya   the mother woke the girl
həkim ne maŋ se ləṛki ko   the doctor had the girl
  jəgvaya   awakened by the mother
məyŋ wrdu pəṛhta huŋ   I am reading, studying Urdu
məwlvi sahəb mere beṭe ko   the Maulvi is teaching my
  wrdu pəṛhate həyŋ   son Urdu
məyŋ məwlvi sahəb se əpne   I am having my son taught
  beṭe ko wrdu pəṛhvata   Urdu by the Maulvi
  huŋ

Formation of Causal Verbs

A causal is formed by making certain changes in the root
of the verb. The root is found by taking off the ending **-na**

of the infinitive, as **bol** from **bolna**, speak; **xərid** from **xəridna**, buy.

Note that :—

(a) The roots of most verbs, other than causals, end in a consonant.

(b) Verbs with roots of more than two syllables have no causals.

(c) Verbs, not themselves causals, with roots ending in **-a**, very rarely have causals. Thus, **pana**, obtain, has no causal; but **bənana**, make, being itself a causal, has one :—

bənna, be made   bənana, make   bənvana, cause to be made

(d) The following verbs have no causals :—

ləlkarna, boast	ana, come	jana, go
cahna, wish	bhana, be agree-	ḍhana, knock
socna, think	able to	down
lana, bring	pəṛna, fall	janna, know
taṛna, see, take in	səkna, be able	pana, find, manage to

Rule I

Verbs with one-syllabled roots ending in a consonant generally form causals by adding **-a** to the root; and if the vowel of the root is long, it is usually shortened : **a** becomes **ə**, **e** and **i** become **y**, **o** becomes **w**.

jəlna, burn (intr.)	jəlana, burn (trans.)
pəkna, be cooked	pəkana, cook
gyrna, fall	gyrana, knock down
swnna, hear	swnana (cause to be heard), relate
khelna, play	khylana, cause to play, invite to play
bolna, speak, make a sound	bwlana, cause to speak or make a sound, call

D

Rule 2

Intransitive verbs ending in a short vowel followed by a consonant sometimes form their causals by merely lengthening the vowel, ə being lengthened to **a**, **y** to **e**, **w** to **u**.

kəṭna, be cut	kaṭna, cut
lədna, be loaded	ladna, load
khwlna, open (intr.)	kholna, open (trans.)
chydna, be perforated	chedna, perforate

On these verbs see further, p. 63.

Rule 3

Verbs with two-syllabled roots ending in a consonant, and having a short **-ə** in the second syllable, add **-a** to the root, but omit the **-ə** of the second syllable.

pyghəlna, melt (intr.)	pyghlana, melt (trans.)
səməjhna, understand	səmjhana, explain
wləṭna, turn upside down (intr.)	wlṭana, turn upside down (trans.)

Exceptions :—

nykəlna, emerge	nykalna, take out, eject
gwzərna, pass, etc.	gwzarna, spend (time, life)
bygəṛna, be spoilt	bygaṛna, spoil
səmbhəlna, recover oneself, be supported	səmbhalna, look after, set right

If the second vowel is **-y** or **-w**, the verb follows Rule 1.

pəhwŋcna, arrive	pəhwŋcana, cause to arrive

Rule 4

Verbs with two-syllabled roots ending in a consonant, and having the second vowel long, add **-va** to the root, and shorten the second vowel.

xəridna, buy	xərydvana, cause to be bought
nycoṛna, squeeze out	nycwṛvana, cause to be squeezed out

The causal of **ghəsiṭna**, drag, is formed as if the verb were **ghysaṭna**; **ghysəṭvana**, cause to be dragged.

Rule 5

Roots ending in a vowel. Such roots always end in a long vowel, never in a short one. The next two sections, (*a*) and (*b*), do not apply to verbs which are themselves causals.

(*a*) Two-syllabled roots ending in a vowel have no causals.

Exceptions :—

nəhana, bathe   nəhlana, to bathe (someone)

cwrana, steal   cwrvana, to cause to be stolen

(*b*) Some one-syllabled roots ending in a vowel shorten the vowel and add **l** :—

pina, drink   pylana, cause to be drunk, give to drink

sina, sew   sylana, cause to be sewn

chuna, touch   chwlana (also chwvana), cause to be touched

jina, live   jylana, cause to live, make alive

dena, give   dylana, cause to be given

sona, sleep   swlana, cause to sleep

rona, weep   rwlana, cause to weep

khana, eat   khylana, cause to be eaten, give to eat. (Here one would have expected **khəlana**.)

The following do not insert **l**.

gana, sing   gəvana, cause to sing or to be sung

lena, take   lyvana (uncommon), cause to be taken or brought

khona, lose   khwvana (uncommon), cause to be lost

Rule 6

One or two monosyllabic roots ending in a consonant occasionally add **l** in the causal, but the form without **l** is better.

sikhna, learn	sykhana; sykhlana (not so good)
bəyṭhna, sit	byṭhana; byṭhlana (not so good)
dekhna, see, look at	dykhana; dykhlana (not so good)

The form **sykhlana** is becoming common in military circles. There is no objection to the **l** in **kəhlana**, from **kəhna**, say, but the word is often used in a passive sense = to be called.

DOUBLE CAUSALS

Verbs with one-syllabled roots ending in a consonant, or with two-syllabled roots ending in a consonant and having the second vowel short (see Rules 1, 2, and 3 on pp. 59–60), form their double causals by adding **-va** to the root, and shortening the vowel if long. The meaning is to get something done through another person's instrumentality.

Verb :—

pəkna, cook	pəkana, cook	pəkvana, cause to be cooked by some one
bolna, speak	bwlana, call	bwlvana, cause to be called by some one
chydna, be perforated	chedna, perforate	chydvana, cause to be perforated by some one
səməjhna, understand	səmjhana, explain	səməjhvana, cause to be explained by some one
pəhwŋcna, arrive	pəhwŋcana, send	pəhwŋcvana, cause to be sent or brought by some one

Note that **nykəlna**, emerge, an exception to Rule 3 in its first causal, **nykalna** (not **nyklana**), is regular in its second, **nykəlvana** : so **ǵwzərvana**, **byǵəṭvana**.

Verbs coming under Rule 2 generally have three causals, as :—

lədna, be loaded	ladna, load	lədana, lədvana, cause to be loaded
kəṭna, be cut	kaṭna, cut	kəṭana, kəṭvana, cause to be cut

IMPORTANT. When, as in the last two verbs, the same idea runs through all the causals, the second and third do not really differ in meaning, and when the notion of instrumentality is prominent, the form in **-va** is preferred.

qwlioŋ se lədvaya (not   got it loaded by coolies
lədaya)

This holds too when the original verb is transitive and has only two causals with the same idea running through all.

kərna, do   kərana, kərvana, cause to be
                             done

dykhna, be visible, which should belong to Rule 1, follows Rule 2 in its first causal.

dykhna, be visible :   1st causal, dekhna, see, look at
                       2nd causal, dykhana, show
                       3rd causal, dykhvana, cause to be
                       looked at or shown

Note that the idea changes; **dekhna** does not mean " cause to be visible ", nor does **dykhana** mean " cause to be seen ". Since the idea changes, the second and third causals differ in both meaning and use.

When a first causal root ends in **-va**, as under Rule 4, **xərydvana**, **ǵhysəṭvana**, or like the three exceptions at the end of Rule 5, **ǵəvana**, **lyvana**, **khwvana**, there is no second causal.

The verbs in Rule 5 which insert **l** in their first

causals make their second by introducing **v** before **-a**.
Thus :—

pina, drink	second causal	pylvana, cause (a drink) to be given
jina, live		jylvana, cause to be made alive
sona, sleep		swlvana, cause to be put to sleep
rona, cry		rwlvana, cause to be made to cry
khana, eat		khylvana, cause (food) to be given

sina, sew; **chuna**, touch; and **dena**, give, retain the
same idea throughout their causals; therefore **sylvana**,
chwlvana, and **dylvana**, the second causals, do not really
differ from the first causals **sylana**, **chwlana**, and **dylana**.

pylana and **khylana** are not in meaning the true causals
of **pina** and **khana**.

mwjhe pani pylao, **mwjhe kwch khylao**, mean : give
me water to drink, give me something to eat.

There is here no causation or compulsion. Therefore the
second causals differ from the first in meaning.

mwjhe pani pylvao, **mwjhe kwch khylvao**, mean : get
a drink given me by some one, get food given me by some
one, presumably a servant.

The Postpositions of Instrumentality se, ko

The causals of transitive verbs, i.e., of their passives,
involve an intermediary through whose instrumentality
the action is performed. The postposition used with that
intermediary is either **se** or **ko**. How may we know which
it is for the causal of any particular verb? The answer is
that it depends on whether that verb, when compounded,
is compounded with (*a*) **dena**, or (*b*) **lena** (see p. 72).

(*a*) The causal of a verb normally compounded with
dena, i.e., one whose action is directed away from

the doer (p. 74), takes the postposition **se**. In this case the idea of causation is strong.

bəɽhəi ne sənduq bəna dia	the carpenter made the box
məyŋ ne bəɽhəi se sənduq bənvaya	I got a box made by the carpenter

(b) The causal of a verb normally compounded with **lena**, i.e., one whose action is for the benefit of the doer or goes toward the doer (p. 74), takes the postposition **ko**. The idea of causation is now very weak. The idea is rather that of providing some one with the means of doing something, or helping him to do it.

ləɽki ne saɽi oɽh li	the girl put on her sari
ma ne ləɽki ko saɽi wɽhai	the mother helped the girl on with her sari
safə baŋdh lo	put on your turban
ləɽke ko safə bəndha do	help the boy on with his turban
nəwkər se safə bəndhva lo	get the turban put on (your head) by the servant
nəwkər se safə bəndhva do	get the turban put on (the boy's head) by the servant
bwɖɖhe ne ʃərbət pi lia	the old man drank the sherbet
zəmindar ne bwɖɖhe ko ʃərbət pylaya	the farmer gave the old man sherbet to drink

(c) Some transitive verbs may be compounded with both **dena** and **lena**; the two compounds differ in meaning. We must enquire whether the causal belongs to the verb as compounded with **dena** or as compounded with **lena**.

hərkare ne pəta lykh lia	the postman wrote the address (for himself)
moci ne hərkare ko pəta lykhvaya	the cobbler dictated the address to the postman
hərkare ne moci ke vaste karɖ lykh dia	the postman wrote a postcard for the cobbler

moci ne hərkare se karḍ lykhvaya — the cobbler got a card written by the postman

Peculiar Causals

The following causals, rather peculiar in form, should be noted :—

bəṭna, be shared — baŋṭna, bəṭana, bəṭvana. (There is a different verb bəṭna, twist, with causal bəṭana, bəṭvana)

bhigna, get wet — bhygona, bhygvana

bykna, be sold — becna, sell; bykvana

bona, sow — bwvana

chwṭna, chuṭna, escape, etc. — choṛna; chwṭana; chwṛana; chwṭvana; chwṛvana

dəbna, be pressed, etc. — dabna, dəbana; dəbvana

dhwlna, be washed — dhona, wash; dhwlana, dhwlvana

ḍubna, sink — ḍwbona, ḍwbana; ḍwbvana

hona, be, become — hwvana (used only in the phrase hona hwvana, as : hona hwvana kwch nəhiŋ = there will be no result)

khena, row (boat) — khyvana

khycna, khyŋcna, be pulled — kheŋcna, khəyŋcna, khiŋcna; khycvana, khyŋcvana

khwjlana, scratch (oneself, one's body) — khwjvana

lena, take — lyvana (used only in phrase lyva lana, bring a person, or cause something to be brought by someone)

pəhcanna, recognise — pəhcənvana (rare)

pəhynna, put on (clothes) — common causal : pynhana; pəhynana is also found

phəṭna, split, burst — phaṛna, phəṛana, phəṛvana

phuṭna, burst forth, etc. — phoṛna, phwṛana, phwṛvana

pwkarna, call out to — pwkərvana

sena, hatch (eggs)   syvana
ṭuṭna, break (int.)   toṛna, twṛana, twṛvana
                         (Note the dental **t** in
                         the last three.)

THE INFINITIVE

This is derived from two Sanskrit forms which have become one in the Urdu infinitive. This dual origin is seen in its two main uses. Sometimes it is a verbal noun corresponding in some degree to the Latin gerund; sometimes a future participle, always passive in transitive verbs, rather like the Latin gerundive. In the first case, it is a masculine noun ending in **-a**, and belongs to the second declension; in the second, it is an adjective ending in **-a.**

Gerund or Verbal Noun

(*a*) həjamət bənvane ki adət   the habit of getting shaved
     age bəṛhne meŋ kya   what harm is there in going
       hərəj həy?   forward?
     mere valyd ka kəhna   what my father says is right
       bəja həy

(*b*) to express purpose; verbal noun inflected with or without **ko.**

     voh zəmin xəridne gəya   he went to buy land
     jys vəqt jua khelne   when they (will) sit down to
       bəyṭheŋge   gamble
     sabyt kərne ko   in order to prove

Negative purpose with **ka** :—

     məyŋ əpni beyzzəti   I am not going to let myself
       kərane ka nəhiŋ   be insulted

(*c*) with **-vala.**
     kwʃti ləṛne vale   wrestlers

Gerundive

See also p. 96, and Sentences, Lessons 12, 13, 14.

(*a*) Necessity, duty, desirability :—

yəriboŋ ki pərvəryʃ kərni lazym thi	it was right to support the poor
mwjhe ap roṭi pəkani pəṛi	I had to cook the food myself
qəydi ko maf kərna zəruri həy	the prisoner must be pardoned
twmheŋ tin kytabeŋ pəṛhni həyŋ	*tres libri tibi legendi sunt*, you must read three books

(*b*) A command to be obeyed at any time : agent in nominative case. When the infinitive is thus used as an imperative, it is kept masculine singular. This is sometimes a rather polite present imperative.

twm khyṛki nə kholna	don't open the window (no time specified)

nə kholo would be used if you saw some one about to open the window, and called out, " Oh, don't open the window ! "

dekhna, sahəb ji, dekhna	look, Sahib, look ; be careful, etc.

(*c*) Used as complement to other verbs :—

gaṛiaŋ ani jani ʃwru huiŋ	carriages began to come and go
ws ne məzduri kərni choṛ di	he gave up doing daily (manual) work
məyŋ ne bhəyŋs xəridni cahi	I wished to buy a buffalo
ajyzi se ərz kərni cahie	one should make petition with humility

səkna, be able. Rules

1. It is joined to the root of verbs.
2. It does not take **ne** in past tenses.

3. It never occurs alone; the other verb must be mentioned.

meri beṭi nə ja səki	my daughter could not go
pəṛh səkte ho? haŋ, pəṛh səkta huŋ	can you read? Yes, I can

Here for " I can " **səkta huŋ** would be wrong; it must be **pəṛh səkta huŋ**.

4. It is generally wrong to use it with compound verbs; thus it is correct to say :

əgər voh choṛ səkeŋ	if they can leave it

but it is wrong to say :—

əgər voh choṛ de səkeŋ

Inability may be expressed by the negative passive of any verb, transitive or intransitive, or by an interrogative tantamount to a passive, along with **se**, by, governing the word signifying the person who is unable.

mwjh se yeh kytab pəṛhi nəhiŋ jati	I can't read this book (lit. by me this book is not being read)
mwjh se əysa jəvab kəb dia jaega	I shall never be able to give such an answer
mwjh se nəhiŋ bəyṭha jata	I can't sit down

cwkna, to finish, to have finished.   Rules as for **səkna**.

1. It is joined to the root of verbs.
2. It does not take **ne** in past tenses.
3. It cannot be used alone; the other verb must be repeated.
4. It should not be used with compound verbs.

Note that the idea of finishing in **cwkna** is weak. It often corresponds to " already " in English.

məyŋ kha cwka	I have already eaten, or, I have finished eating
meri bəhyn kytab pəṛh cwki həy	my sister has already read the book

jəb hysab təiyar kər cwkoge, mwjhe dykhana	when you have got the account ready, show it to me

The transitive use of **cwkna** as an auxiliary verb must be distinguished from the intransitive use of it as an independent verb meaning : to be finished off, or paid.

qərz cwk gəya	the debt has been paid

This has a causal **cwkana**, to pay, finish off.

ləgna, begin.   Rules

1. It is used with the infinitive (verbal noun) inflected in **-e**.
2. It does not take **ne** in past tenses.
3. It cannot be used alone; the other verb must be repeated.
4. It is not usual with compound verbs.
5. It is often nearly meaningless; the idea of commencing is almost absent.

becari (bycari) rone ləgi	the poor woman began to cry
gidəɽ dekhte hi bhagne ləge	the jackals began running away immediately on seeing him

ləgna is generally used with past or pluperfect tenses; less often with present, indicative or imperfect, rarely with the future, and never with the imperative or infinitive.

pana, manage to.   Rules

1. It is used with the infinitive (verbal noun) inflected in **-e** to mean " manage to ", " get the chance of ", and, rarely, " be allowed to ".

meŋh bərsa, məyŋ bahər nykəlne nə paya	it rained, I did not manage to get out
zərur mylne jauŋga jane pauŋ to	I shall certainly go and see him if I get the chance

2. **pana**, meaning "manage to", does not take **ne** in past tenses, but when it means "obtain, find", it does.

3. It usually occurs in negative clauses, or clauses suggesting a negative, as in the second sentence above.

4. It is seldom used with compound verbs.

dena, allow, permit. Rules

dena with the infinitive (verbal noun) inflected in **-e** means "allow to".

ws ne mwjhe dwkan kholne nə di	he did not let me open a shop

Here **di** agrees with **dwkan**, feminine.

məyŋ kəbhi əpne bəcce ko mar khane nə duŋgi	I (feminine) will never let my child be beaten
jane do	let it go; i.e., it does not matter

Note that **kysi ko yəhaŋ bəyţhne nə do**, don't let anyone sit here = **koi yəhaŋ bəyţhne nə pae**, let no one manage to sit here.

COMPOUND VERBS

When two verbs are so joined that they convey a single idea, they become one compound verb. But if the verbs both retain their own meaning, they are two verbs. Thus each of the following sentences contains two verbs, not one compound one :—

voh jəvab nə de səka	he could not answer
voh mwjhe do rwpəe ynam de gəya	he gave me a reward of two rupees as we went

But the following contain one compound verb each. True compounds have their action strictly limited; see below.

bəyţh jao	sit down
həm ne rəkh lia	we kept it, or, have kept it

Compound Verbs

These are formed by prefixing the root of a verb to certain auxiliary verbs which lose their proper meaning. With intransitive verbs the commonest auxiliary verb is **jana**; with transitive verbs the commonest auxiliary verbs are **dena** and **lena**.

thək jana, get tired	bhər jana, be filled
dykha dena, show	swna dena, relate
kha lena, eat	swn lena, listen to

Intransitive Verbs

jana. Most, but not all, intransitive verbs can be compounded with **jana**. When so compounded, they indicate a single action or occasion, involving change of state, finality or completeness; there is no idea of a continuing process. If the simple verb has two or three allied ideas, the compound with **jana** limits itself to one, and refers to only one occasion. Sometimes these compounds are practically passives in meaning.

Owing to the emphasis on reaching a final state, we usually find that the state can also be expressed by the past participle with **hua**. Thus to take verbs from the list below, we may say:—

voh leṭ gəya, he lay down	*therefore*, leṭa hua həy, he is lying down (resting)
voh bəyṭh gəya, he sat down	*therefore*, bəyṭha hua həy, he is now seated
pani khəwl gəya, the water came to the boil	*therefore*, pani khəwla hua həy, the water is in the state of having been boiled, it is boiled water
sona, sleep, go to sleep	so jana, go to sleep
jagna, be awake	jag jana, wake up
ghysna, rub (int.)	ghys jana, get rubbed away
khəwlna, be boiling, boil	khəwl jana, come to the boil
phyrna, turn (various senses)	phyr jana, turn back, become retrograde

letna, lie .... let jana, lie down
bəythna, get into a sitting ..... bəyth jana, sit down
  position
hylna, move, shake (int.) .... hyl jana, be shaken (said of
                           thing at rest)
ɾəhna, stay .... rəh jana, stay for good, be
                           left behind

Verbs which show a continuing process and cannot indicate arriving at a final state are not compounded with **jana**. Such are :—

khelna, play .... təyrna, swim
kwɾkwɾana, grumble .... cyllana, cry out, call out
kəhlana, be called or .... rona, weep
  named .... həŋsna, laugh

The verb **jana** is not compounded with the root of **jana**; we cannot say **ja jana**.

It is important not to confuse a single compound verb having **jana** as its auxiliary element, with two verbs of which the second is **jana**. Thus **wɾh jana** is not a compound verb, whereas **bəyth jana** is; **wɾh jana** means rise and go away, hence move into another house, etc.; **jana** here has its own meaning. The same holds of **wɾ jana**, fly away. The test simply is whether there is any idea of going or going away in the **jana**; if there is, we have two verbs, not one single compound verb.

lena is sometimes compounded with intransitive verbs to express (i) doing a thing as much as one feels inclined, and (ii) performing an action to be immediately followed by another. Their action is limited as described above under **jana**, p. 72.

ro le dyl kholkər .... weep thy fill
voh ws ke sath ho lia .... he accompanied him
voh ws ke piche ho lia .... he followed him
voh a le to —— .... let him come first, and then
                          —— (do so and so)
mwjhe bəyth lene do .... first let me sit down, and
                          then, etc.

dena is compounded with a few intransitive verbs and conveys the idea of a certain amount of suddenness.

voh ro dia	he began to cry; almost = **ro pəṛa**
voh həŋs di	she burst out laughing; almost = **həŋs pəṛi**
voh cəl di	she went off; almost = **cəl pəṛi**

Transitive Verbs (Compound)

With transitive verbs the commonest auxiliary verbs are **lena** and **dena**. **lena** is used when the action has special reference to the doer or is for his benefit; **dena** directs the action towards some one else or away from the doer. More briefly, **lena** suggests connection with the agent, **dena** separation from him. Thus we have :—

pəhyn lena, put on (clothes)	pi lena, drink
swn lena, listen to	

but :—

pynha dena, pəhyna dena	help some one on with his clothes
pyla dena, give drink to	swna dena, relate

One must not lay too much stress on *benefit* to the doer in **lena** verbs; e.g., **pi lena** might be used of drinking poison, and **swn lena** of listening to something distressing.

Sometimes there are interesting differences of meaning according to which auxiliary verb is used.

rəkh lo, keep it for yourself	rəkh do, put it down
baṇt lo, distribute it and keep your share	baṇt do, distribute it among others
lykh lo, write it down for your own use	lykh do, write it for me (because I am illiterate)
məyŋ ne wse byṭha lia, I seated him by my side, beside myself	məyŋ ne wse byṭha dia, I seated him anywhere

məyŋ ne wse səmjha lia, I explained it to him (for my advantage)

məyŋ ne wse səmhja dia, I explained it to him (for his advantage)

Limitation of action in transitive compound verbs :—

lena and **dena** compounded with transitive verbs limit the action in a manner very similar to that of **jana** with intransitive verbs, imparting an idea of finality or completeness, and confining the action to one occasion.

məyŋ ne tin məhine goʃt khaya, phyr choɽ dia
I ate meat for three months, and then gave it up

məyŋ ne sara goʃt kha lia
I ate up all the meat (one occasion) •

dwkandar ne wse dəs dəfə tənxah di
the shopkeeper gave him his pay ten times

wse tənxah de di
paid him his wages (one occasion)

jana with transitive verbs :

We have seen that compounded with intransitive verbs **jana** does not mean "go"; with transitive verbs, however, it is nearly always a separate verb and does mean "go".

bəndər khyɽkiaŋ toɽ gəya
the monkey broke the windows and went off

məyŋ twmheŋ təsvireŋ dykha jauŋga
I shall show you the pictures as I go

There are exceptions to this rule, which we may put in three classes :—

(a) **kərna** used with a noun to form an intransitive compound, as :—

yeh ws meŋ syrayət kər gəya
this penetrated into it

pəwda ws meŋ jəgəh pəkəɽ gəya
the plant has taken root in it (lit. seized a place)

(b) Verbs meaning "understand", "take in", etc. :—

həm səməjh gəe
we took it in

| həm jan gəe | we took it in, *or* have taken it in |
| həm taɽ gəe | we took it in |

(c) Verbs of eating and drinking :—

| sari roʈi həzm kər gəya (kha gəya, cəʈ kər gəya, nygəl gəya) | he ate up (gobbled up) all the food and went off, *or simply*, ate or gobbled it up |
| sara ʃərbət pi gəya | he drank the sherbet and went off, *or* drank it all up |

In these three cases (a), (b), and (c) the auxiliary **jana** need not have the meaning of going, indeed in (a) and (b) it cannot have it.

Other auxiliary verbs used to form compound verbs are **pəɽna**, **wʈhna**, **ḍalna**, **bəyʈhna** and **rəhna**. The limitation of meaning mentioned above occurs also in these.

1. **pəɽna** and **wʈhna** are added to a few intransitive verbs to express suddenness :—

ləɽki ro pəɽi	the girl burst out crying
mere dada ka paoŋ physəl pəɽa	my grandfather's foot suddenly slipped
meri valdə bol wʈhi	my mother suddenly spoke. [It does not mean " spoke up "]
donoŋ bwḍḍhe ghəbra wʈhe	both the old men suddenly got confused

2. **ḍalna** is joined to transitive verbs to express vigour or even violence :—

| marna, *either* beat *or* kill | mar ḍalna, *only* kill |
| kaʈna, cut | kaʈ ḍalna, cut down |

3. **bəyʈhna** suggests force or insistence :—

| voh malyk bən bəyʈha | he became owner by force or usurpation |
| voh ws ko mar bəyʈha | he beat him without reason |

4. **rəhna** with the roots of intransitive verbs sometimes

means doing a thing of set purpose, but probably in this case the idea of " remaining " is present, and if so we have two verbs, not one compound verb.

roz yəhaŋ ake bəyṭh rəhta həy	he comes daily and plants himself down here
jao mər rəho	go off and die
məyŋ ləwṭke so rəhuŋga	I shall go to sleep when I return

TWO VERBS CLOSELY JOINED, BUT NOT FORMING A COMPOUND

The root of a verb joined to another verb, both verbs retaining their meaning, is a shortened conjunctive participle. In this case the two verbs are much more closely connected than when the first is a full conjunctive participle.

ləṛka bhəyŋs pər cəṛh bəyṭha	the boy got up on the buffalo
bhəyŋs pər cəṛhke bəyṭha	he got up on the buffalo and sat down
məyŋ ne jəgəh rok rəkkhi həy	I have booked a seat
məyŋ ne əlmari meŋ rəkh choṛa	I have put it away in the cupboard

IMPORTANT. Further rules about compound verbs and close combinations of two verbs should be noted. In addition to the fact that they all have the limitation of meaning described on p. 72, we must observe :—

1. They are not used in straightforward negative clauses.

kha lia ? has he eaten it up?　nəhiŋ khaya, he has not

but we might get :—

məyŋ ne kha to nəhiŋ lia	I have not *eaten* it (though you seem to think I have, *or*, but I have thrown it away)

2. They are rarely joined to a third verb; thus we cannot say :—

baɳʈ de səkta həy   he can distribute it

it should be :—

   baɳʈ səkta həy

3. They are rarely used with the conjunctive participle. It is wrong to say **rəkh lekər** or **rəkh dekər**.

PERSIAN AND ARABIC VERBS

Nearly all Urdu verbs are of Indo-Aryan origin. A very few have been formed from Persian and Arabic words.

Persian

bəxʃna	forgive (a sin or fault)
xəridna	buy
gwzərna	pass
fərmana	command, say
azmana	test, try
ʃərmana	feel ashamed *or* shy
tərəsna and ləlcana	feel a longing (for, **ko**). These are intransitive, but **ləlcana** is also transitive, make some one feel a longing (for, **ko**). The transitive of **tərəsna** is **tərsana**

Arabic

bədəlna (trans. and intrans.)	change, exchange
bəhəsna	argue; commoner : **bəhəs kərna**
qəbulna	accept; commoner : **qəbul kərna**

VERBS FORMED FROM ADJECTIVES AND NOUNS

Verbs composed of (a) Adjective and Verb, and (b) Noun and Verb

Before discussing these we must mention verbs of Indo-Aryan origin formed directly from adjectives and nouns; such are :—

əpnana, make one's own, assimilate (from **əpna,** own)
ləngɽana, walk lame (from **ləngɽa,** lame)
bətana, show, tell (from **bat,** matter, word, etc.)

. A very large number of verbs are formed by prefixing a noun or adjective to **kərna**, make, and **hona**, be, become, or **hojana**, become; occasionally to one or two other verbs, such as **dena**, give; **lena**, take; **marna**, beat; **khana**, eat; **pana**, obtain.

It is difficult to say whether such verbs are real verbs or are two distinct ideas. Thus in Urdu for " praise him " we find " make his praise ". But in English too we can say either " praise him " or " sing his praises ". We do not call the latter a real verb, yet it is as much so as the Urdu " make his praise ". Other examples in English are " wash it " and " give it a wash "; " straighten it " and " make it straight ".

Adjective

With an adjective the verb is almost always **kərna**, make, for the transitive, and **hona** or **hojana**, become, for the intransitive. **kərna** with an adjective takes a direct object.

məyŋ wse əccha kəruŋga   I will make him well
voh əccha ho gəya   he became well

Noun

With **kərna, dena, marna, khana, lena, pana**, etc. See also separate section under **ləgna, ləgana,** pp. 110–12.

IMPORTANT NOTE.—In each case the noun joined to one of these verbs, though it may be regarded as governed by it, can never have the accusative form with **ko**. It must always have that accusative form which is the same as the nominative. Thus we can say :—

> məyŋ ne ws ki tarif ki   I praised him

But we may not say :—

> məyŋ ne ws ki tarif ko kia.   So with all the others

A. kərna with a noun. Three cases arise :—

> (i) *First Construction :* the two are joined so closely as to become one word, and the gender of the noun does not matter. Thus with feminine nouns :—

yad kərna, learn by heart, remember
ws ne əpna səbəq yad kia, he learnt his lesson

jəma kərna, collect
bəhwt mal jəma kia, collected much property

The same construction is found with other feminine nouns, as :—

tələb kərna, summon
tələʃ kərna, search for [also (ii)]

fətəh kərna, conquer
rwxsət kərna, send off, say goodbye

malyʃ kərna, rub [also (ii)]
tamir kərna, build [also (ii)]

talim kərna, give religious instruction to [also (ii)]; *see* **talim dena**

So too with masculine nouns. The gender does not affect the construction.

> (ii) *Second Construction :* noun with **ka**, **ki**, according to gender.

> (*a*) Feminine Nouns :—

tarif kərna, praise
məyŋ ne ws ki tarif ki, I praised him

mynnət kərna, beseech
məyŋ ne ws ki mynnət ki, I besought him

maly∫ kərna, rub

məyŋ ne ws ki ţaŋg ki maly∫ ki, I rubbed his leg [also (i)]

ki tazim kərna, honour

ki təhqir kərna, despise

ki tərbiət kərna, train, etc.

ki hyfazət kərna, protect

ki nygrani kərna, protect

ki rəhnwmai kərna, guide

ki fərmanbərdari kərna, obey

ki hyqarət kərna, despise

ki bəɽai kərna, exalt

ki bwrai kərna, speak evil of

ki pərvəry∫ kərna, support, rear

ki təla∫ kərna, search for [also (i)]

ki mədəd kərna, help; also with **dena**

ki nygəhbani kərna, protect

ki hydayət kərna ⎱ give religious instruction to; [also (iii)];
ki talim kərna   ⎰   also with **dena**

(b) Similar are masculine nouns, as :—

ka bəndbəst (bəndobəst) kərna	arrange for
ka yntyzam kərna	arrange for
ka fəyslə kərna	decide

(iii) *Third Construction :* this is like (i), but with this important difference, that the gender of the noun affects the verb. This is seen in the past tenses of the verb, whèn the noun is feminine. There are not so many in this class as in (i).

wse məlamət ki, rebuked him

ws ne wse takid ki, he urged him

ws ne wse təmbih ki, he punished him

wse tadib ki, punished him

ws ne wse nəsihət ki, he gave him advice

ws ne wse hydayət ki, gave him orders.

Cf. **hydayət kərna** in (ii) and see **hydayət dena** below

B. dena with a noun. Two classes :—

(i) The verb made up of **dena** and a noun takes its object in the dative case with **ko**. Pronouns may of course take their short forms, **mwjhe**, **wse**,

wnheŋ, etc. The noun joined to **dena** cannot take **ko**.

twm ne wse (*or* wsko) dhokha dia — you deceived him

twm ne ws ko ys bat ka bədla dia — you rewarded him for this or paid him out for this (i.e., both good and bad meaning)

Cf. **bədla lena** below under **lena**. So also with feminine nouns.

wse ʃykəst di, defeated him — do ʃəxsoŋ ko səlib di, crucified two men

Others are :—

talim dena — teach; *see* **talim kərna**
tərjih dena — prefer
mədəd dena — help; *also* **mədəd kərna**
hydayət dena — instruct about religious matters; *see* **hydayət kərna** in (ii) and (iii) above

(ii) The noun and **dena** are treated like one single verb, and the gender of the noun does not affect the verb. There are very few in this class.

tərtib, fem., arrangement, gives us :—

kytab ko tərtib dia — compiled the book
kytab is accusative here, not dative.

qərar dena — fix, decide
jəlse ka dyn qərar do — fix the day of the meeting

C. **Nouns with marna.** The noun joined to **marna** cannot take **ko**.

juti marna, strike with a shoe — bed marna, cane
koɽa marna, whip

laṭhi marna, strike with a big stick

ws ne mwjhe juti mari

yotə marna, dive (purposely; *see infra* yotə khana)

he struck me with a shoe

D. khana, eat (with noun which cannot take ko). This almost always means " to suffer or experience something unpleasant ".

dhokha khana, be deceived
yəm khana, be grieved
mar khana, be beaten
koṛa khana, be whipped
qəsəm khana, take an oath
yotə khana, sink in water, be almost drowned; *see supra* yotə marna

ṭhokər khana, stumble
bed khana, be caned
juti, jutiaŋ khana, be beaten with shoe
pəlṭi khana, turn a somersault
ʃykəst khana, be defeated

Common, but peculiar, is **cwyli khana**, speak against, slander :—

ws ne meri cwyli khai

he spoke against me, *or* he slandered me

E. lena, take (with noun which cannot take ko).

mol lena, buy, with direct object :—

məyŋ ne ek kytab mol li   I bought a book

bədla lena, take vengeance (on, **se**), pay out (**se**, of object) :—

voh twm se ys bat ka bədla leŋge

they will pay you out for this

F. pana, obtain (with noun which does not take ne).

hydayət pana, reform (intr.)

ws ne hydayət pai, he reformed, gave up evil ways

qərar pana, be decided; does not take **ne** in past participle tenses :—

yeh bat qərar pai   this matter was decided

But note that **qərar pana**, obtain rest, does take **ne** with past participle tense :—

axyr wnhoŋ ne qərar paya   at last they obtained rest

ADVERBS

Adverbial ideas are usually expressed in Urdu by means of abstract nouns and a postposition. Some adjectives are used as adverbs, and some words are both postpositions and adverbs.

Place

pas, near	nice, below
qərib, near	upər, upwards
age, ahead, in front	piche, behind
par, on the other side	bahər, outside
əndər, inside	bhitər, inside

tərəf (*feminine*), direction, helps to form adverbs :—

ys tərəf	over here, in this direction
kys tərəf	where, in what direction?
caroŋ tərəf	on all sides, in all directions
yəhaŋ, here, hither	vəhaŋ, there, thither
kəhaŋ, where, whither?	jəhaŋ, where, whither (relative)
kəhiŋ, somewhere	kəhiŋ nə kəhiŋ, somewhere or other
kəhiŋ kəhiŋ, here and there	jəhaŋ kəhiŋ, wherever

yəhiŋ, **vəhiŋ**, and **jəhiŋ** are emphatic forms of **yəhaŋ**, **vəhaŋ**, **jəhaŋ**. **jəhiŋ** is uncommon.

ydhər, hither, here	wdhər, thither, there
kydhər, whither, where?	jydhər, whither, where (relative)

In the case of these last four, the sense of motion to, hither, thither, etc., is commoner than that of rest in, here, there, etc.

Time

aj, to-day
kəl, to-morrow, yesterday
pərsoŋ, the day after to-mor-row, *or* day before yester-day.

tərsoŋ (rare), the day after or before **pərsoŋ**
nərsoŋ (rare), the day after or before **tərsoŋ**

In place of **tərsoŋ** and **nərsoŋ** it is more usual to say **cəwthe dyn**, **paŋcveŋ dyn**.

The words given above are used only from the stand-point of to-day. From the standpoint of the past or the future "the next day" would be: **dusre dyn**, and "two days after": **tisre dyn**. "The day before" would be: **ek dyn pəhyle**, and "two days before": **do dyn pəhyle.**

Other adverbs connected with time are :—

ahystə, slowly (and softly)
əb, now
jəb, when (relative)
jəb se, since
jəb tək, until
kəb, when?
kəb se, since when?
kəbhi, sometimes
kəbhi kəbhi, occasionally
kəbhi nə kəbhi, some time or other
hote⸴ hote, gradually

əb se, from now (looking either forward or back)
təb, then, after that (often correlative to **jəb**)
jhət ⎫ at once, immedi-
fəwrən ⎬ ately
fylfəwr ⎭
jəb kəbhi, whenever
rəftə rəftə, gradually
jəldi jəldi, quickly

əbhi, **jəbhi**, **təbhi** are emphatic forms of **əb**, **jəb**, **təb**. **jəbhi** and **təbhi** usually mean: for that reason, that is why. See notes on **əb**, **əbhi**, pp. 120–1; on **jəb**, **jəbhi**, **jəbtək**, **jəb to**, pp. 121–2.

aj kəl, in these days

dyn dyn ⎫ day by day
dyn bə dyn ⎬ day after day
roz bə roz ⎭ gradually

bar bar ⎫ frequently
ghəɽi ghəɽi ⎭ over and over again

həɾ roz (or simply, **roz**), every day

səvere, early
dəfətən, suddenly
əcanək, suddenly

fylhal, at present, in the meantime

bylfel, almost the same as **fylhal**

Manner

tərəh (*fem.*), manner, is used for adverbs of manner.

ys tərəh, in this way
əcchi tərəh, well
yuŋ, thus
tuŋ, tyuŋ, vuŋ (correlative to **juŋ**) so

kys tərəh, how?

juŋ, as (relative)

juŋ tuŋ kərke, with difficulty

yuŋhi, **juŋhi**, emphatic forms of **yuŋ** and **juŋ**. For notes on **juŋ**, **juŋhi**, **juŋjuŋ**, **juŋtuŋ**, see p. 122.

yuŋhi often means "without any reason", "causelessly".

əyse, so, thus
jəyse, as (relative)
kyoŋkər, how? (especially in rhetorical questions, often suggesting impossibility)

kəyse, how?
vəyse, so (correlative to **jəyse**)

Other adverbs :—

əlbəttə	of course, certainly
əlɣərəz, ɣərəz	in short
ənqərib	nearly
bəhwt	very
bəxubi	well
baqi	after all, in any case
bəɽhkər	more, to greater extent
befʃək	without doubt

bhəla	well then
bhi	also, even; see pp. 127–8
bylkwl	altogether
fəqət	only, that is all
haŋ	yes
hərgyz (used only with negative) :	never
hi	adverb of emphasis; see pp. 123–4
hote hote	see under Adverbs of Time
kəhiŋ	much (in comparison)
kəm se kəm, kəm əz kəm	at least
koi	approximately
kyoŋ	why?
xaskər	especially
xwsusən	especially
lyhaza	therefore, accordingly
məslən	for example
mət	don't (with imperative)
nə	not, no
nahəq	unwarrantably, unreasonably
nəhiŋ	no, not
nyhayət	extremely
niz	also
phyr	then, again
qərib, qəribən	nearly
rəftə rəftə	see under Adverbs of Time
səxt	very (of unpleasant things)
syrf	only
tək (with negative)	not even (emphasising preceding word)
to	indeed, then
yttyfaqən	by chance
zərur	certainly, of necessity
zyadə	more

kəhiŋ, much, as in **kəhiŋ əccha** *or* **behtər** : very much better.

koi, approximately; **koi dəs mil ka faslə**, a distance of about 10 mls.

mət is used with imperatives only when the person is addressed as **tu** or **twm**.

tək in negative clause means " not even "; as :—

ghəɽa tək nə choɽa	he did not leave me even a water vessel

It will be noticed that **tək** is not a postposition since we do not have **ǵhəɽe tək.**

POSTPOSITIONS

Postpositions generally follow the noun or pronoun or adverb which they govern. Nouns or pronouns are governed by postpositions in the ordinary oblique case.

Etymologically postpositions are in most cases nouns in the locative case, sometimes old nouns, sometimes nouns in current use. Sometimes they directly follow the word they govern, but more often the word for " of ", **ke** or **ki**, intervenes. This brings out the fact that they are nouns and have gender, **ke** being used when they are masculine, and **ki** when they are feminine.

Postpositions immediately following the word governed :—

* ka, ke, ki, of ; see note	pər, upon
ko, for, to	meŋ, in, into
se, from, with, than, by	ne, by
tək, up to, till	səmet, along with

Postpositions following the word governed, but preceded by **ke** :—

ke pas, near, with	ke lie, for, for the sake of
ke piche, behind, after	ke nice, under
ke upər, over, above	ke age, in front of, before
ke nəzdik, near	ke sath, along with
ke bhitər, inside	ke əndər, in, inside

* This is both a postposition and an adjective; it becomes **ke** before a masculine noun in the plural and in the oblique singular. Before all feminine nouns, it is **ki**.

ke pəre, beyond

ke vaste, for, for the sake of

ke syre, at the end or extremity of

ke bəɣəyr, without

ke mwtabyq, according to

ke mare, through, on account of

ke mafyq (mwafyq), according to, suitable to

ke sypwrd, in charge of

ke həvale, in charge of

ke bəjae, instead of

ke bərəks, the opposite of

ke layq, suitable for

ke dərmyan, in the middle of

ke bays, on account of

ke qabyl, worthy of, fit for

ke xylaf, ke bərxylaf, in opposition to

ke əlavə, besides, in addition to

ke zymme, in the responsibility of

ke bədle, in exchange for

ke gyrd, ke yrd gyrd, round about

ke qərib, near

ke par, on the other side of, beyond

ke haŋ, at or to the house or place of

ke hath, by the hand of

ke samne, in front of

ke bəmujyb, according to

ke byna, without

ke bahər, outside of

ke bərabər, equal to, on a level with

ke rubəru, face to face with

ke bavwjud, in spite of

ke mwtəəllyq, connected with

ke evəz, instead of

ke dərpəy, in pursuit of

ke səbəb, on account of

ke vəsile, by means of, through

ke as pas, round about and near

ke bad, after (in time)

ke qəbl, before (in time)

ke zərie, by means of

ke syva, besides, in addition to

ke caroŋ tərəf, on all sides of

The following come after their noun or pronoun, but are preceded by **ki** :—

ki tərəf, towards

ki xatyr, for the sake of

ki manynd, like

ki nysbət, than

ki janyb, towards

ki babət, concerning

ki mysl, like

ki jəgəh, in place of

ki maryfət, by means of, through

ki tərəh, in the manner of

ki bədəwlət, thanks to, through (of good things)

ki zəbani, by the mouth of

Occasionally one of these postpositions is separated from **ki** and comes before its noun or pronoun. In this case **ki** is changed to **ke**, as :—

> manynd ws ke   like him

There are a few Arabic and Persian postpositions which precede their nouns or pronouns. Some of these are used only in certain fixed phrases, and their meanings as postpositions do not arise. The following are worth recording :—

dər, in	be, without
ba, with	əz, from, by (of author)
ma, along with	fi, per ; as :—
ta, up to, till	fi sədi, per cent.

Except **be** and **ma**, all are used only in Persian and Arabic expressions.

NOTES

1. donoŋ, tinoŋ, caroŋ, etc. (with postpositions)

The following sentences show how to attach postpositions to these numerals :—

tinoŋ ne lykha	the three of them wrote
donoŋ ko dykhao	show it to both
caroŋ admioŋ ne kəha	all four men said; cf. **caroŋ admi ae**, all four **men** came
tisra hərf zəbər əwr peʃ se donoŋ tərəh həy	the third letter can be written with short **a** and short **u**, both ways
rastbazoŋ əwr narastoŋ donoŋ ki qyamət hogi	there will be a resurrection of both the righteous and the unrighteous
ws ne hynduoŋ əwr mwsəl-manoŋ donoŋ pər ylzam ləgaya	he blamed both Hindus and Muhammadans

mwrdoŋ əwr zyndoŋ donoŋ
ka xwdavənd

Lord of both the dead and
the living

donoŋ beṭoŋ meŋ se hər ek
ko dwa di

he blessed both his sons

2. Two or three postpositions may be used together

wn ke bic meŋ se	from among them
yn meŋ ka	(one) of them
meri tərəf se kəhna	say from me, on my behalf
mez pər se gyra	it fell off the table (from on)
yn meŋ se ek ne kəha	one of them said (from in)
ghər ke samne ka dərəxt	the tree in front of the house
ws ke pas se cəla gəya	he went away from him

" From " of motion from a *person* cannot be expressed
by **se** alone. This sentence would more naturally be : **wse
choṛkər cəla ġəya**.

CONJUNCTIONS

əwr, and
o, and (Persian)
lekyn, but
pər, but
bəlky, but (not so and so,
but so and so); on the
contrary; say rather
əgər, if
hərcənd, although
to, then, indeed
cuŋky, since
pəs, so, in short, accordingly
nəhiŋ to, if not, otherwise
taky, in order that
ya . . . ya, either . . . or
xah . . . xah, whether . . .
or; either . . . or

cahe . . . cahe, caho . . .
caho, whether . . . or;
either . . . or
ya, or
ky, that
məgər, but
tahəm, nevertheless, yet
təwbhi, nevertheless, yet
go, go ky, although
halaŋky, although
phyr, then
cwnaŋcy, accordingly, so
kyoŋky, because
vərnə, if not, otherwise
aya, whether
kya . . . kya, whether . . .
or; both . . . and
nə . . . nə, neither . . . nor

NOTES

1. **aya**, whether : is used at the beginning of noun clauses; it is often followed a few words farther on by **ya**, or :—

jake pucho (ky) aya twm ana cahte ho ya nəhiŋ	go and ask him whether he wishes to come or not

In this sentence, **ya nəhiŋ** may be omitted.

2. **kya . . . kya** : separates words, but not clauses :—

kya bəṛe kya choṭe	whether great or small; i.e., both great and small

3. **xah . . . xah** : separates both clauses and words :—

xah swneŋ xah nə swneŋ	whether they listen or not
xah choṭe xah bəṛe	whether small or great, but not both (*see* **kya . . . kya**)

4. **cahe . . . cahe** : usually separates clauses :—

cahe dudh pio cahe ləssi pio	drink either milk or butter-milk
cahe kwch hi ho	no matter what happens; lit., whether anything may be, with " or not " understood. In this case the second **cahe** is omitted

If the nominative is **twm**, as in the first sentence under **cahe**, we may change **cahe** to **caho**, you wish—**caho dudh pio caho ləssi**.

5. **cahe . . . cahe, caho . . . caho, xah . . . xah** : all mean either one alternative or the other, but not both alternatives. On the other hand, **kya . . . kya** means both the one and the other.

6. **lekyn, məgər, pər**, and **bəlky**.
bəlky is distinct from the others. It expresses English " but ", " in fact ", etc., in phrases like the following : not

so, but on the contrary; not only so but more; not that, in
fact not even this; so, in fact even more than that.

lomɽi nəhiŋ bəlky gidəɽ	not a fox but a jackal
yəhiŋ nəhiŋ bəlky wlṭa xəfa hua	not only so, but on the contrary he got angry (wlṭa = upside down)
car kya? bəlky ek bhi nəhiŋ aya	four? why, not even one came
haŋ, wse nəwkər rəkhuŋga, bəlky ghər bhi duŋga	yes, I will take him as a servant; in fact I shall give him a house in addition

lekyn, məgər, and **pər** all mean " but " in adversative
clauses. There is little difference. **lekyn** is the strongest,
məgər the next, and **pər** is the weakest. **pər** can
never be stressed; the other two can. In most cases one
may use any one of the three. Indian grammars say that
məgər marks exceptions. There is not much in this.

səb ae məgər kərim nə aya	they all came, but Karim did not come
twm ʃayəd rənjida ho, pər bole bəγəyr kəyse rəhuŋ?	you will perhaps be annoyed, but how can I refrain from speaking?
məyŋ ne səxt hwkm dia lekyn ws ne meri ek nə mani	I gave strict orders, but he paid no attention to a single thing I said

The difference is very slight.

INTERJECTIONS

hae, hae hae, alas !	əfsos, what a pity !
vah va, how splendid !	ʃabaʃ, bravo !
əre (*fem.* əri), O !, used in addressing some one; it implies the pronoun **twm** or **tu**	kaʃ, kaʃ ky, would that !

We may include here nouns of address :—

ji	sir, madam; may be said to any one who is addressed as **ap**
ji haŋ	yes, sir
ji nəhiŋ	no, sir

jənab, **hwzur**, **sərkar** are very respectful terms of address, meaning "sir" or "madam". **jənab** may be used in any highflown conversation for " sir " or " madam ". **hwzur** is used chiefly by servants, but also occasionally by others as an exaggerated term of respect. **sərkar**, literally the Government of a state or country, is rather obsequious ; it is rather common among villagers, but rare among servants.

vala has the sense of being connected with, being in charge of, belonging to, possessing. With a verbal noun or gerund it is an agent, one doing or about to do something. It is used as a suffix to nouns, including verbal nouns, and to some adverbs and postpositions. Nouns of the Second Declension, ending in **-a**, including verbal nouns, or **-ə**, change **-a** or **-ə** to **-e** before **-vala**. It cannot be used with an adjective.

dwpəṭṭevala	the man with a shawl
bəkrivala	the goatherd
voh aj janevali həy	she's about to go to-day; she is starting to-day
həm car khanevale həyŋ	we are four eaters; my family consists of four
bicvala	the middle one
parvala	the one on the other side

-vala can be suffixed to the following adverbs of time and postpositions or adverbs of place :—

aj, to-day	tərsoŋ ⎱ (rare) (see under
kəl, to-morrow, yesterday	nərsoŋ ⎰ adverbs of time)
pərsoŋ, day after to-morrow, day before yesterday	əb, now

pas, near

qərib, near

nəzdik, near

par, on the other side

bad, after

bic, middle

dərmyan, middle

nice, below

upər, above

sath, along with

samne, in front

pəhyle, before, formerly

bahər, outside

əndər, bhitər, inside

piche, behind

age, before

pəre, beyond

bərabər, on a level with

-vala must not be used with adjectives; thus, referring to **topiaŋ**, caps :—

ap kali cahte həyŋ ya lal?
məyŋ kali luŋga

do you want the black one or the red? I will take the black one

It would be wrong to say **kalivali**; still more so, **kala-vala**.

NECESSITY, ADVISABILITY, DUTY

These ideas are expressed by either :—

1. The infinitive with one of the verbs **hona**, **həy**, **tha**, together with some adjective (or even noun) meaning necessary, proper, advisable, duty, etc. [On this infinitive see below, p. 96.]

2. One of these adjectives or nouns with the conjunction **ky**, that, followed by the present subjunctive or past conditional.

The adjectives generally used are **zəruri**, **zərur**, necessary; **mwnasyb**, suitable, proper; **vajyb** or **lazym**, right, proper; **fərz**, a noun meaning "duty" is also quite common.

Examples of (1) and (2) :—

(1) jana mwnasyb həy

jana mera fərz tha

(2) lazym həy ky məyŋ jauŋ

lazym tha ky voh jata

it is proper to go

it was my duty to go

it is right that I should go

it was right that he should go

3. The idea of necessity, must, etc., may also be expressed by one of the verbs **hona**, **həy**, **tha**, **pəɽna** without the word **zərur**, necessary.

mwjhe jana pəɽega	I shall have to go
mwjhe jana həy	I have to go

4. The idea of duty, advisability, ought, etc., may also be expressed by :—

   (i) **cahie**, it is advisable or desirable or right, with the infinitive, or, in the past tense, with the infinitive and **tha**.

   (ii) **cahie** alone for the present tense, or with **tha** followed by the conjunction **ky**, that, and the present subjunctive or past conditional.

mwjhe jana cahie	I ought to go
mwjhe jana cahie tha	I ought to have gone
cahie tha ky məyŋ jata	I ought to have gone

It will be noticed that although **cahie** by itself means " it *is* desirable ", it can be used with **tha**, and then **cahie tha** means " it *was* desirable ".

Gerundive Infinitive

In the above cases the infinitive is almost always the gerundive infinitive (see p. 68), i.e., it is an adjective agreeing with the object if there is one (except in case (*b*) explained below). We must remember that in reality this object is generally the grammatical nominative. As will be seen below, the gerund is sometimes used.

The rules for the construction of the gerundive infinitive are as follows :—

   (*a*) If there is no object the infinitive is masculine singular.

   (*b*) If there is an object followed by **ko** the infinitive is masculine singular.

   (*c*) If there is an object without **ko** the infinitive agrees with it in gender and number.

(*d*) The person who has to or ought to perform the action mentioned, or for whom it is necessary, is put in the dative case with **ko**. In English this person is usually in the nominative case.

Examples :—

həmeŋ əpni bhul manni cahie	we should admit our fault
wse naʃpatiaŋ xəridni pəɽeŋgi	he will have to buy pears
twmheŋ əpni amdəni ko gəɲvana mwnasyb nəhiŋ	it is not proper for you to throw away your income
mwjhe cyṭṭhi ḍak meŋ ḍalni thi	I had to post a letter

For the subjunctive after **ky** the rule is that the present subjunctive is used for present and future time, and the past conditional for past time.

ap ka fərz həy ky ədəb se jəvab deŋ	it is your duty to answer politely
lazym həy ky voh vərzyʃ kəre	it is right that he should do physical exercise
mali ko cahie tha ky nimbu nycoɽta	the gardener should have squeezed out the lemons
həmeŋ vajyb tha ky pəhyle se təiyari kərte	we should have prepared beforehand

Gerund or Verbal Noun

This is sometimes used instead of the gerundive, but not often if there is an object.

mera fəwrən ləwṭ ana lazym bəlky fərz həy	it is right, in fact a duty, for me to return at once (my immediately returning is right, in fact a duty)
ap ka ys tərəh jhuṭ bolna mwnasyb nə tha	your telling lies like this was improper

HABIT

Habit can be expressed to some extent by the Present and Imperfect tenses, but to emphasise the habitual nature of an action, the verb **kərna** is used with what appears to be the past participle of the required verb. It is not certain that this is a past participle, but beginners will remember the rule more easily if they consider that it is. It has the same form as the masculine past participle for every verb except **jana**, which takes the form **jaya**. The form does not vary for gender or number.

ws ke dəftər meŋ nə bəyʈha kəro	do not make a habit of sitting in his office
məyŋ ʃam ke vəqt ʈəhla kərta tha	I used to go for a walk at sunset

CONTINUANCE, ETC.

rəhna : remain, reside, when used with another verb, has two meanings :—

1. **rəha**, the past participle, joined to the root of another verb, expresses doing or being something at the moment spoken of. We have already seen this in the conjugation of the verb.

pi rəha	drinking at the moment
wʈ rəha	flying at the moment
ʃerni jəngəl meŋ pani pi rəhi thi	the tigress was drinking water in the forest
wqab asman meŋ wʈ rəhe həyŋ	eagles are flying in the sky

2. **rəhna** with the present participle of any verb means to go on doing something, keep on doing, continue to do. This closely resembles the English idiom.

sari rat jua khelte rəhe	they gambled all night
meri bivi rəfu kərti rəhti həy	my wife keeps on darning

Beginners find a difficulty in the use of **kərna** (see last section) and **rəhna**, when used with other verbs, and still more when used with each other. The following should be studied :—

richni seb kha rəhi həy	the she-bear is eating apples
richni seb khati həy	the she-bear eats apples
richni seb khati rəhti həy	the she-bear keeps on eating apples
richni seb khaya kərti həy	the she-bear makes a habit of eating apples

Compare also :—

məlkə xemoŋ meŋ rəha kərti həyŋ	the queen makes a habit of living in tents
məlkə kam kərti rəhti həyŋ	the queen keeps on working
məlkə kam kər rəhi həyŋ	the queen is working just now

CONDITIONAL SENTENCES

The method of expressing conditions depends on whether the fulfilment of the condition is (a) assumed, (b) doubtful, but possible, (c) impossible :—

(a) When the fulfilment is assumed as at least extremely probable, the indicative is generally used.

əgər ap ki əysi mərzi həy to zərur jauŋga	if this is your will, I shall certainly go
əgər nəwkər se yeh bhul hui to ws se bəɽa qwsur hua	if the servant made this mistake, he committed a great fault
ap der se aeŋge to ap ka kam nə bənega	if you come late you will not obtain your purpose (your work will not be made)

(b) If the fulfilment is possible but doubtful, the protasis (the if-clause) has the present subjunctive. The other may be either indicative or present subjunctive. The latter implies more doubt. The apodosis (second clause) sometimes has the verb in the imperative, which is only a form of the present subjunctive.

ʃayr ho to ʃer bhi kəhega nə	if he is a poet, he will make up verses, won't he?
əgər ʃer pynjre meŋ phəŋs gəya ho to əccha həy	if the tiger has been caught in the trap it is a good thing
xəbərdar twm ne gali di to pəchtaoge	take care, if you use bad language you will be sorry
hwkm dijie to məyŋ əb jauŋ	give the order and I will go
əgər yjazət myle to kam ʃwru kəruŋ	if I get permission I shall (or can) begin the work
age bəɽhe to məre	if you go forward you are a dead man; (lit. if you went forward you died)

(c) Fulfilment not possible; both clauses in past conditional or pluperfect conditional.

əgər ləɽke ke bap ko xəbər hoti to bəɽa ghəbrata	if the boy's father knew, he would be much distressed (or had known . . . would have been)
ys koɽhɽi ki səfedi nə ki gəi hoti to məwlvi sahəb səxt naraz nə hote?	if this room had not been whitewashed, would the maulvi not have been very angry?
zəra bhi durəndeʃi kərte to əysi bevəqufi twm se sər- zəd na hoti	if you had exercised the least foresight, you would not have committed such folly
ap wse dərgwzər kərte to əccha hota	if you had forgiven him, it would have been a good thing

For examples of the pluperfect conditional, see sentences, Lesson 27, pp. 210–12.

SOME PARTICIPIAL CONSTRUCTIONS

Types :

> (i) phəṭa jata həy.
> (ii) pəṛhta jata həy.
> (iii) pəṛhe jata həy.
> (iv) jata rəha.
> (v) kəhe deta həy.
> (vi) aya cahta həy.
> (vii) roya ki

(i) Past participles of intransitive verbs are used with tenses formed from the present participle of **jana** to indicate being on the verge of or rapidly approaching some condition.

mera dyl phəṭa jata həy	my heart is just breaking
məyŋ məri jati huŋ	I am almost dead (i.e., exhausted, greatly distressed)
mera gəla bəyṭha jata tha	my throat was sitting down, i.e., I was rapidly becoming so hoarse that I could not speak
mere roŋgṭe khəṛe hue jate the	the hairs (on my body) were ready to stand on end (through alarm, etc.)
məyŋ əccha hua jata huŋ	I am rapidly getting well, am almost well

Note that **hota jata huŋ** would mean "gradually getting well".

(ii) When the present participle of any verb, transitive or intransitive, is used with **jana** as an auxiliary verb, three cases arise :—

(a) The verb **jana** may retain its sense of "going". In this case there are two distinct verbs :—

voh həŋsta jata tha	he was going along laughing
gwṛia leti ja	take the doll with you (*fem.*)
ca pite jao	have some tea before you go

(*b*) If the first verb is purely neuter, not expressing action of any kind, the meaning is " gradually becoming ".

voh buṛha hota jata tha   he was gradually becoming old

Note that in example 4 under (i) above, **khəṛa hona** is not a neuter verb, though **hona** by itself is.

(*c*) If the first verb is transitive or intransitive (but not neuter), the two verbs together mean " keep on doing " with the action limited to one occasion at a time. It implies intention, and therefore is confined to sentient beings, including inanimate things personified. Arising out of the intention implied there is often a suggestion of " in spite of something going on at the same time, possibly tending to hinder it ". It sometimes seems to say " he went on, and would not give up ". The meaning does not differ greatly from that given below under **pəṛhe jana**, but in this case the first verb may be intransitive as well as transitive.

voh cahe lakh məna kərta   although he used (on various
tha məyŋ əpna kam kərta   occasions) to forbid me
jata tha   strongly, yet (on each oc-
                           casion) I went on with my
                           work (lit. he used to
                           forbid me 100,000)

(iii) The past participle of transitive verbs, inflected in the masculine singular oblique form, is used with **jana** to indicate " keep on doing ". The action is generally limited to one occasion at a time. Like **pəṛhta jana**, dealt with in the previous section, this implies intention, is confined to sentient beings, and has a suggestion of something else going on at the same time, possibly tending to hinder it.

phuloŋ ko kyoŋ choṛe jate   why do you go on leaving
ho   out the flowers?

(**choṛ jate ho** would mean " leave them and go off ".)

saŋp wse nygle jata tha	the snake kept on swallowing it up
ləɽka əpna səbəq pəɽhe jata tha	the boy kept on at his lesson (on that occasion)

(**pəɽhta rəha** might mean he worked for some months.)

ram ka nam rəʈe jao	keep on repeating Ram's name (do not mind what is going on at the same time)
ws ne bəhwt məna kia, pər məyŋ əpna kam kie gəya	he tried hard to stop me, but I went on with my work

This is like the case discussed under (ii), but here the first verb must be transitive.

(iv) **jata rəhna** means :—

> (*a*) disappear,
> (*b*) die,
> (*c*) keep on going.

ys ʃəhr ki sari rəwnəq jati rəhi	the liveliness of this town has disappeared, i.e., few people are left in it
voh vəhaŋ do məhine bərabər jata rəha	he continued going there for two months

(v) The past participle of a transitive verb (inflected in the oblique masculine singular) is joined to **dena**, rather less commonly to **lena**, still less commonly to **ḍalna**, and least commonly to **bəyʈhna**, to show definite decision. This use is confined to tenses formed from the present participle.

məyŋ saf kəhe deta huŋ	I tell you plainly
məyŋ əbhi dhoe ḍalta huŋ	I will wash it in a moment
məyŋ əpna dwpəʈʈa lie leta huŋ	I will take my shawl

(vi) The uninflected past participle of a verb (or what looks like a past participle) is joined to the tenses formed

from the present participle of **cahna** to express the idea of
" about to do something ".

gaṛi aya cahti həy   the train is just coming

With **jana** the form **jaya** (not **gəya**) is used. See p. 66.

(vii) The past participle (or what looks like the past
participle) of any verb may be used with the past tense of
kərna (which in this case does *not* take **ne**) to mean continuous action.

voh chəy məhine tək myṭṭi   they were carrying earth for
   ḍhoya kie   six months
bwṛhia der tək roya ki   the old woman kept on
                      weeping for a lonɜ time

This should be compared with the use of the past participle of a verb along with all tenses of **kərna** *except* those
formed from the past participle to express habitual action.

The methods of expressing the passive may be summarised
as follows :—

> (i) By turning the sentence round so as to make the
>   verb active. See above.
> (ii) By the passive voice—not so common as in
>   English. See above.
> (iii) By an intransitive verb having what seems to us
>   a passive sense. Thus an angry schoolmaster
>   says :—

ləṛko xamoʃ ! nəhiŋ to   boys, be quiet ! or you will
   pyṭoge   get the cane (lit. be
                      beaten)

> The transitive verb implies intention; there-
> fore a servant breaking a plate is right in saying
> " **pleṭ ṭuṭ gəi** ", the plate has got broken.
> " **məyŋ ne toṛi** ", I have broken it, suggests
> deliberate breaking. Gross carelessness would
> count as intentional.

ws ne əpna sara mal wṛa dia   he squandered all his pro-
                                     perty

(iv) By using an adjective with a passive sense, such
as an Arabic passive participle, with **hona** or
ho jana :—

nəwkər məwquf ho gəya   the servant was dismissed

Notes on the Use of the Passive Voice

1. Many kinds of transitive verbs made up of two or
more words can be used in the passive. Such are the
following :—

(i) Compound verbs, e.g., verbs with **dena, lena,
ḍalna, rəkhna**, as their second element.

təmam dərəxt kaţ ḍale gəe   all the trees were cut down

(ii) Verbs composed of noun or adjective and verb.

moţər mol li gəi   the motor-car was bought
səbəq yad kia gəya   the lesson was learnt

A remarkable thing is that this sometimes
occurs when the active verb does not take the
direct object.

ʃəhr ke qərib bəhwt se admi   many men were crucified
səlib die gəe   near the city

The active voice of this verb takes the dative.

(iii) **ləgna, səkna** and **cwkna** can be used along with
the passive.

joţa sia ja cwka   the suit of clothes has been
                                 made (sewn)
əb voh wstadoŋ meŋ gyna   now he has begun to be
jane ləga   counted among the mas-
                                 ters
bəyl jota nə ja səka   the bull could not be yoked

(iv) Verbs used in expressions signifying necessity,
duty, etc.

ws vəqt cyţţhi lykhi jani thi at that time a letter had to
                                 be written

    (v) Along with **rǝhna** and the present participle which show continuity :—

paejamǝ sia jata rǝhega   the trousers will continue being made

    (vi) Two verbs used together as a form of repetition.

vǝhiŋ pala posa gǝya   it was there he was brought up and looked after

    (vii) A very peculiar use is the impersonal passive with the logical nominative governed by **ko**, which means " as for, with regard to, etc. ".

ws ko bǝr tǝrǝf kia gǝya   with regard to him it was dismissed, i.e., he was dismissed

ws ko xub piṭa gǝya   he was soundly beaten

ws ko byṭha dia gǝya   he was seated, i.e., he was given a chair

        Students should not attempt to copy this usage till they have become very familiar with it. The straightforward passive is also correct and quite common : **voh bǝr tǝrǝf kia ǵǝya**, he was dismissed.

    (viii) The negative passive expresses inability, cannot, could not, etc. See p. 69.

SPECIAL POINTS
The use of ne

[See p. 49.]

    (*a*) *Compound Verbs.* A compound verb requires **ne** if both the verbs of which it is composed would take **ne** when used alone. If either of the verbs would not take **ne** when used alone, the compound verb will not take **ne**.

    E.g., **kǝh dena**; both verbs take **ne**, therefore **kǝh dena** takes **ne**.

mǝyŋ ne saf kǝh dia   I said plainly

But **ro dena**, weep; **həŋs dena**, laugh; **cəl dena**, go off; **ho lena**, accompany, etc.; **ro lena**, weep—have in each case one verb which does not take **ne**; therefore the compound verbs do not take it.

ləṛki ro di	the girl burst out crying
donoŋ sypahi cəl die	both the sepoys went off

So also :—

voh le aya, he brought	voh le gəya, he took away

(b) The following verbs which are or can be transitive do not take **ne** :—

*bolna, speak	bhulna, forget
*bəkna, talk nonsense	ləgna, begin
*jənna, give birth to	cwkna, finish
lana, bring (probably con-	kərna, expressing continu-
tracted from **le-ana**)	ance : as **voh roya ki**, she
dykhai dena, be visible	kept on crying
swnai dena, be audible	phaŋdna, leap over
pana, succeed in, manage to,	
be allowed to	

(c) The following verbs can be either transitive or intransitive. They take **ne** when they are transitive; otherwise they do not.

bədəlna, change	bhərna, fill, become full, be
jhwləsna, scorch, be	filled
scorched	rəgəṛna, rub
pələṭna, return	wləṭna, turn upside down
qərar pana, obtain rest	pwkarna, call out
qərar pana ne, be decided	pwkarna ne, call to some one
	for help

pəṛhna : learn, read, recite; and **sikhna** : learn to do

* These, when the object is expressed, may take **ne**. Thus :—

ws ne [or voh] behudə bəka	he talked great nonsense
ws ne [or voh] jhuṭ bola	he told a lie

For " what did he say? " we may not use **ws ne**; it is **voh kya bola ?**

something, should both have **ne**, but occasionally occur without it.

səməjhna, even when transitive, is better without **ne**, but occasionally has it.

(*d*) The following never have **ne** when there is no object, but when there is one they may either have it or omit it.

harna, lose, be defeated   jitna, win

When they have an object such as **bazi**, game; **ʃərt**, bet; **mwqəddyma**, lawsuit, they may either take or omit **ne**.

cahna, wish, omits **ne** if the nominative is **dil**, **ji**, heart; otherwise it takes **ne**.

bəhəsna, argue; **cyllana**, call out, do not take **ne**; **sath dena**, accompany, does.

(*e*) The following intransitive verbs take **ne** :—

thukna, spit   həgna, mutna, perform the
chiŋkna, sneeze   offices of nature
jhaŋkna, peep

thukna can be transitive, meaning despise :—

sare ʃəhr ne wse thuka   the whole city despised him

but it takes **ne** whether it is transitive or not.

həy, hota həy, hota tha, tha, hua

In this connection the following should be noted :—

həy and **tha** mean " is " and "was on one occasion ".
hota həy and **hota tha** mean " is " or "was as a rule, generally ".

The same idea is found in the present and imperfect tenses of other verbs. Finally, the form described on pp. 97–8 means " make a practice of ".

Examples:

ys bəkre ka ek hi siŋ həy   this goat has only one horn
bəkroŋ ke do siŋ hote həyŋ   goats have two horns
bhalu məkəi khate həyŋ   bears eat Indian corn (maize)

dekho bhalu məkəi kha rəha həy — look, the bear is eating the maize

ek bhalu pəhaɽ meŋ rəhta həy, jo hər roz həmari məkəi ko khaya kərta həy — a bear lives in the mountain which makes a daily practice of eating our maize

tha, hua:

tha means simply " was "; **hua** suggests " became ".

voh xəfa tha — he was angry
voh xəfa hua — he got angry
ws ka fəyslə yeh tha — this was his decision
fəyslə hua ky . . . — it was decided that (decision became that)

kya bat thi — what was the matter?
kya hua — what has happened?

mylna, mylana

See also p. 15.
mylna (intransitive), accrue, come to, meet, agree with, join with, mix with.

1. Of things :—

   Be obtained, accrue. The word for the thing is in the nominative, and that for the person who obtained it in the dative.

wn ko tin tin pəyse myle — they got three pice each (to them three pice each accrued)

2. Of persons :—

   Meet, join ; with **ko**, by accident ; with **se**, by design.

voh mwjhe rəste meŋ myla — I met him on the road (Urdu has " he met me ")

səb se myl lo — shake hands with everyone (lit. meet everyone)

əb to ap bhi wdhər hi ja myle — now you too have joined their party (lit. have gone and joined there)

məyŋ ws se jake myla	I went and had a talk with him
voh mwjhe kəhiŋ nəhiŋ mylta	I cannot find him anywhere
voh mwjh se kəbhi nəhiŋ mylta	he never comes to see me
voh meri mwxalyfət ke lie myl gəe	they have conspired to oppose me
3. mylkər, together	səb mylkər khao, eat altogether
myla jwla, mixed up	myla jwla pəṛa həy, it is lying all mixed up

mylana : to compare, make agree, introduce to, mix, joined :—

yn donoŋ xətoŋ ko mylao	compare these two letters
təhsil ki ghəṛi se məyŋ ne əpni jeb ghəṛi mylai	I set my watch by the Tahsil clock (or simply compared it)
kəl məyŋ bəṛe sahəb se myla; kys ne mylaya?	yesterday I had an interview with the head (of any particular department). Who introduced you?
xwda hi ne twjh se mylaya mwjhe	it is God that has united us (made me meet with you)
kysi ne ys ʃərbət meŋ zyadə qənd mylai	some one has put too much sugar in this sherbet
ws ne haŋ meŋ haŋ mylai	he agreed to everything (mixed yes with yes)
həm wse əpni tərəf myla leŋge	we shall get him to join our party (mix him with our side)

ləgna, ləgana

We have already noticed the use of **ləgna** with verbal nouns, p. 70. It means literally "to be attached, to stick" (intransitive). The following sentences will illustrate its various meanings. See also the sentences on pp. 163–4.

səxt dhup ləgi	the sun was very hot (severe sunshine attached)
ap ko coṭ nəhiŋ ləgi nə?	you did not get hurt, did you? (**coṭ**, *f.*, blow, hurt)
mwjhe lohe se ṭhokər ləgi	I knocked my foot against a piece of iron
meri juti ləgti həy	my shoe pinches
səfər meŋ pəndrə dyn ləgeŋge	the journey will take a fortnight
bis admioŋ ki nəwkəri ləgti həy	they employ twenty men
mwjhe hər roz barə bəje bhuk ləgti həy	I get hungry every day at twelve (hunger attaches to me)
kəl mwjhe do bəje pyas ləgi	yesterday I felt thirsty at two
voh mera bhai ləgta həy	he is, one might say, my brother, i.e., my cousin, oldish nephew, etc., almost my brother
ws ka ɣəyr mwlk meŋ dyl (*or* ji) nəhiŋ ləgta	he is not happy in a foreign country (his heart does not stick there)
kytni der ləgegi?	how long will it take?
jənab ap ke nam pər dhəbba ləgega	sir, your name will be disgraced (**dhəbba** = stain)
wn ka kəhna mwjhe bwra ləga	what they said hurt me (attached as evil)
yeh safə ws ko əccha nəhiŋ ləgta	this turban does not suit him, or, he does not like it
ap ke hath kya ləga?	what did you get (what attached to your hand)?
yeh cabi qwfl meŋ nəhiŋ ləgti	this key does not fit the lock
ghər meŋ ag ləg gəi	the house caught fire
mere bap kam meŋ ləge rəhte həyŋ	my father is always at work

mwjhe ws se bimari ləgi	I caught his illness
twmheŋ mwjh se khaŋsi ləgi	you have caught my cough
dostoŋ meŋ məyŋ kyoŋ ghəbrane ləga ?	why should I feel embarrassed (or confused or shy) among friends ?
wse mwŋh nə ləgne do	do not let him become forward with you (or, too familiar with you)
təlvar mwjhe ləgi (occasionally **mere ləgi**)	the sword struck me
dərəxtoŋ meŋ bəhwt phəl ləga həy	there is a lot of fruit on the trees

Some ideas expressed intransitively with **ləgna** can be expressed transitively by **ləgana**. This is true of the following taken from the sentences just given :—

səfər meŋ pəndrə dyn ləgana	take a fortnight over the journey
der ləgana	take a long time over
dhəbba ləgana	to disgrace
cabi ləgana	try the key in the lock
ghər meŋ ag ləgana	set fire to the house
dəs admioŋ ki nəwkəri ləgana	to put ten men to the work

The postpositions are the same as for the intransitive form. Others are :—

ws ne kayəz pər mohr ləgai	he sealed the paper
məyŋ ne dərvaze ki cyțxəni (*or* cəțxəni) ləgai	I bolted the door

cahna, ʃwru kərna, ʃwru hona, xətm kərna, xətm hona

cahna, wish; **ʃwru kərna**, begin; **xətm kərna**, finish, are used with the gerundive infinitive. The rules for this infinitive are :—

   (i) If there is no object, the infinitive is masculine singular.

(ii) If there is an object governed by **ko**, the infinitive is masculine singular.

(iii) If there is an object not governed by **ko**, the infinitive agrees with it.

ʃayr ne nəzm pəṛhni cahi	the poet wished to read a poem
ws ʃəxs ne ag swlgani ʃwru ki	that man began lighting a fire
mere valyd do həveliaŋ bənvani cahte həyŋ, məgər tisri həveli ko bənvana nəhiŋ cahte	my father (plural of respect) wishes to have two houses built, but does not wish to get the third house built

ʃwru hona, begin (intransitive) and **xətm hona**, be finished, are sometimes used with a similar construction of the gerundive infinitive.

təb cyṭṭhiaŋ ani jani ʃwru huiŋ	after that, letters began to come and go (i.e., to pass between them)

cahna = be about to

cahna in its present and imperfect tenses is used with what seems to be a past participle (see p. 97 under Habit) to express " be about to ".

sahəb əbhi aya cahte həyŋ	the gentleman is just about to come
ghoṛi məra cahti thi	the mare was about to die

But note :—

bwḍḍhi bycari mərna cahti thi	the poor old woman wished to die

This apparent past participle is invariable in form. See pp. 98, 104.

cahie

cahie, desirable, comes from **cahna**; its use with verbs has been explained on p. 96. With nouns the rule is as follows :—

> The word for the person who desires a thing is in the dative, the thing desired is in the nominative. In the plural **cahie** changes to **cahieŋ** when used by itself without another verb.

mwjhe kəl car qwli cahieŋ	I want four coolies to-morrow
ḍakṭər ko əcchi dəvaeŋ cahie thiŋ	the doctor wanted good medicine

kəhna, bolna, bətana (bətlana), jətana (jətlana)

kəhna

(i) To say :—

ws ne kəha	he said

(ii) To call :—

yse kya kəhte həyŋ	what do they call this (say to this)?
ws ko kərim kəhte həyŋ, jahyl kəhte həyŋ	they call him Karim—call him ignorant !

(iii) To tell :—

məyŋ ne ws se kəh dia	I have told him

(iv) To command :—

nəwkər se kəho gaṛi təiyar kəre	tell the servant to get the carriage ready
jəyse wn ke bap ne wn ko kəh dia tha	as their father had ordered them

bolna

(i) Speak (occasionally, say) :—

nə bolo ; bolo mət	do not speak
voh boli	she said

(ii) To sound (intransitive) :—

yeh rwpəya bolta nəhiŋ   this rupee does not ring (it is bad)

(iii) To tell (a lie or the truth) :—

| jhuṭ bolna | tell a lie |
| səc bolna | tell the truth |

bətana (less common, **bətlana**) : show, tell, inform.

| məyŋ ap ko rəstə bətata huŋ | I will show you the way |
| mwjhe koi kam bətaə | give me some work to do (show me some work) |

jətana (another form : **jətlana**) is practically the same as **bətana**, but is much less common.

pana and mylna

For **mylna** see details on pp. 109–10.

pana : find, obtain.

twm   ne   kəhaŋ   paya?   where did you find it?
   (= twmheŋ kəhaŋ myla?)
ws ne bəhwt dwkh paya   he suffered much

For being given money one should use **mylna** with the dative :—

     twm ko kya myla?   what did you get?

For **pana**, manage to, which does not take **ne** in past participle tenses, see p. 70.

maŋgna and cahna

See also pp. 112–13.

maŋga is "ask for"; it never means to "want something".

ys ke do hi rwpəe maŋge   he asked only two rupees for this

maŋgkər laya	he has asked for it and brought it (i.e., borrowed it)
bhik maŋgta həy	he begs (asks for alms)

cahna: wish for, desire, love. For construction of **cahna**, see p. 96; for **cahie**, see pp. 96, 114. With a subject denoting an animate being, **cahna** takes **ne** in past participle tenses, but with **dyl** or **ji**, heart, it does not.

mera ji caha	my heart wished
məyŋ ne caha	I wished
kya cahte ho?	what do you want?
ws ki maŋ wse bəhwt cahti həy	his mother loves him very much

cahe, cahe . . . cahe, see p. 92.

gyrna, leṭna, pəṛna

ġyrna: ordinary word for " fall ", also metaphorical.

meri jan gyri jati həy	I am greatly depressed (my life is falling)

leṭna, lie down; **leṭa hua**, lying down

jake leṭ rəho	go and lie down

pəṛna :

(i) Fall, of dew, sunshine, rain, snow, hail, drops of water, etc., but not of things falling off a table, etc.

(ii) Metaphorical, e.g., **afət pəṛi**, calamity befell; **zərurət pəṛi**, necessity befell.

(iii) **pəṛa, pəṛa hua**, lying down.

pəṛa tha	was lying, or lying down
məkan pəṛa hua həy	the house is lying empty
khet pəṛe hue həyŋ	the fields are lying fallow

(iv) Various phrases :—

yəhaŋ pəṛ rəho	sleep here, spend the night here

voh bimar pəɽa	he fell ill, became ill
ws ka gəla pəɽ gəya	he became hoarse (gəla = throat)
voh dur ja pəɽa	it (tottered along, etc., and) fell at a distance
bic meŋ (or, mamle meŋ) kyoŋ pəɽte ho	why do you interfere, intervene?
pəɽe pəɽe	while lying down, or while idle or out of work
ws ka nam kəllu pəɽ gəya	he came to be called Kallu

(v) With infinitive, to have to, see p. 96.

TO HAVE

The English word " have " is expressed in several ways according to the nature of the thing possessed :—

(a) Relatives, human beings : the genitive with **ka** and the corresponding possessive pronouns, **mera**, **twmhara**, etc.

meri car bəhneŋ həyŋ	I have four sisters
ap ke kytne mədədgar həyŋ	how many helpers have you ?

For sons and daughters the old oblique in **ke** used to be heard, but is now almost obsolete.

babu ke əwr koi bəccə nəhiŋ — the babu (clerk) has no other child

On the analogy of this one got also : **mere, tere, həmare, twmhare**. It must be remembered that this **ke** is an old oblique case ; no word is understood.

(b) Parts of the body : generally **ka**.

wn ki aŋkheŋ to həyŋ məgər dekhte nəhiŋ — they have eyes but do not see

Theoretically the old oblique in **ke** may be used, but it is very rare nowadays. Here, too, no word is understood.

(c) Property, especially movable property : **ke pas**.

dukandar ke pas bəhwt mezeŋ əwr kwrsiaŋ həyŋ	the shopkeeper has a lot of tables and chairs
mere pas do mwrəbbe həyŋ	I have two squares of land

But for property like land, which is not movable, we may have **ka** or **mera**, etc.

mere do mwrəbbe həyŋ	I have two squares of land

(d) Abstract nouns : the dative in **ko** of the person ; the abstract noun is in the nominative with the verb " to be ".

raja ko bəɽa ʃəwq tha, *or* bəɽi xahyʃ thi	the rajah had a great desire
mwjhe ylm nəhiŋ, *or* xəbər nəhiŋ	I have no knowledge, I do not know

If these are personal qualities (a) the genitive in **ka**, or (b) **-vala**, or (c) rarely, the verb **rəkhna** is used.

ws ki bəɽi lyaqət həy	he has great ability
xwda qwdrətvala həy, *or* qwdrət rəkhta həy	God has great power.

(e) Diseases : either use the verb " to be " with the dative, or say " he has contracted " the disease, for which : **hona, hojana, ləgna, ana**, are used ; for fever **cəɽhna** is common ; and for cough **wt̤hna** ; **ləgna** often occurs with the meaning of " catching " an infectious disease.

wse bwxar cəɽh gəya	he has got fever
wse səxt mərəz ho gəya	he has got a serious disease
bəcce ko zwkam hua	the child has a cold
meri valdə ko sərdi ləg gəi	my mother has caught cold
wse hər roz khaŋsi wt̤hti həy	he coughs every day
mwjhe ws se bimari ləgi	I got the disease from him
mwjhe ws se khaŋsi ləgi	I caught my cough from him

TO WEAR

" To wear " is expressed by verbs meaning "put on ".
The following sentences show how :—

safə baŋdhta tha	he used to tie (i.e., put on, therefore wear) a turban
koṭ pəhyne aya	he came with a coat put on (i.e., wearing a coat)
ws ne cadər oṛhi thi	she had put on a shawl (i.e., was wearing a shawl)

But it must be remembered that these words mean " put
on ", not " wear ", and the sentences must be turned with
this in mind.

pəhynna is used of coat, overcoat, waistcoat, cap, hat,
shoes, boots, gloves, trousers, *bwrqa*, etc.

oṛhna is used of shawl, quilt, and similar garments.

baŋdhna, tie, is used of turbans, dhotis, and similar
things.

Some say : **dhoti pəhynna**. Of the sari it has been
remarked :—

əwrteŋ saṛi ko adhi baŋdhti adhi oṛhti həyŋ	women tie half the sari round their waists and pull half of it over themselves

TO KNOW

"To know" is expressed by **janna**, know ; **xəbər**, *f.*, news ;
and **malum**, known, etc.

məyŋ janta huŋ	I know
mwjhe xəbər nəhiŋ	I do not know
xəbər bhi həy?	don't you even know? (said to find fault or threaten)

malum means "known", "seeming", "appearing",
according to the following rules :—

> **malum**, known, when used with the present or imper-
> fect of **hona**, be *or* become, means seem *or* appear ;

with other tenses generally to be known, sometimes to seem; with any part of **hojana**, become, and with **həy**, is, and **tha**, was, it always means to be known.

həmeŋ malum hota həy	it seems to us
wnheŋ malum hota tha	it seemed to them
həmeŋ malum hua	it became known to us, or, it seemed to us
həmeʃə malum hojata həy	it always becomes known
ap ko malum həy	you know, you are aware
wn ko bəxubi malum tha	they knew quite well
ap ko malum hoga	you will know, i.e., no doubt you know

PARTICLES

nə and nəhiŋ

For " no " **nəhiŋ** is commoner, but **nə** is also used. With the meaning of " not " they are chiefly connected with verbs expressed or understood.

nəhiŋ is used with the present indicative.

nə with subjunctive and conditional tenses, and the imperative. **nəhiŋ** is very occasionally used with the imperative.

nəhiŋ and **nə** are both used with the imperfect, future and pluperfect. Both are found with the past tense, but with a distinction in meaning not always maintained.

nə gəya	he did not go
nəhiŋ gəya	he has not gone (therefore = present perfect)

The most important thing is to use **nəhiŋ** in the present indicative and **nə** in subjunctive and conditional tenses.

voh nəhiŋ jata	he is not going, will not go
voh nə jata	he would not have gone

əb, əbhi

əb means now, nowadays, in future.

əb əgle se wstad kəhaŋ ?	where nowadays are teachers like the former ones ?

əccha məyŋ ne twmheŋ maf kia (əb əysa nə kərna) — all right, I have forgiven you, do not do so in future

əb ki bat əpne hath; jəb ki bat jəb ke sath — the present is in your power, the past is past

əb ki dəfa — this time

əbhi means now, at once, soon, so far, recently, still; yet (in negative clause).

əbhi cəle jaoge? əbhi rat nəhiŋ gwzri (swbəh əbhi dur həy) — are you going so soon? the night is not over yet (morning is still far away)

voh to əbhi əbhi yəhaŋ rəhne ləga — he has only recently begun to live here

əbhi kya həy? əbhi ap ki dwkan əwr cəmkegi — nothing has happened yet (lit. what is it so far?), soon your shop will get on much better (shine more)

jəb

jəb, when (relative; also: **jəb ky**) :—

jəb məyŋ ne swna — when I heard

jəb se, since (of time) :—

jəb se məyŋ ne yeh bat swni — since I heard this

jəb tək

jəb tək : (i) until; (ii) so long as.

(i) **jəb tək**, until, inserts a negative which we should not expect :—

jəb tək məyŋ nə auŋ meri rah dekho — wait for me till I come

jəb tək bəccə rota nəhiŋ, maŋ dudh nəhiŋ deti — the mother does not give the child milk until it cries

(ii) **jəb tək**, so long as, does not insert this negative :—

jəb tək jan meŋ jan həy — so long as one lives (so long as life is in life)

| jəb tək dəm həy təb tək yəm həy | as long as there is breath there is sorrow |

jəb to, **jəbhi**, mean " that is why ".

| jəbhi xəfa hua | that is why he got angry |

juŋ

juŋ, as, when.

juŋ tuŋ, or **juŋ tuŋ kərke**, somehow or other, with difficulty.

| həm juŋ tuŋ kərke ghər pəhwŋc gəe | we got home with difficulty |

juŋ ka tuŋ, **juŋ ki tuŋ**, **juŋ ke tuŋ**, exactly as before.

| məyŋ ne ws ko juŋ ka tuŋ rəkh dia | I put it down just as it had been |

juŋhi, **juŋhiŋ**, as soon as, so far as, etc.
juŋ juŋ, the more, as by degrees.

| mərəz bərhta gəya juŋ juŋ dəva ki | the disease got worse the more they treated it |

Other pronunciations (less good) : **jyuŋ**, **joŋ**, **jyoŋ**; **toŋ**, **tyoŋ**.

səhi

səhi is a word in constant use, often overlooked by foreigners. It means : admitted, I agree, very well then, so be it. With an imperative it means : do not hesitate, why are you delaying? do it, won't you? It can never begin a clause.

Examples :—

purchaser : do hi duŋga	I will give only two
seller : əccha do hi səhi	all right, I agree to two
dəs rwpəe nə səhi əth hi səhi	very well then, if not ten, then eight

jhyɽki səhi, əda səhi, cin e jybiŋ səhi, yeh səb səhi, pər ek nəhiŋ ky nəhiŋ səhi	rebuke—very well; airs—all right; frowns—so be it; I agree to all this, but one thing I do not agree to—your saying "no"
twm nəhiŋ əwr səhi əwr nəhiŋ əwr səhi	very well then, if not you, then some one else, if not that someone, then some-one else again
dykhao to səhi	just show it to me, won't you?
ek dəfə dekhie to səhi	(why hesitate?) look at it once anyway

It can of course be used in threats, but it does not itself contain such an idea :—

phyr ek bar tu mwjhe gali de to səhi to dekhega bəs	just swear at me once again, and you will see; that is all

hi

hi is used to emphasise the word which it immediately follows. It cannot begin a sentence or clause. To say merely that it is emphatic is misleading, for it has several senses, and its use is complicated.

A. Form and Position

When **hi** is added to **mwjh, twjh, həm, voh, yeh, ws, ys**, the **h** is omitted, and we get : **mwjhi, twjhi, həmiŋ, vohi, yehi, wsi, ysi**. The **i** of **hi** is nasalized when it follows **həm, twm, wn, yn**; thus, **həmiŋ, twmhiŋ, wnhiŋ, ynhiŋ**; it is frequently nasalized after **yuŋ** and **juŋ**, thus : **yuŋhiŋ, juŋhiŋ**. **wnhiŋ, ynhiŋ** stand for both **wn-hi, yn-hi**, and **wnhoŋ-hi, ynhoŋ-hi**.

hi is joined to **kəb, jəb, təb, səb, həm, twm, voh, yeh, ws, ys, wn, yn**, so as to make a single word, as : **jəbhi, səbhi, həmiŋ, vohi, ynhiŋ**. **yəhaŋ**, here, and **vəhaŋ**, there,

F

become **yəhiŋ**, **vəhiŋ**. **kəhaŋ**, where? becomes **kəhiŋ**, but means " somewhere ".

When it is desired to emphasize a word with a postposition after it, some latitude is observed, and **hi** is often written after the postposition. **məyŋ ne** and **tu ne** almost always take **hi** after **ne** (**məyŋ ne hi**, **tu ne hi**), but in other cases **hi** usually precedes the postposition, as: **mwjhi se**, **sahəb hi ne**.

B. Meaning

When its force is emphatic, the emphasis may be laid either on the actual word immediately preceding, or on the fact as a whole. Sometimes the stress is laid on an act, suggesting that it was just about to begin, or was just going on, or had just finished. Sometimes it means " only ", " merely " or " at least ", or again it may mean " finally ", or " with difficulty "; and lastly there is the use with " neither . . . nor ".

(i) *Emphasis on the Preceding Word :—*

pas hi həy	it is quite close
twmhiŋ bətao	you say it
dəs hi səhi	very well, ten then
wsi ko lykha	wrote it to *him*
məyŋ hi tha	it was I (no one else)
twmhiŋ the	it was you
kəl hi səhi	all right, to-morrow
məyŋ ne hi lia	it was I who took it
cəɽhai kəysi hi ho	however severe the ascent may be
ʃayəd hi əysa ynam wse myla ho	it is barely possible he may have got the reward
aŋkh hi se nə ʈəpka to ləhu ka kya zykr?	if no tears dropped from your eyes, what is the use of talking of blood (being stirred)?
əgərcy məyŋ mara hi kyoŋ nə jauŋ	even if I were to be killed

bəlky voh tu hi tha	it was not so-and-so, but it was *you*
dusre hi dyn məyŋ cəla aya	the very next day I came away
ws ne mwjhi se dylvaya	he had it given through *me*
pəhyle hi jwmle meŋ	in the very first sentence
nəwkər hi ne ghəɽi cwrai	it was the servant that stole the watch
əccha məyŋ nəhiŋ jata vohi jae	very well, I won't go; let *him* go
kərmu hi ko bwlaya	it was Karmu that he called
voh janta hi nəhiŋ	he does not even know
ys bat ka jəvab hi nəhiŋ	there is no answer to this (it is unanswerable)

(ii) *Emphasis on the Fact* :—

yeh to həy hi	this certainly is
voh jata hi nə tha bəɽi mwʃkyl se bheja	he would not go, it was with great difficulty that I sent him
həm qimət to le hi leŋge	we *will* obtain the price
cytthi həm ne lykh hi li	we *did* write the letter
məyŋ kər hi cwka tha hwkm dene ki kya zərurət pəɽi?	I had already done it; what was the good of ordering me to do it?
əysa to ho hi ga	it will certainly be so (**ho hi ga = hoga hi**)

(iii) *Emphasis on the Act or Time of the Act.*

Many of these cases have the form " I was actually doing something when something else happened ".

məyŋ mwŋh hath dho hi rəha tha ky ap ae	I was in the act of washing my face and hands when you came
məyŋ bəytha hi nə tha ky voh jhəgɽa kərne ləga	I had not even sat down when he began to quarrel
məyŋ bəythne hi ko tha ky saŋp nykəl aya	I was just about to sit down when a snake came out

məyŋ ap ko lykh hi cwka tha ky ap ka xət aya	I had just finished writing to you when your letter came
pəhwŋcte hi	at the very time of arrival
swnte hi	at the time of hearing, upon hearing

(iv) *Only, merely, at least :—*

mere pas do hi kytabeŋ thiŋ	I had only two books
dəs hi the	$\begin{cases}(a) \text{ there were only ten} \\ (b) \text{ yes, ten was the number}\end{cases}$
hath hylane hi se ws ne wnheŋ dəraya	by the mere shaking of his hand he frightened them
lahəwr hi tək pəhwŋca hoga	he will have got only as far as Lahore
yəhiŋ nəhiŋ	not only so (but)
məyŋ hi nəhiŋ sara ʃəhr ws ko thukta tha	not only I but the whole town despised him
ek hi do həfte to ṭhəyrie nə?	stay one or two weeks at least, won't you?

(v) *Finally, with difficulty :—*

mənane se man hi lega	by persuasion he will finally agree

Contrast :—

nəhiŋ nəhiŋ zərur manega	no, no, he will certainly agree
bhuk ləgi hogi to kha hi lega	(a) he must be hungry, so he will eat it (b) he will eat it . . . if he is hungry
ws ke dam meŋ a hi gəya	he finally fell into his snare (he was wheedled)

(vi) *Neither . . . nor :* note the position of **hi** in the following :—

nə ram hi aya nə mohən	neither Ram nor Mohan came

bhi

bhi, like **hi**, immediately follows the word with which it is associated. Consequently it cannot begin a clause.

(i) *The commonest meaning of* **bhi** *in affirmative clauses is " also ".*

cəlo məyŋ bhi sath cəluŋga	come along, I will go too
tənxah ke sath twmheŋ ghər bhi duŋga	with your pay I will give you a house too

(ii) **bhi . . . bhi**, *both . . . and :—*

yeh bhi mənzur voh bhi mənzur	both this and that are agreed to

Sometimes they insert a **bhi** where in English we omit the corresponding word: also, too, etc.

voh bhi gəe twm bhi jao	they (also) went, you go too

(iii) **bhi** *with the imperative gives a sense of hastiness or irritation.*

əre lykh bhi lo	write it, won't you?
cəlo bhi der ho gəi	do come along, it is getting late
kəhiŋ mər bhi	oh get out of the way! (lit. oh, die somewhere)

(iv) **koi bhi, kwch bhi, əwr bhi**.

koi bhi	any one at all
koi bhi ae	let any one come
kwch bhi	anything at all
kwch bhi dykhao	show anything at all
əwr bhi	still more
mwjhe əwr bhi do	give me still more
əwr bhi bələnd	still higher

(v) *With a negative it means either " not even " or " also not ".*

The context will show which meaning is the right one.

ek bhi nəhiŋ	not even one
ws ka nam o nyʃan bhi nəhiŋ	not a trace of him (name and sign)
məyŋ bhi nəhiŋ gəya	I too did not go
ws jəngəl meŋ ynsan ka kya zykr həyvan bhi nə tha	in that jungle there was not even a wild beast, let alone a man
admi bhi nə the həyvan bhi nə the	there were no men, there were also no animals
mere ghər meŋ voh bəyʈha bhi nəhiŋ	he did not even sit down in my house

Motion to Anything

The idea of going to a person or thing is expressed in different ways. When the postposition is omitted, the noun is in the locative case, which is the same as the oblique.

1. To a person or animal : **ke pas**.

ws ne sahəb ke pas jakər kəha	he went to the Sahib and said

2. To a room, garden, field, plain : **meŋ**.

gol kəmre meŋ aie	come to the drawing-room

3. To a house or building : **ko**, **pər**; or, if the idea of " into " is prominent, **meŋ**.

mere ghər pər jake puchie	go to my house and ask

When **ghər** means home the postposition is generally omitted.

mali ghər gəya	the gardener went home

4. To a country, city or village : **ko**, **meŋ**, or omit postposition. **meŋ** is common if " into " can be substituted for " to ".

5. To a well or tomb : **pər**.

donoŋ qəbr pər dəwʈe gəe	both of them went running to the tomb

6. To a point of the compass : **ki tərəf, ko.**

ʃymal məɣryb ko [*or* ki tərəf]   to the north-west
wttər pɛcchym ko [*or* ki tərəf]   ,,   ,,

7. To an isolated object, such as a tree, pillar, door, window, cupboard, table : **tək, ke pas.**

> əlmari tək gəi   she went to the cupboard
> mez ke pas gəi   she went to the table

8. Sometimes the postposition is left for the second clause, as :—

jakər mez pər cəʈh bəyʈha   he went over to the table and
                                              sat on it

9. With **pəhwŋcna**, arrive, the postposition may be omitted or **meŋ** or **tək** may be used. **ko** is not used.

10. With a verb meaning " send ", as in " send a letter, parcel, box, etc., to some one " : **ko.**

məyŋ ne ws ko xət (parsəl,   I sent him a letter (parcel,
bəkəs) bheja   box)

" Send a telegram " is usually **tar dena**, but **bhejna** is also right.

məyŋ ne wse tar dia (*or*   I sent him a telegram
bheja)

For " a letter, etc., came to me ", we must not say : **mwjh ko aya.**   It should be : **mere pas aya** *or* **mwjhe myla.**

11. Sell something *to* some one is : **ke hath.**

məyŋ ne əpni sari zəmin ws   I sold him all my land
ke hath beci
ws ne car kytabeŋ mere hath   he sold me four books
beciŋ

12. In English we can say " swim " or " crawl " or " fly " or " run to a place ".   The corresponding verbs in

Urdu are not so often followed *directly* by **ko** or other postpositions of motion.

təyrak dərya ke par təyrke gəe	the swimmers swam across the river
saŋp əpne byl meŋ reŋgta gəya	the snake crawled into its hole
kəbutər əpni kabək ki tərəf wɽe cəle ae	the pigeons flew home to the pigeon house

REPETITION OF WORDS

In Urdu words are repeated :—

(a) To indicate distribution over time or space. This holds of the vast majority of instances.

(b) Occasionally to express niceness or pleasantness. When a word can have either a pleasant or an unpleasant meaning, the repeated word has the pleasant one.

(c) Without any real meaning, repetition being due to mere habit.

Repetition is almost confined to short words. It will be found that on an average out of every thousand :—

370 or 37 per cent. occur in words of one syllable.
610 or 61 per cent. in words of two syllables.
20 or 2 per cent. in words of three syllables.

The number of cases in words of more than three syllables is negligible.

In verbs it is confined to the present, past and conjunctive participles, and means " keeping on doing a thing " or " doing it repeatedly ".

bəɽe bəɽe ʃəhr əwr choṭe choṭe gaoŋ	big towns and little villages
ahystə ahystə bolo	speak softly (all the time)
wn ko do do ane myle	they got two annas each

voh to əbhi əbhi aya həy	he has only just come, or, come recently
che che fwt gəhra	six feet deep (all over)
thəndi thəndi həva	a nice cool breeze (not a piercing cold wind)
lal lal rwxsareŋ	nice rosy cheeks (not of a hectic red colour)
wn ka gəla cyllate cyllate bəyth gəya	they became hoarse through shouting (lit. their throat sat down)
dəwri dəwri a rəhi həy	she is coming along running
soc soc ke kam kəro	work thoughtfully, carefully (all the time)

Connected with repetition, but expressing other ideas, are the following :—

   (a) Placing together two almost synonymous adjectives ;
   (b) attaching to a word a jingling repetition of it ; this generally follows it ;
   (c) joining to a word another which either is not used by itself, or has no meaning in this connection ;
   (d) joining a verb to its causal.

Notes on the Above with Examples:

(a) The two adjectives often suggest intensity :—

kala syah, very black	saf swthra, very clean
gora cytta, very fair, like an Englishman (**cytta** is not used alone in Urdu)	

(b) The jingling repetition often implies rather careless or even jocular reference. It would not be much used in speaking of something sacred or solemn.

meri lərki khati vati kwch nəhiŋ	my girl eats nothing
amne samne = samne	in front (there is nothing jocular in this word)

baje gaje	musical instruments of various sorts
ṭhik ṭhak = ṭhik	correct or right
soc soc ke = soc ke	having thought, i.e., carefully

(c) An ordinary word is often coupled with another which is not proper Urdu, though perhaps found in dialects, or is not used alone, or has another meaning when used alone. Contrary to (b), the two words do not imply flippancy, and they may be employed in solemn speech on solemn subjects.

rəha səha = rəha	remaining, i.e., what is left over (not much)
ws ke rəhe səhe həvas wṛ gəe	his remaining senses flew away; he became utterly confused

dekh bhalkər, having examined; but **dekh dekhkər** means having looked repeatedly *or* all the time, i.e., taking great care

dyn dyhaṛe = dyn ko	by day, in broad daylight, in the sight of all

In the above sentences **səha** by itself means " suffered ", but here simply accompanies **rəha**; **bhalna** and **dyhaṛa** have the same meanings as the words they follow, but are not used alone in Urdu.

(d) The past participle of a verb is often used with the past participle of its causal to express the idea of all ready for use.

bəsa bəsaya, occupied, inhabited

bəna bənaya, ready made

səja səjaya, all ready adorned

kəsa kəsaya, ready tightened; said of a saddle or other article ready fastened on

syla sylaya, ready sewn

pəka pəkaya, ready cooked

kəta kətaya, all ready cut

kətra kətraya, all ready snipped or cut out

The ease with which a causal can be introduced leads to its being employed with little meaning. Thus :—

de dylakər	having given or caused to be given
swni swnai bat	a thing heard and related, i.e., hearsay
hona hwvana kwch nəhiŋ	nothing will happen; (lit. nothing is to be or caused to be)

CEREMONIOUS OR RESPECTFUL SPEECH

There is a good deal of this in the Urdu of educated Indians. The following words are very common in the conversation of people of good position :—

ap	you, with verb in third plural
jənab *or* sahəb	which might be translated " your honour " or " sir ", but means no more than " you "

Servants and others to show exaggerated respect use **hwzur**, **sərkar** (or even : **xwdavənd**).

A speaker uses one set of words for things connected with the person he is speaking to, and another set for himself.

For the person spoken to		*For himself*
to say :	**fərmana** (command)	**ərz kərna** (make petition); **kəhna**, say
son :	**sahəbzadə**	**beṭa**
daughter :	**sahəbzadi**	**beṭi**
house :	**dəwlətxanə** (house of wealth)	**ɣəribxanə** (poor man's house)
sit down :	**təʃrif rəkhna**	**bəyṭh jana**
be present :	**təʃrif lana** *or* **rəkhna**	**hazyr hona**
come, go :	**təʃrif lana, lejana**	**hazyr hona, ana, jana**

hazyr means " present in a subordinate capacity ".

məyŋ zərur hazyr huŋga	I shall certainly come (and be at your service)
kytne ləɽke hazyr həyŋ ?	how many boys are present (in school, etc., where they are in a subordinate position) ?
məyŋ hazyr kəruŋga	I shall bring it *or* him

Yet the Arabic **hazyrin**, plural of **hazyr**, used in Urdu with the meaning of people present in a meeting, has no sense of subordination.

mere əziz hazyrin	my honoured audience !

məwjud, present, is colourless :—

ap bhi məwjud the?	were you there too?
ap bhi təʃrif lae the?	did you come too? (ceremonious)

The student may freely use all these expressions in their proper places, except **hwzur, sərkar, xwdavənd**, and he should perhaps avoid **hazyr hona**.

EXPRESSIONS OF TIME, O'CLOCK, ETC.

bəjna, to sound or strike, expresses time. It is used not only for gongs and striking clocks, but also for watches— in short, for time in general.

ek bəj gəya	one has struck, it is one o'clock
səva tin bəje həyŋ	it is a quarter past three
saɽhe car bəj cwke həyŋ	it is already half past four
əbhi pəwn bəjnevala həy	it is almost three quarters, i.e., 12.45

At a certain time is expressed by the locative case of some noun denoting time, or by **bəja**, past participle of **bəjna** inflected in -e. There are also other methods, as will be shown below.

səva bəje ya pəwn bəje ya ʃayəd ek bəje	at one and a quarter o'clock or three quarters o'clock (i.e., 1.15 or 12.45) or perhaps one o'clock
məngəl ke dyn	on Tuesday
ws dyn	on that day
ws vəqt	at that time
ws ghəṛi	at that moment
dyn dyhaṛe	in broad daylight, in sight of all

ghəṛi denotes an indefinite but very short time :—

ek ghəṛi dyn ḍhəle	one ghəṛi (say half an hour) after sunset

dyn ḍhəlna means " sun declining ".
pəhər, watch, three hours, rather indefinite. **pəhər** is masculine, but **do pəhər**, noon, is feminine.

tisre pəhər	at the third watch, in the afternoon
ek pəhər rat rəhe	with one watch of the night remaining

When minutes are mentioned, we get expressions like the following :—

nəw bəjne meŋ barə mynəṭ pər	at twelve minutes to nine

Or, not quite so common :—

nəw bəjne se barə mynəṭ pəhyle (or, peʃtər).

aṭh bəjne meŋ sat mynəṭ baqi həyŋ	it is seven minutes to eight
panc bəjke pəccis mynəṭ pər	at twenty-five minutes past twelve

p.m., and a.m., are expressed by **dyn ko**, by day; **rat ko**, by night; **ʃam ko**, in the evening; **swbəh ko**, in the morning.

che bəje ʃam ko	at six in the evening
nəw bəje swbəh	at nine a.m.

Or, as follows :—

rat ke ɖhai bəje	at 2.30 a.m.
dyn ke tin bəje	at 3.0 p.m.

LESSON I

DECLENSION OF NOUNS, ADJECTIVES, IS, ARE, WAS, WERE, KE, POSTPOSITIONS ; QUESTIONS

See Grammar, pp. 1–16, 16–20, 38–9, 88–91.

Nouns ending in **-a** or **-ə** are generally masculine. Such are **kəmra** = room; **kona** = corner; **nəqʃə** = map. The plural is **kəmre, kone, nəqʃe**. The oblique singular is the same, **kəmre, kone, nəqʃe**.

Nouns ending in **-i** are generally feminine. Such are **kwrsi** = chair. The plural is **kwrsiaŋ**. The oblique singular is the same as the nominative singular.

Nouns with any other ending may be masculine or feminine. If they are masculine, the nominative plural is the same as the singular, as **qələm** = pen; **qələm** = pens. If they are feminine, the nominative plural ends in **-eŋ**; as **ciz** = thing; **cizeŋ** = things; **pynsəl** = pencil; **pynsəleŋ** = pencils.

Adjectives ending in **-a** generally change **-a** to **-e** when agreeing with a noun in the nominative plural or oblique singular, as **məyla qələm** = a dirty pen; **məyle qələm** = dirty pens; **məyle qələm se** = with a dirty pen. These adjectives end in **-i** when agreeing with feminine nouns, whether singular or plural, as **kali pynsəleŋ** = black pencils.

The following verbs occur in the lesson :—

həy = is; **həyŋ** = are. No change for gender. In a negative sentence **həy, həyŋ** may be omitted. See sentence No. 12.

tha = was; **the** = were; the feminine is **thi** = was; **thiŋ** = were.

A possessive adjective is often formed by adding **-ka**, as **ap**, you; **ap ka** = your, yours. This adjective agrees with its noun like other adjectives ending in **-a**.

Postpositions nearly always follow the noun they govern.

Questions usually have the same form as affirmations, see Nos. 1, 8, 11, 15, 21, etc.

1. yeh kya ciz həy?	What is this thing?
2. yeh kwrsi həy.	This is a chair.
3. voh kytab həy.	That's a book.
4. yeh ləmbi kwrsiaŋ həyŋ.	These chairs are long ones.
5. voh do kytabeŋ meri həyŋ.	Those two books are mine.
6. yeh qələm əccha həy.	This pen's good.
7. voh qələm ap ke həyŋ.	Those pens are yours.
8. meri pynsəl kəhaŋ həy?	Where's my pencil?
9. ap ki pynsəl mez pər həy.	Your pencil's on the table.
10. voh meri kwrsi nəhiŋ həy.	That's not my chair.
11. voh qələm ap ke həyŋ?	Are those pens yours?
12. nəhiŋ, mere nəhiŋ.	No, not mine.
13. ap ki kytni kwrsiaŋ həyŋ?	How many chairs have you?
14. yeh pərcə kəl kəhaŋ tha?	Where was this paper yesterday?
15. kya, yeh cizeŋ kəl vəhaŋ thiŋ?	Were these things there yesterday?
16. voh nəqʃə pəhyle yəhaŋ tha.	At first that map was here.
17. əb voh nəqʃe yəhaŋ nəhiŋ həyŋ.	Now those maps are not here.
18. kəl kəmra məyla tha	Yesterday the room was dirty.
19. aj kəmre meŋ mezeŋ həyŋ.	To-day there are tables in the room.
20. kəmre ke kytne dərvaze həyŋ?	How many doors has the room?
21. kytab ka kaɣəz əccha həy?	Is the paper of the book good?
22. nəqʃe kəhaŋ the?	Where were the maps?
23. mez pər kytni cizeŋ thiŋ?	How many things were on the table?
24. kytab pər qələm əwr pynsəleŋ thiŋ.	There were pens and pencils on the book.

LESSON 2

PRESENT AND IMPERFECT INDICATIVE, PRESENT PARTICIPLES, INTERROGATIVE AND OTHER PRONOUNS

Grammar illustrated in Lesson 2. See pp. 26–43.

There are two present participles. One ends in **-ta**, as **khata** = eating; **pita** = drinking; **lykhta** = writing. This gives some idea of habit; thus **məyŋ khata huŋ** means " I eat ", not " I am eating ".

Another construction has **rəha** and always means doing *or* being something at the moment; therefore **kha rəha huŋ** means " I am eating ", not " I eat ".

The two constructions with **-ta** and **rəha** are declined like adjectives in **-a**. Both are used with **huŋ, həy, həyŋ, tha, thi, the, thiŋ** = am, is, are, was, were.

Note that interrogative pronouns and adverbs follow the subject of the sentence. In English they precede it. See Lesson 1, nos. 8, 14, 22; Lesson 2, nos. 8, 15, 17, 18.

twm kəwn ho ?	It's none of your business.
ap kyoŋ nəhiŋ jate ?	Why don't you go ?

Interrogative adjectives like **kytna, kəysa**, may agree with nouns, and then naturally they precede them. See Lesson 1, nos. 1, 13, 20, 23.

Before **ka** and other postpositions **yeh, voh, kəwn**, become **ys, ws, kys**, in the singular, so that we get : **ys ka, ws ka, kys ka**.

The plural of nouns ends in **-oŋ** before postpositions, as **kytaboŋ se** = from books.

1. məyŋ həmeʃə ʈhəndạ pani pita huŋ.	I always drink cold water.
2. məyŋ gərm dudh pi rəha huŋ.	I'm drinking warm milk.
3. bylli goʃt kha rəhi həy.	The cat's eating meat.
4. sare nəwkər kam kər rəhe həyŋ.	All the servants are working.
5. yeh mere bap həyŋ, məyŋ yn ka beʈa huŋ.	This is my father; I'm his son.

6. voh twmhara bhai həy twm ws ki bəhn ho.

He's your brother; you're his sister.

7. voh kəwn tha əwr kys ki nəwkəri kərta tha?

Who was he, and whose servant was he?

8. ap kəhaŋ ja rəhe the?

Where were you going?

9. voh kytab dekh rəhi həy əwr məyŋ lykh rəhi huŋ.

She's looking at the book and I am writing.

10. məyŋ kəh rəha tha əwr ap swn rəhe the.

I was speaking and you were listening.

11. meri bat koi nəhiŋ swnta.

No one listens to me.

12. jo ap kəhte həyŋ məyŋ swnta huŋ.

Whatever you say I listen to.

13. jəhaŋ maŋ cahti thi vəhaŋ məyŋ jati thi.

I went (used to go) where mother wished.

14. koi kwch lykhta tha koi kwch pəṛhta tha.

One was writing something, another reading something.

15. twm kəwn ho əwr kya cahte ho?

Who are you and what do you want?

16. voh koi kam nəhiŋ kərti.

She does no work.

17. ap pəhyle kəhaŋ rəhti thiŋ, əwr əb kəhaŋ rəhti həyŋ?

Where did you live formerly, madam, and where do you live now?

18. jate kyoŋ nəhiŋ, yəhaŋ kyoŋ bəyṭhe ho?

Why don't you go, why do you stay here?

19. əysi batoŋ se məyŋ bəwht xwʃ hota huŋ.

Such things please me very much.

20. jo jata həy voh dekhta həy.

Whoever goes sees it.

LESSON 3

FUTURE

Grammar illustrated. See pp. 44–5.
The future tense is as follows :—

məyŋ kəruŋga	həm kəreŋge
tu kərega	twm kəroge
	ap kəreŋge
voh kərega	voh kəreŋge

The feminine is the same except that the ending is **-i** throughout. The first plural feminine is by some made the same as the masculine when the subject is a pronoun without a noun in apposition, as **həm kərenge**; but if a noun is mentioned, the ending is **-ģi**, as: **həm tinon əwrəten jaenģi**.

Present Presumptive : see grammar, p. 44.

koi = someone, anyone, becomes **kysi** before postpositions. Note the difference between **kysi ka** = anyone's, and **kyska** = whose?

jo becomes **jys** : **jo koi** is in the nominative case; the postposition case is **jys kysi**.

The relative clause usually precedes the principal clause, as **jys ki laţhi ws ki bhəyns** = whose the stick, his the buffalo, i.e. might is right.

Singular nouns sometimes take the plural for respect, as **sahəb jate həyn** = the sahib is going.

1. məyn aj nə jaunga, kəl jaunga.

   I shall go to-morrow, not to-day.

2. yeh kam twm kərogi ya koi əwr kərega?

   Are you going to do this, or will someone else do it?

3. voh pəhyle roţi pəkaegi, phyr khaegi.

   She'll first cook her food, then eat it.

4. həm nə kəbhi kəpŗe lejaenge əwr nə kəbhi dhoenge.

   We won't either take away the clothes or wash them.

5. nə məyn lykhungi əwr nə məyn pəŗhungi.

   I will neither write nor read (you are wasting time on me).

6. mystri aj sənduq bənaega əwr kəl le aega.

   The carpenter will make the box to-day and bring it to-morrow.

7. jəb kəbhi aunga ap ke ghər ţhəyrunga.

   Whenever I come, I shall stay with you.

8. kya voh admi jo kəl yəhan kam kər rəha tha kəl vapəs cəlajaega?

   Will the man who was working here yesterday go back to-morrow?

9. jys ki laṭhi ws ki bhəyŋs.   Might is right.
10. yeh kys ki ghoṛi həy?   Whose is this mare?
11. malum nəhiŋ kysi ki hogi.   I don't know; it'll be someone's.
12. jo aega ap ws se puchəŋge nə?   You'll ask whoever comes, won't you?
13. haŋ jys kysi ko dekhuŋga, ws se puchuŋga.   Yes, I shall ask whoever I see.
14. voh do pəyse deta tha.   He offered two pice.
15. jəb ləwṭoge, mere liye kya laoge?   What'll you bring me when you come back?
16. nə voh dega, nə məyŋ luŋga.   Neither will he give it, nor I take it.
17. sahəb kəhiŋ jaeŋge? nəhiŋ, kəhiŋ nəhiŋ.   Will the sahib go anywhere? No, nowhere.
18. rəddi kaɣəz kəhaŋ rəkhoge?   Where will you put the waste paper?
19. voh bəttiaŋ jəlaegi.   She will switch on the lights.
20. ws ke lie bhi kwch kəroge?   Will you do anything for him too?

LESSON 4

IMPERATIVE, PAST TENSE

Grammar illustrated in Lesson 4. See pp. 40–1, 45, 50.
The Imperative used in addressing servants and young people ends in **-o**; for those whose age or position gives them higher rank, the ending is **-ie**.

jao or **jaie** = go; **bətao** or **bətaie** = show.

From **kərna**, " do ", we get **kəro**, and an irregular **kijie** or **kije**. See No. 6.
The direct object is either the same as the nominative, or is the oblique with **ko** after it. The latter is more definite. Thus, in No. 16 **ləkṛi ko** = the wood; **ləkṛi** alone would be simply " wood ".

The past participle is formed by adding **-a** to the root; when the verb is transitive, this is passive.

bəyʈha = seated; **dekha** = seen.

This participle can be finite, **dəwɽa** = he ran.

The nominative of an intransitive verb agrees with its past participle used as a finite verb in the past tense, as **voh dəwɽi** = she ran.

When the verb is transitive, a passive construction is used, and the object becomes the nominative, as No. 14: **ʃykari ne lomɽi mari** = a fox was killed by a hunter. But if what we think of as the object has **ko** after it, the verb becomes impersonal, as in No. 18: **wnhoŋ ne tinoŋ dərvazoŋ ko khola** = they opened all the three doors.

lana, leana = bring, have the intransitive construction; see next lesson, No. 16.

1. jao, dekho, kya ho rəha həy.

   Go and see what's happened.

2. khyɽki kholo, dərvaza bənd kəro.

   Open the window and shut the door.

3. ydhər aie, mere pas bəyʈhie.

   Come here and sit by me.

4. ap ləɽke ka nam bətaie.

   Tell me the boy's name.

5. kysi nəwkər ko bwlaie əwr mere pas bhejie.

   Call a servant and send him to me.

6. ap əpna kam kijie məyŋ əpna kəruŋga.

   You do your work, and I'll do mine.

7. mali əpni bivi ke samne bəyʈha.

   The gardener sat in front of his wife.

8. twmhara bap cəla gəya twm bhi cəle jao.

   Your father's gone away, you go too.

9. səb log əpne gaoŋ se nykle.

   All the people went out of their village.

10. kwtta əwr bylli apəs meŋ ləɽe.

    The dog and the cat had a fight (together).

11. əbhi to koi nəhiŋ aya lekyn rat ko kəi admi aeŋge.

    No one has come yet, but a good many'll come tonight.

12. cor dur tək dəwṛa.	The thief ran a long way.
13. məyŋ bəhwt xwʃ hui.	I (*fem.*) was extremely pleased.
14. ʃykari ne aj ek lomṛi mari.	The hunter killed a fox to-day.
15. ws ki bəhyn ne kwch bhi nə dekha.	His sister saw nothing at all.
16. mali ne ləkṛi ko wṭhaya.	The gardener lifted up the wood.
17. dhobi ne səb kəpṛe dhoe.	The washerman washed all the clothes.
18. wnhoŋ ne tinoŋ dər-vazoŋ ko khola.	They opened all the three doors.
19. twm ne ws bətti ko kyoŋ jəlaya?	Why did you switch on that light?
20. xansamaŋ ne həmare vaste bəhwt əcchi cəpatiaŋ pəkaiŋ.	The cook made some very good chapatis for us.

LESSON 5

CONJUNCTIVE PARTICIPLE : IMPERATIVE AND PAST CONTINUOUS

Grammar illustrated in Lesson 5 : see pp. 40, 43.

The conjunctive participle ends in **-kər** or **-ke**, which is added to the root. It has three meanings :—

    (*a*) Having done something, as : **khakər** = having eaten. Nos. 5, 6, 13, 17.

    (*b*) An adverbial sense, as : **dəwṛke** = quickly, **socke** = thoughtfully. Nos. 7 and 8.

    (*c*) Although, in spite of, as : **hoke**; in spite of being, **hoke-**. No. 19.

For " understand me ", etc., we must say " understand my word "; see No. 10.

Note that **lana, leana** = bring, do not take **-ne**; No. 16.

əlmari in No. 1 means bookcase, cupboard, linen- or clothes-press.

The **-kər** or **-ke** is sometimes omitted; see No. 4.

1. meri bəhyn ne əlmari meŋ do rumal rəkhe həyŋ.

My sister has put two hand-kerchiefs in the cupboard (linen-press, etc.).

2. wn əŋgrezoŋ ne pəhyle hi məzduri di thi.

Those Englishmen had already paid the wages.

3. malykoŋ ne jys ko dekha (jo aya) wse ynam dia.

The masters rewarded whoever they saw (or whoever came)

4. twm zəra dekh ao nə?

Just go and look, won't you?

5. məyŋ əbhi khakər aya huŋ.

I had a meal just before I came.

6. voh bərtən saf kərke hi gəi thi nə?

She cleaned the vessels before she went, didn't she?

7. dəwṛke jao nəhiŋ to naraz huŋga.

Go quickly, or I shall be annoyed.

8. meri ləṛki ne xub socke kam kia.

My girl did the work very thoughtfully.

9. qwlioŋ ne khaya piya hoga.

The coolies must have eaten and drunk (feasted themselves).

10. meri bat koi nə səmjha.

No one understood me.

11. jəb kəbhi zərurət pəṛi məyŋ ne ap ki mədəd ki.

I helped you whenever you needed help.

12. wnhoŋ ne jəhaŋ kəhiŋ həmeŋ dekha həmeŋ mədəd di.

They helped us wherever they saw us.

13. ws ne kya kia? khana khake cəli gəi hogi.

What did she do? She must have had dinner and gone.

14. jys ne kytab pəṛhi həyran hogəya.

Whoever read the book was amazed.

15. yeh juti kahe ki bəni hui həy?

What's this pair of shoes made of?

16. swno nə, yeh təsvir bylkwl rəddi həy; mere pas kyoŋ lae?

Just listen; this picture's quite worthless; why did you bring it to me?

17. bənie ke beṭe ne cyṭṭhi The grocer's son wrote and
  lykhkər ḍak meŋ ḍali. posted a letter.
18. ap ki xatyr məyŋ yəhaŋ For your sake I remained
  bəyṭha rəha. sitting here.
19. twm wstad hoke bhi yeh You, a teacher, and do not
  nəhiŋ jante? know this?

LESSON 6

COMPOUND VERBS, VERBS COMPOUNDED WITH LENA AND DENA ; COMPARISON

See Grammar, pp. 64–5, 71–7, 19.

Two verbs so joined as to express a single idea form a compound verb. The action is limited to one occasion.

Verbs compounded with **lena** and **dena** are generally transitive. It is always the root that is prefixed to **lena** and **dena**. Compounded with **lena** they suggest an action for the benefit of the doer; with **dena** they indicate action moving away from the doer, perhaps for someone else's benefit or injury.

For the contrast between **lena** and **dena** see specially Nos. 3, 4, 12.

Comparison : see Nos. 15–21; Grammar, pp. 19–20.

There are no forms for the comparative or superlative. Than is expressed by **se**, than ; *or* **ki nysbət, ke mwqabyle meŋ** = in comparison with.

1. twm beʃək pəta lykh lo. By all means write down the
   address.
2. khana kha lo bad meŋ Have your food and then
  əpni kytab pəṛh lena. read your book.
3. yeh pəyse apəs meŋ baŋṭ Divide this money among
  lo. (or between) yourselves.
4. yeh rwpəe wn meŋ baŋṭ Divide this money among
  do. them.
5. həspətal ka ḍakṭər ap The hospital doctor will give
  ko dəvai de dega. you medicine.

6. məyŋ ap ke məkan meŋ car taq bəna duŋga.

I'll make four niches in your house.

7. məyŋ əpne yhate meŋ phaṭək bəna luŋga.

I'll make a gate in my compound.

8. mere lie karḍ lykh dije.

Write a card for me.

9. gae ghas kha legi.

The cow'll eat the grass.

10. masṭər ne chwri rəkh li.

The teacher kept the knife.

11. ẅs jəvan ne ṭopi wtar li əwr koṭ pəhyn lia.

That young man took off his cap and put on his coat.

12. mere dost ne kapi rəkh di əwr safə ṭrənk meŋ rəkh lia.

My friend put down the notebook, and put the turban in his trunk.

13. əwrət ne ynkar kər dia.

The woman refused.

14. ws ne wse bəɽi takid kər di.

He strongly urged him.

15. alu aluce se bəɽa hota həy.

A potato is bigger than a plum.

16. yeh pəhaɽ to bələnd həyŋ lekyn həmare mwlk ke pəhaɽ əwr bhi bələnd həyŋ.

These hills are high, but the hills of our country are higher still.

17. evərəsṭ pəhaɽ ki coṭi dwnya meŋ səb se bələnd həy.

The summit of Mt. Everest is the highest in the world.

18. məyŋ ne ws se zyadə koʃiʃ ki.

I tried harder than he.

19. ləndən ki nysbət (*or* ke mwqabyle meŋ) lahəwr meŋ zyadə gərmi pəɽti həy.

Lahore is hotter than London.

20. twm ne ʃəkər kəm ḍali (or thoɽi ḍali) əwr məkkhən zyadə ḍala.

You've put in too little sugar, and too much butter.

21. əqəl meŋ məyŋ ws se kəm huŋ.

I'm not so wise as he is.
Or,
I am inferior to him in wisdom.

LESSON 7

CAUSAL VERBS

Grammar illustrated in Lesson 7; see Grammar, pp. 57–67.

Causal verbs are a marked feature of Urdu. Causals of intransitive verbs are transitive; cf. the English fall, fell; the tree fell; he felled the tree.

Causals of transitive verbs mean " cause the action to be performed ", i.e., they are causals of the passive of the transitive. When the original transitive verb is normally compounded with **lena**, the causal means "help some one to do something "; see Nos. 2 and 7, helped the scholars to study, and gave the girl something to eat and drink. It is not real causation.

When the original transitive verb is normally with **dena** the causal of its passive shows actual causation—cause something to be done by someone. The postposition for "by" is **se**, whereas for the **lena** verbs the corresponding postposition is **ko**.

For causals of intransitive verbs see **pəkana** in No. 5, **becna** in No. 6, **torna** in No. 9.

Double causals are frequent, see Nos. 5, 6, 9—**pəkvana**, **bykvana** and **twrvana**.

1. məyŋ xət xwd nəhiŋ lykhta kysi se lykhvata huŋ.

   I don't write letters myself, I get them written by some one else.

2. wstad ne pəhyle xwd səbəq pərha; bad meŋ ʃagyrdoŋ ko pərhaya.

   The teacher first studied the lesson himself, and then taught it to the scholars.

3. yeh tala yuŋhi nəhiŋ khwla, ya to bəccoŋ ne khola, ya wn ki maŋ ne khwlvaya.

   This lock didn't open of itself; either the children opened it, or their mother had it opened.

4. əgər voh phəl ke dam kəl nə dega, to pərsoŋ swbəh məyŋ ap dylva-uŋga.

   If he doesn't pay for the fruit to-morrow, I shall get it paid for in the morning of the day after.

5. aj kəl meri roṭi ghər meŋ pəkti həy; meri bivi pəkati həy; lekyn pəhyle məyŋ bazar se pəkvakər khata tha.

Now my meals are cooked at home; my wife cooks them; but last year I got them cooked in the bazaar.

6. ys dwkan pər lohe ki cizeŋ bykti həyŋ; əksər dwkandar ap becta həy; vərnə kysi nəwkər se bykvata həy.

At this shop iron things are sold; generally the shop-keeper sells them himself; otherwise he gets them sold through a servant.

7. ləṛki kyoŋ roti həy? twm ne wse rwlaya hoga; kwch khylao pylao nəhiŋ to der tək roegi.

Why's the girl crying? You must have made her cry. Give her something to eat and drink; otherwise she'll cry for a long time.

8. ws buṭhe yərib ne babu se pəŋc cyṭṭhiaŋ lykh-vaiŋ.

That poor old man got the clerk to write five letters for him.

9. botəl kəyse ṭuṭi? kys ne toṛi? sahəb ne twṛvai.

How did the bottle break? Who broke it? The sahib had it broken.

10. qənd zyadə ḍəlvaie to əccha hoga. əccha sahəb. xansaman, twm ne qənd kəm ḍali.

It'll be a good thing if you have more sugar put in it. Very well. Cook, you put too little sugar in it.

11. bəhwt zyddi həy mənata huŋ manta nəhiŋ.

He's very obstinate; I persuade him, but he doesn't agree.

12. bəhwt swst həy; səm-jhata huŋ, səməjhta nəhiŋ.

He is very dull; I explain to him, but he does not understand.

13. swni swnai bat həy.

It's hearsay.

14. bəni bənai ṭokri.

A ready-made basket.

15. bhəyŋs ko bhusa khyla do.

Feed the buffalo with chaff.

16. zəmindar ne hərkare se cyṭṭhi lykhva li.

The farmer got the postman to write a letter for him.

17. wstani ne skul ki ləṛki-oŋ ko kwch lykhva dia.

The schoolmistress dictated something to the girls.

LESSON 8

FURTHER COMPOUND VERBS

The grammar illustrated in Lesson 8; see Grammar, pp. 71–7.

Intransitive verbs compounded with **jana**, **pəṛna**, **wṭhna**, and transitive verbs with **ḍalna**. The meaning of these compounds is usually limited to a single occasion. **pəṛna** and **wṭhna** indicate suddenness.

Transitive verbs joined to **jana** do not as a rule form true compounds. They are merely two verbs, and **jana** retains its own meaning of going.

Transitive verbs with **ḍalna** are true compounds, and suggest vigour or even violence.

1. tinoŋ mwsafyr gaṛi se wtər gəe.	All three travellers got out of the train.
2. lomṛi əwr gidəṛ donoŋ bhag gəe.	The fox and the jackal both ran away.
3. nə bhai, nyʃan myṭ jaeŋge.	My dear sir, the marks will come out.
4. bəhu jit gəi, sas har gəi.	The daughter-in-law got the better of her mother-in-law.
5. meri dastan swn jao.	Hear my story before going.
6. mwjhe yjazət de gəya.	He gave me permission before going.
7. voh bədmaʃ twmhara sara mal luṭ le jaega.	The scoundrel will rifle all you have before he goes.
8. bəccə kicəṛ meŋ physəl gəya.	The child slipped in the mud.
9. bhuka becarə həŋs pəṛa.	The poor hungry fellow burst out laughing.
10. kueŋ meŋ kud pəṛi.	She jumped into the well.
11. bəhwt mehnəti həy, sari kytab pəṛh ḍali.	He works hard, he's finished off the whole book.
12. hakym ne əpne tinoŋ dwʃmən mərva ḍale.	The chief had his three enemies killed.
13. ʃolə bhəṛək wṭha.	The flame flared up.

14. raja ka nam swnkər ghəbra wṭha. — He lost his nerve on hearing the raja mentioned.
15. rani jag wṭhi. — The queen woke up.
16. ləṛki cylla wṭhi. — The girl called out.
17. koi ʃayr yeh ʃer kəh gəya həy. — Some poet has said this in a verse.
18. a gəi həy? nəhiŋ ai. — Has she come? No, she hasn't.
19. zəhr khake behoʃ ho gəya? nəhiŋ hua. — Was he unconscious after taking the poison? No.
20. aŋdhi ne cyraɣ ko bwjha dia? bylkwl nəhiŋ. — Did the storm put out the lamp? Not in the least.
21. dekho, ʃərbət meŋ məkkhi gyr pəṛi. nəhiŋ, nəhiŋ gyri. — Look, a fly's fallen into the sherbet. No, it hasn't.
22. twm ne əxbar pəṛh lia? nəhiŋ. — Have you read the newspaper? No.
23. dekhna! bəndər dərəxt pər cəṛh jaega. — Look out! The monkey'll go up the tree.
24. cyuŋṭi pələng ke nice dəb gəi. — The ant was squashed under the bed.
25. am ke pətte jhəṛ gəe. — The mango's lost its leaves.

LESSONS 9 and 10

PRESENT SUBJUNCTIVE OR CONDITIONAL

Lessons 9 and 10 illustrate the uses of the Present Subjunctive; see Grammar, pp. 46–7.

1. Wish or desire that something may or may not happen. Nos. 1, 2, 5, 6.

2. Conditions. Nos. 3, 4.

3. The questions: shall I, shall we, shall he or they, etc. Nos. 3, 4.

4. Ceremonious Imperative, Nos. 9, 10, 11, 12.

5. Whether this or that, whatever may be, as if, Nos. 7, 8, 13, 14.

6. Let this or that happen, Nos. 6, 8.

7. It may be, Nos. 15–19.

8. In order that, No. 10.

9. A form of narrative, rather like the present indicative, but with the idea of " just to think that such a thing happens or should happen ". Nos. 20, 21.

10. Subordinate clause after command that, wish that, it is right or proper or customary that. Nos. 23–8.

11. Would that ! Nos. 29, 30.

12. Whenever, however or wherever may be. Nos. 31–5.

Further sentences involving the present subjunctive will be found under Conditional Sentences in Lessons 26 and 27, and under Necessity and Duty in Lessons 12 and 13.

1. nə koi bahər jae əwr nə koi əndər ae.

Let no one go out or come in.

2. məhina bhər nə rəheŋ, kəm se kəm pəndrə dyn to rəheŋ.

If they won't stay a full month, at least let them stay a fortnight.

3. sare mwlk meŋ tufan məc jae, to həm log kya kəreŋ ?

If a storm breaks all over the country, what are we to do ?

4. yəhaŋ məkan meŋ bəy- thke kam nə kəruŋ, to kya sərək pər jakər bəythuŋ ?

If I mayn't sit and work here in the house, am I to go and sit on the road ?

5. bəs, əb se twm meŋ se mere khet meŋ koi admi kam nə kəre.

Well then, in future none of you are to work in my field.

6. jys kysi ka jo ji cahe so pəhyne.

Everyone may wear what he likes.

7. rəkh leŋ, choṛ deŋ həmeŋ kya ?

What do we care whether they keep it or leave it ?

8. dam kwch hi hoŋ, koi nə koi gahək mol hi jaega.

Whatever the price some one or other will buy it.

9. əccha ji, əb mwaf * kəreŋ, məyŋ mwŋh hath dho luŋ əwr khana kha luŋ.

Very well, my man ; now excuse me ; I'll wash my face and hands and have dinner.

* mwaf : generally pronounced məaf or maf—though more fas-tidious speakers use a back quality of a, or a slight back on glide.

10. ap fəyslə zəra jəldi kəreŋ taky ws ki jan na jae.

You should decide rather quickly so that his life may be saved.

11. ap nədi ke kynare pwl ke nice jake ḍhuŋḍheŋ.

You might go and look by the bank of the river under the bridge.

12. ap mwjh se xəfa nə hoŋ.

Don't be angry with me.

13. pətte əyse jhəɽ rəhe həyŋ, jəyse ole bərəs rəhe hoŋ.

Leaves are falling as if it were hailing.

14. ys tərəh qədəm wṭhata həy jəyse bwxar cəɽha ho.

He's walking as if he had fever.

15. ʃayəd bij bote hoŋ.

Perhaps they're sowing.

16. ʃayəd pəwda wga ho.

Perhaps the plant may have begun to grow.

17. ws ne ʃayəd kho dia ho.

He may have lost it.

18. xəyr, dekhie, qysmət meŋ kya lykha ho.

Well, we shall see what fate may have in store for us.

19. ʃayəd məvəyʃi pərli tərəf cər rəhe hoŋ.

The cattle might be grazing on the far side.

20. kysi ka ghər jəle, əwr koi ag tape.

Taking advantage of another's misfortune.

21. koi etyraz kəre, koi nə kəre.

Some may object and some may not.

22. hwkm həy ky dəftər meŋ koi bhi daxyl nə ho.

No one may enter the office. By order.

23. wnheŋ cahie ky voh ek dusre ko gali nə deŋ.

They shouldn't abuse one another.

24. yeh əccha həy ky hər qysm ka səwda ʃəhr meŋ byke.

It's a good thing that all kinds of things should be sold in the city.

25. yəhaŋ dəstur həy ky mərd safə bandheŋ, əwrəteŋ cadər oɽheŋ.

It's the custom here for men to wear turbans and women shawls.

26. voh ləɽki fəwrən cəli jae.

That girl is to go away at once.

27. meri xahyʃ həy ky ws tərəf bəyṭhuŋ.

I should like to sit over there.

28. donoŋ ki mərzi həy ky hysab ki pərtal kəreŋ.	They both wish to inspect the account (or audit).
29. kaʃ jəld ae, vərnə bat bygəɽ jaegi.	I hope he'll come soon, otherwise things'll be in a mess.
30. jytni jəldi ho səke.	As quickly as possible.
31. jəhaŋ kəhiŋ myle.	Wherever you can get it.
32. jəb kəbhi nəzər ae.	Whenever you see it.
33. jys tərəh bən pəɽe.	However you can manage it.
34. jəhaŋ tək mwmkyn ho.	So far as possible.
35. meri məjal həy ap ki mwxalyfət kəruŋ?	Could I ever oppose you?

LESSON II

PAST CONDITIONAL

See Grammar, pp. 47–8.

This tense is used chiefly :—

1. In conditional sentences; see Nos. 1, 2, 4–7, 11, 13. The word " if " may or may not be expressed.

2. In clauses following phrases like " it was necessary or advisable that (something should take place) "; see No. 3.

3. In clauses containing "would that (something had happened) "; see No. 8.

No. 12 is a conditional sentence with the if-clause suppressed.

No. 8 closely resembles Lesson 9, Sentence 29, and should be carefully compared with it.

Further sentences involving the past conditional will be found under Necessity and Duty, Lessons 12 and 13, and under Conditional Sentences, Lessons 26 and 27.

1. meŋh nə bərəsta, to həm bhig nə jate.	We shouldn't have got wet if it hadn't rained.
2. memsahəb mwjhe rəstə bətatiŋ to məyŋ kəb ka pəhwŋc jata.	If the English lady'd shown me the way, I should have got there long ago.

3. cahie to yeh tha ky bəɽhəi ap hi bəkəs bə-nata.

The carpenter should have made the box himself.

4. ys se lapərvahi nə hoti to ytna nwqsan nə wɽhata.

If he hadn't been careless, he wouldn't have suffered such a loss.

5. əb se do car dyn pəhyle ylaj kərvata, to kya hi əccha hota.

What a good thing it would have been if he'd got treated three or four days ago.

6. bəɽe sahəb ko fwrsət hoti to həm se mwlaqat kərte.

The boss (etc.) would have seen us if he'd had time.

7. neki kərta hoſyar rəhta to kamyab ho jata.

He'd have had success if he'd done good and been careful.

8. kaſ jəld ata, mwamylə nə bygəɽta.

I wish he had come sooner, then things would not have got into such a mess.

9. əpne qwsur ka yqrar kərta, to ſayəd mwaf kər dete.

If only he'd admitted his fault, they might have forgiven him.

10. ws ki təbiət əysi səxt nə hoti, to log ws se nə dərte.

He was so bad-tempered; people wouldn't have feared him otherwise.

11. əgər mere pas kafi saman hota to məyŋ karxanə kholta.

If I'd had sufficient stock, I should have opened a factory.

12. həm yeh səlah to na dete; baqi ap mərzi ke malyk həyŋ.

We shouldn't have advised it, but after all, you can do as you please.

13. gədha cwp rəhta, to log wse ſer hi mante.

If the ass hadn't brayed, they'd have thought him a tiger.

G

LESSONS 12, 13, 14

NECESSITY, DUTY, ETC.

The Infinitive. See Grammar, pp. 95–7.

Sentences expressing necessity, duty, etc., fall into two main classes, corresponding to the two English types :—

    (i) it is necessary to go,

    (ii) it is necessary that I should go.

The former has one single clause with an infinitive; the latter has two clauses.

Sentences containing a word like **lazym**, **vajyb**, **mwnasyb**, **fərz**, **cahie** or **zəruri** can be expressed in both ways. When there are two clauses, if the verb of the main clause is present indicative, that of the second will be present subjunctive; if the verb of the main clause is past, that of the second clause will be past conditional.

The following examples illustrate this : Lesson 12, Nos. 5, 6, 11, 3; Lesson 14, No. 16; Lesson 13, No. 7—contain each one single clause, but they may be expressed in two clauses as follows :—

12, 5 : zəruri həy ky əmir myskinoŋ ki pərvəryʃ kəreŋ.	It is necessary that the rich should support the poor.
12, 6 : lazym tha ky log cyraɣ rəwʃən kərte.	It was proper that people should light the lamps.
12, 11 : mera fərz tha ky jəvab deta.	It was my duty that I should give an answer.
12, 3 : cahie ky həm Xwda se dwa maŋgeŋ.	We ought to pray to God.
13, 6 : əgər cahie ky səvere jageŋ, to jəldi so jaie.	If you want to wake up early, then go to bed soon.
14, 16 : cahie tha ky ʈhekedar məzduroŋ pər mehrbani kərta.	The contractor should have been kind to the workmen.

In the same way in the remaining sentences below, when the idea of necessity, duty, etc., is expressed by the infinitive and a single clause, it can be changed, as in the six examples just given, to two clauses—the second of which contains the present subjunctive or past conditional.

An analysis of these lessons shows the following methods of expression :—

Necessity by **həy, tha**, or the simple verb **hona** :—

> Lesson 12, Nos. 1, 2, 8, 15, 16.
> Lesson 13, Nos. 5, 6.

by **pəɽna** :—

> Lesson 12, Nos. 1, 4, 7.
> Lesson 13, Nos. 1, 3, 11.

by **zəruri** :—

> Lesson 12, Nos. 5.
> Lesson 13, No. 15.

Advisability, duty, etc., by **cahie** :—

> Lesson 12, Nos. 3, 14.
> Lesson 13, Nos. 2, 12, 13.
> Lesson 14, Nos. 14–19.

by **lazym** :—

> Lesson 12, Nos. 6.
> Lesson 13, No. 14.

by **vajyb** :—

> Lesson 13, No. 9.

by **mwnasyb** :—

> Lesson 12, No. 10, 13.
> Lesson 13, No. 4.
> Lesson 14, No. 9.

by **fərz** :—

> Lesson 12, Nos. 11, 12.
> Lesson 13, Nos. 7, 8.

The use of the infinitive is illustrated in the following :—

Gerundive infinitive for necessity, duty, etc. :—

> Lesson 12, Nos. 1–4, 6–9, 11–16.
> Lesson 13, Nos. 1–3, 5–7, 11–15.
> Lesson 14, Nos. 14–19.

Gerundive as an imperative :—

> Lesson 14, Nos. 20, 21.

Gerundive, other uses :—

> Lesson 14, Nos. 4, 5, 10.

Gerund or verbal noun : Lesson 14, Nos. 1–3, 6–13.
This expresses purpose in Lesson 14, No. 6; negative intention in Lesson 14, No. 7; agent in Lesson 14, No. 13.

LESSON 12

1. əgər twmheŋ jəldi pə-hwŋcna həy, to rel meŋ səfər kərna pəɽega.

   If you want to get there quickly, you must travel by train.

2. mwjhe aj bəyan lykhna həy.

   I have to write the report (narrative) to-day.

3. Xwda se həmeŋ dwa mangni cahie.

   We should pray to God.

4. bis ke bəjae tis rwpəe xərc kərne pəɽe.

   Rs. 30 had to be spent instead of Rs. 20.

5. əmiroŋ pər myskinoŋ ki pərvəryʃ zəruri həy.

   The rich must support the poor.

6. hər gəli kuce meŋ cyraɣ rəwʃən kərne lazym the.

   Lamps should have been lit in all the lanes and alleys.

7. dhup meŋ wnheŋ həl nə jotna pəɽe.

   (I) hope they won't have to plough in the sun.

8. (əre), bətao to səhi, kəhaŋ jana həy.

   Tell me any way where you have to go.

9. əgər wse aj səhn meŋ jhaṛu nəhiŋ deni, to kəl səhi.

If he doesn't want (or hasn't got) to sweep the courtyard to-day—very well then, to-morrow.

10. mwnasyb tha ky voh rich ko goli marta.

He should have shot the bear.

11. jəvab dena mera fərz tha.

It was my duty to give an answer.

12. təklif wṭhana ynsan ka fərz həy.

It's one's duty to take trouble over a thing.

13. lekyn təklif deni mwnasyb nəhiŋ.

But one shouldn't give trouble.

14. jys vəqt nəmaz pəṛhni cahie ws vəqt pəṛhe.

One should say prayers at the proper time.

15. Hynduoŋ ke syva əwr kysi ko nəhiŋ bwlana hoga.

No one is to be called besides the Hindus.

16. bəs Brəhmənoŋ ko hi roṭi khylani thi.

Only the Brahmans had to be fed.

LESSON 13

1. twmheŋ bazuoŋ əwr ṭaŋgoŋ ki malyʃ kərni pəṛegi.

You'll have to rub arms and legs.

2. wse Xwda ka ʃwkr kərna cahie.

He ought to thank God.

3. mwjhe caŋdi choṭi ḍybia meŋ chwpani pəṛi.

I had to hide the silver in the little box.

4. kysi ke lie mwnasyb nəhiŋ ky samp ko nənge hath se pəkṛe.

No one should seize a snake with bare hands.

5. jəb kəbhi zin baŋdhni ya peṭi kəsni ho, to mwjh se kəhie.

Tell me whenever you want the saddle put on or the girth fastened.

6. səvere jagna ho to jəldi so jae.

If he wants to wake early, he should go to bed soon.

7. xah əndhe hoŋ, ya bəhre, ya ləŋgṛe, səb ko palna fərz həy.

It's a duty to support them all, whether blind or deaf or lame.

8. ynsan ka fərz həy ky əpne bədən ko saf rəkkhe.

It's man's duty to keep his body clean.

9. kya vajyb nə tha ky hər gəli kuce meŋ dhəndhora pyṭvate?

Wasn't it right to have it proclaimed all over the town?

10. haŋ cahie tha ky həm kəm se kəm yʃtyhar chəpvate.

Yes, at least we should have had a notice printed.

11. kwch hi ho jae, bhari bojh dəhne hath se əwr həlka baeŋ se wṭhana pəṛega.

Be that as it may, the heavy load will have to be lifted with the right and the light one with the left hand.

12. həmeŋ həlal həram meŋ fərq kərna cahie nə?

Mustn't we make a distinction between lawful and unlawful?

13. twmhare buṭ myṭṭi se bhər gəe, bədəlne nəhiŋ cahieŋ?

Your shoes are all muddy, shouldn't you change them?

14. sari rəpəṭ hərf bəhərf səcci honi lazym thi.

The proper thing was that the whole report should be true.

15. twmheŋ səza pani zəruri thi.

It was necessary for you to be punished.

LESSON 14

1. bhyʃti pani bhərne ka kam kərta həy.

The water-carrier draws water.

2. dekhne meŋ koi hərj nəhiŋ.

There's no harm in looking.

3. janvəroŋ ko marna bwra kam həy.

It's a dreadful thing to beat animals.

4. ws ne lal syahi xəridni cahi.
He wanted to buy red ink.

5. məyŋ ne sukhi ləkṛi kaṭni ʃwru ki.
I began to cut dry wood.

6. mali dudh lene gəya.
The gardener went to get milk.

7. voh yuŋhi chati piṭne ki nəhiŋ.
She's not going to mourn without reason.

8. ap ka kəhna səhih həy.
What you say is right.

9. mera bar bar vəhaŋ jana mwnasyb nəhiŋ.
It's not proper for me to go there constantly.

10. əb cyṭṭhiaŋ ani jani ʃwru huiŋ.
Now letters began to pass (between them).

11. wnhoŋ ne dərzi se qəmiz sine ko kəha.
They told the tailor to make a shirt.

12. məllah dərya par kərne ko təiyar ho gəya.
The sailor (or boatman) prepared to cross the river.

13. həm chəy khanevale həyŋ.
There are six of us to feed.

14. hər roz twmheŋ aṭh səfhe xətm kərne cahieŋ.
You should finish eight pages a day.

15. wse dəs dyn ki chwṭṭi leni cahie.
He should take ten days' leave.

16. ṭhekedar ko məzduroŋ pər mehrbani kərni cahie thi.
The contractor should have been kind to the workmen.

17. ws mərd ko əysi gəndi bateŋ muhŋ se nə nykalni cahie thiŋ.
That man shouldn't have allowed such foul language to pass his lips.

18. ʃəwhər ko bivi se həmeʃə nek swluk kərna cahie.
A husband should always treat his wife well.

19. əsbab ladnevale ko bəhwt xəbərdar rəhna cahie.
A man should be very careful in loading goods.

20. meri koṭhi pər jana əwr jhəṭ ləwṭ ana.
Go to my house and return at once.

21. cori nə kərna, xun nə kərna.
Do not steal or commit murder.

LESSON 15

səkna = to be able ;
cwkna = to finish, to have finished

See Grammar, pp. 68–70.

1. bərsat ke dynoŋ meŋ kysan asani se zəmin jot səkte həyŋ.

Farmers can easily plough the ground during the rains.

2. voh ḍər ke mare cylla bhi nə səki.

She was so frightened, she could not even cry.

3. əgər wse pəhcan səka, to bhej duŋga.

If I can recognise him, I shall send him.

4. mwjh se yeh nəhiŋ ho səkta.

I can't do this.

5. əgər ho səka, hazyr huŋgi.

I shall come if possible.

6. jəb tək wṭh nə səkoge, kam kəyse xətm kəroge ?

Until you're able to get up, how can you finish the work ?

7. ji nəhiŋ, məyŋ kha cwka.

No, I've already eaten.

8. bəndobəst ho cwkega, to xəbər kəruŋga.

When everything's ready, I'll let you know.

9. baryʃ ho cwkne pər həva bhi thəm gəi.

By the time the rain stopped, the wind had ceased.

10. badəl ki vəjəh se gyrja dykhai nəhiŋ de səkta.

Because of the clouds, one can't see the church.

11. ghənṭa bəjne ke səbəb ws ki avaz swnai nə de səki.

Because of the gong, one couldn't hear his voice.

12. əlbəttə jəgəh dəryaft ho səkti, to məyŋ bhi ja məwjud hota.

Of course, if I could have found the place, I should have gone too.

13. jəb beṭi nəzdik akər khəṛi hui, maŋ kəhiŋ nə kəhiŋ ja cwki thi.

When the daughter came and stood near, her mother had gone somewhere or other.

14. ho səkta to məyŋ ap ki dərxast mənzur kərta.

If it had been possible, I should have granted your request.

15. zəxmi sypahi bhəla kəb   Well, how long could a
    tək səbr kər səkta?   wounded sepoy remain
                                   patient?

16. cwhia yəhaŋ tək ḍəri ky   The mouse got such a
    byl meŋ nə ghws səki.   fright that she couldn't
                                   get into her hole.

LESSON 16

ləgna = begin ; and other uses of ləgna

See Grammar, p. 70 and pp. 110–12.

1. rəssa kheŋcne ləga.   He began pulling the rope.
2. voh thər thər kaŋpne   She began trembling vio-
   ləgi.   lently.
3. voh kəhne ləge həmare   They said : " There is no
   bərabər koi pəhlvan   wrestler equal to us."
   nəhiŋ.
4. mere pwkarne pər səb log   When I call, everyone be-
   piche həṭne ləgte həyŋ.   gins moving back.
5. bəccoŋ ko ḍərao mət, rone Don't frighten the children,
   ləgeŋge.   they'll cry.
6. dhup ki gərmi ləge, to sae If the sun's hot, rest in the
   meŋ aram kijie.   shade.
7. jəb bərf pəṛne ləgi,   When it began to snow,
   bheṛoŋ ka kəhiŋ pəta na   there was no trace of the
   ləga.   sheep.
8. jhaṛi ki jəṛ se wse bwri   He stumbled badly against
   ṭhokər ləgi.   the root of a bush.
9. jəb se meri nəwkəri ləgi   Since I got work, my
   məyŋ əwr mere bal bəcce   children and I have never
   bhi bhukhe nə rəhe.   been hungry.
10. sadhu ko səxt bhukh əwr   The sadhu seems to be very
    pyas ləgi malum hoti   hungry and thirsty.
    həy.
11. do pəhr ko hər roz pyas   One gets very thirsty every
    ləgti həy.   day at noon.

12. təmam qəwm pər ys xun ka dhəbba ləgega.

The whole community will be stained by this murder.

13. vəhaŋ jane se həmeŋ kəhiŋ khaŋsi ya koi əwr bimari nə ləgjae.

I hope that by going there we shan't contract a cough or some other ailment.

14. coṭ ləgi, jəb hi kəhne ləga ky mera dyl yəhaŋ nəhiŋ ləgta.

It was when he got hurt that he began saying that he was not happy there.

15. khane meŋ der nə ləgao vərnə jane meŋ der ləgegi.

Don't delay about your food or you'll be late in going.

16. wn ke hath kwch nə ləga.

They got nothing.

17. yeh paejamə həmeŋ əccha nəhiŋ ləgta.

These trousers don't suit us : or, we don't like them.

18. salən degci meŋ ləg gəya.

The curry's got burnt and stuck to the pot.

19. meri aŋkh ləgi thi ky ws ne jəga dia.

I had just got to sleep when he woke me up.

LESSON 17

dena = permit ; pana = manage to

See Grammar, pp. 70–1.

1. voh bətti gwl kərne nə pae ky ap hi əndhera ho gəya.

It got dark before they'd put out the lamp.

2. əgər səyr kərne pauŋ to kəruŋga.

I shall take a walk if I can manage it.

3. voh zevər pəsənd kərne bhi nə pai thi ky ɣayb ho gəya.

The jewel vanished before she had time to choose it.

4. koi səfed joṛa pəhynne nə pae.

Don't let anyone wear a white suit.

5. kysi ko səbz rəng ki cadər oɽhne nə do.

Don't let anyone wear a green-coloured shawl.

6. əccha, jane do.

Very well, let it pass; or : never mind.

7. voh hərgyz sais ko ghoɽa phyrane nə dega.

He'll certainly not let the groom walk the horse about.

8. mwmkyn həy ky fəjr ko nəhane pae.

He may manage to bathe at sunrise.

9. ʃiʃe ko nice gyrne nə dia.

He didn't let the glass fall on the ground.

10. jəhaŋ tək ho səkega həm wse bimar nə hone deŋge.

As far as possible, we shan't let him get ill.

11. choʈe bəccoŋ ko gəhri jhil meŋ təyrne nəhiŋ dena cahie.

You shouldn't let little children swim in the deep lake.

12. bəyl, bəkri, vəɣəyrə ko ys məydan meŋ nəhiŋ cərne dena.

Don't let bulls, goats, etc., graze on this plain.

13. əgərcy hath se koi chune nəhiŋ pata, məgər cwp-cap bəyʈhkər ankhoŋ se dekhne to dete həyŋ ?

Though one may not touch, they do let one watch quietly, don't they?

LESSON 18

HABIT

Habit is expressed by **kərna** = to do, with what is probably the past participle of other verbs. No. 15 shows that for **jana**, the form used is **jaya**; not the usual past participle **gəya**.

1. The schoolboys are always throwing balls.

   mədərse ke ləɽke geŋd pheŋka kərte həyŋ.

2. Don't make a practice of walking in the veranda.

   bəramde meŋ nə phyra kəro.

3. They eat and drink in the drawing-room.

   gol kəmre meŋ khaya pia kərte həyŋ.

4. Make a habit of working hard.

   xub mehnət kia kəro.

5. The Maulvi conducts prayers on Fridays.

   jwme ko məwlvi sahəb nəmaz pəɽhaya kərte həyŋ.

6. Your work is to wipe the chairs with a duster.

   twmhara kam yeh həy ky jhaɽən se kwrsiaŋ poŋcha kəro.

7. If you always do difficult work carefully, your master will be pleased with you.

   mwʃkyl kam socke kəro to malyk xwʃ hoga.

8. Village girls easily get confused and cry.

   gaoŋ ki ləɽkiaŋ jəldi ghəbraya əwr roya kərti həyŋ.

9. Those who walk slowly do not slip.

   jo ahystə cəla kərte həyŋ wn ka paoŋ physəlta nəhiŋ.

10. Wild animals come here all night.

    yəhaŋ rat bhər jəngli janvər aya kərte həyŋ.

١   مدرسہ کے لڑکے گیند پھینکا کرتے ہیں ۔

٢   برآمدہ میں نہ پھرا کرو ۔

٣   گول کمرے میں کھایا پیا کرتے ہیں ۔

٤   خوب محنت کیا کرو ۔

٥   جمعہ کو مولوی صاحب نماز پڑھایا کرتے ہیں ۔

٦   تمہارا کام یہ ہے کہ جھاڑن سے کرسیاں پونچھا کرو ۔

٧   مشکل کام سوچ کے کرو تو مالک خوش ہوگا ۔

٨   گاؤں کی لڑکیاں جلدی گھبرایا اور رویا کرتی ہیں ۔

٩   جو آہستہ چلا کرتے ہیں ان کا پاؤں پھسلتا نہیں ۔

١٠   یہاں رات بھر جنگلی جانور آیا کرتے ہیں ۔

11. Not only I but everyone complains about him.

syrf məyŋ hi nəhiŋ səb ws ki ʃykayət kia kərte həyŋ.

12. In those days ghi used to be sold dear.

wn dynoŋ meŋ ghi məhŋga byka kərta tha.

13. In future it will be obtained cheaply.

əb se səsta myla kərega.

14. The result of this examination used to be good.

ys ymtyhan ka nətijə əccha hua kərta tha.

15. Let them go wherever they feel inclined.

jəhaŋ ji cahe jaya kəreŋ.

11   صرف میں ہی نہیں سب اس کی شکایت کیا کرتے ہیں ۔

12   ان دنوں میں کبھی مہنگا بکا کرتا تھا ۔

13   اب سے ستا ملا کرے گا ۔

14   اس امتحان کا نتیجہ اچھا ہوا کرتا تھا ۔

15   جہاں جی چاہے جایا کریں ۔

LESSON 19

CONTINUANCE, DOING A THING AT THE MOMENT, HABIT

For continuance, see Grammar, pp. 42–8; for doing a thing at the moment, pp. 42–5; for habit, pp. 97–9, and Lesson 18.

1. My eye's swelling up.

   meri aŋkh suj rəhi həy.

2. He kept on telling lies.

   jhuʈhi bateŋ bəkta rəha.

3. There's always a difference between a good and a bad rupee.

   khəre khoʈe rwpəe meŋ fərq hua kərta həy.

4. Sinners keep on sinning.

   gwnəhgar gwnah kərte hi rəhte həyŋ

5. Mongooses become tame if you love them.

   nevle pyar se hyl jaya kərte həyŋ.

6. He kept on swearing great oaths.

   voh bəɽi qəsmeŋ khata rəha.

7. The canal's very broad and boats will go on it.

   nəhr bəhwt cəwɽi həy. ws meŋ kyʃtiaŋ cəlti rəheŋgi.

8. All day motors keep going on the main road.

   dyn bhər pəkki səɽək pər moʈəreŋ cəlti rəhti heyŋ.

9. You worked an hour and now it's finished?

   ghənʈa bhər kam kərte rəhe, əwr əb xətm ho gəya?

10. Don't drink strong tea, or you'll spoil your digestion.

    tez cae nə pia kəro vərnə hazmə xərab ho jaega.

١   میری آنکھ سوج رہی ہے۔

٢   جھوٹی باتیں بکتا رہا۔

٣   کھرے کھوٹے روپیہ میں فرق ہوا کرتا ہے :

٤   گنہگار گناہ کرتے ہی رہتے ہیں۔

٥   نیولے پیار سے ہل جایا کرتے ہیں۔

٦   وہ بڑی قسمیں کھاتا رہا۔

٧   نہر بہت چوڑی ہے۔ اس میں کشتیاں چلتی رہیں گی۔

٨   دن بھر پکی سڑک پر موٹریں چلتی رہتی ہیں۔

٩   گھنٹہ بھر کام کرتے رہے اور اب ختم ہو گیا ؟

١٠   تیز چائے نہ پیا کرو' ورنہ ہاضمہ خراب ہو جائے گا۔

11. Keep on stirring the milk with a spoon or a fork.

cəmce ya kaŋțe se dudh hylate jao.

12. The scent of the flowers perfumes the whole house.

phuloŋ ki xwʃbu se təmam məkan məhək jata həy.

13. The river flows through the year.

sal bhər dərya bəhta rəhta hy.

14. For fifteen days the moon will get bigger; and after that will in the same way get smaller.

pəndrə dyn tək caŋd bəṛhta rəhega phyr bad meŋ vəyse hi ghəțța jaega.

15. Look, the stars are shining.

dekhie tare cəmək rəhe həyŋ.

16. He kept on doing mischief.

voh ʃərarət kərta rəha.

17. He used to do good.

voh neki kia kərta tha.

18. She was asking a question.

voh səval kər rəhi thi.

19. She used to live in the jungle.

jəngəl meŋ rəha kərti thi.

11   چمچے یا کانٹے سے دودھ ہلاتے جاؤ۔

12   پھولوں کی خوشبو سے تمام مکان مہک جاتا ہے۔

13   سال بھر دریا بہتا رہتا ہے۔

14   پندرہ دن تک چاند بڑھتا رہے گا پھر گھٹتا جائے گا۔ بعد میں ویسے ہی

15   دیکھئے تارے چمک رہے ہیں۔

16   وہ شرارت کرتا رہا۔

17   وہ نیکی کیا کرتا تھا۔

18   وہ سوال کر رہی تھی۔

19   جنگل میں رہا کرتی تھی۔

LESSON 20

SPECIAL NUMBERS AND TIME

See Grammar, pp. 20–26, 134–6.

1. It'll be half a mile or three-quarters.

ek adh mil ka fasələ hoga.

2. I want one-and-a-half sers of flour.

ḍeṛh ser aṭa cahie.

3. It'll take an hour and forty-five minutes.

pəwne do ghənṭe ləgeṅge.

4. It must weigh two and a half to two and three quarter maunds.

ys ka vəzən ḍhai ya pəwne tin mən hoga.

5. This seems to be three and a quarter or three and a half yards high

yeh səva tin ya saṛhe tin gəz uṅca malum hota həy.

6. It's now half past one; I shall bring lunch at a quarter to two.

ḍeṛh bəj gəya həy məyṅ pəwne do bəje lənc lauṅga.

7. This town has two thousand two hundred and fifty to two thousand five hundred inhabitants.

ys qəsbe meṅ səva do ya ḍhai həzar baʃynde həyṅ.

8. London has about nine million inhabitants.

Ləndən meṅ koi nəvve lakh log rəhte həyṅ.

9. In the first hartal three quarters of the shops were shut.

pəhli həṛtal meṅ tin cəwthai dwkaneṅ bənd thiṅ.

10. To-day I got breakfast at eighteen minutes past eleven.

aj mwjhe hazyri gyarə bəjkər əṭṭharə mynəṭ pər myli.

١   ایک آدھ میل کا فاصلہ ہوگا۔

٢   ڈیڑھ سیر آٹا چاہیئے۔

٣   پونے دو گھنٹے لگیں گے۔

٤   اس کا وزن ڈھائی یا پونے تین من ہوگا۔

٥   یہ سوا تین یا ساڑھے تین گز او پچھا معلوم ہوتا ہے۔

٦   ڈیڑھ بج گیا ہے' میں پونے دو نے لنچ لاؤں گا۔

٧   اس قصبہ میں سوا دو یا ڈھائی ہزار باشندے ہیں۔

٨   لندن میں کوئی نوے لاکھ لوگ رہتے ہیں۔

٩   پہلی ہڑتال میں تین چوتھائی دوکانیں بند تھیں۔

١٠ آج مجھے حاضری گیارہ بج کر اٹھارہ منٹ پر ملی۔

11. The day before yesterday I had my morning tea at nineteen minutes to six.

pərsoŋ məyŋ ne choṭi həzyri chəy bəjne meŋ wnnis mynəṭ pər khai.

12. London's nine times as big as Birmingham.

Ləndən Bərmyŋghəm se nəw gwna bəṛa həy.

13. The population of India is three hundred and fifty millions.

Hyndostan ki abadi pəyŋtis kəroṛ həy.

14. The population of Delhi is five times the population of Multan.

Dylli Mwltan se paŋc gwni həy.

15. It is 12.45; he was to begin the work at 12.45.

pəwn bəj gəya həy; wse pəwn bəje kam ʃwru kərna tha.

16. There cannot be more than 750 people in our village.

həmare gaoŋ meŋ saṛhe sat səw se zyadə admi nə hoŋge.

17. A third of the ships were lost in the battle.

ləṛai meŋ ek tyhai jəhaz bərbad hue.

١١   پرسوں میں نے چھوٹی حاضری چھ بجے میں انیس منٹ پر کھائی ۔

١٢   لندن برمنگھم سے نو گنا بڑا ہے ۔

١٣   ہندوستان کی آبادی پینتیس کروڑ ہے ۔

١٤   دلّی ملتان سے پانچ گنی ہے ۔

١٥   پون بج گیا ہے ۔ اسے پون سنے کام شروع کرنا تھا ۔

١٦   ہمارے گاؤں میں ساڑھے سات سو سے زیادہ آدمی نہ ہونگے ۔

١٧   لڑائی میں ایک تہائی جہاز برباد ہوئے ۔

LESSON 21

THE PASSIVE

See Grammar, pp. 53–5, 105–6.

1. One plays this instrument with one's finger.

   yeh baja wngli se bəjaya jata həy.

2. If you rub oil on the knee, it'll get well.

   ghwṭne pər tel ləgakər məlo to əccha ho jaega.

3. One meaning of this word was explained.

   ys ləfz ke ek mane bətae gəe.

4. Let it be spread on the floor (or ground).

   zəmin pər bychaya jae.

5. If he's treated harshly, he'll die.

   əgər zwlm kia jae to mər jaega.

6. They'll get lines drawn here by the workmen.

   mystrioŋ se yəhaŋ ləkireŋ khyŋcvai jaeŋgi.

7. Fish are caught with hooks or nets.

   məcchliaŋ kaŋtoŋ ya jaloŋ se pəkṛi jati həyŋ.

8. An advance of two rupees was (had been) given.

   do rwpəe peʃgi die gəe the.

9. To-morrow the marriage will be performed.

   kəl nykah pəṛhaya jaega.

10. Here the Id festival is observed.

    yəhaŋ id mənai jati həy.

۱   یہ باجہ انگلی سے بجایا جاتا ہے ۔

۲   گھٹنے پر تیل لگا کر ملو تو اچھا ہو جائیگا۔

۳   اس لفظ کے ایک معنی بنائے گئے ۔

۴   زمین پر بچھایا یا جائے۔

۵   اگر ظلم کیا جائے تو مر جائے گا ۔

۶   مستریوں سے یہاں لکیریں کھنچوائی جائینگی

۷   مچھلیاں کانٹوں یا جالوں سے پکڑی جاتی ہیں ۔

۸   دو روپئے پیشگی دئے گئے تھے ۔

۹   کل نکاح پڑھایا جائے گا ۔

۱۰   یہاں عید منائی جاتی ہے ۔

11. Agree to whatever price is settled.

qimət jytni thəhrai jae to zərur man lo.

12. It'll be a good thing if he's taught Persian.

əgər wse farsi pəɽhai jae to behtər.

13. The madman was chained.

pagəl zənjiroŋ se jəkɽa gəya.

14. Are you mad?

teri əql mari gəi?

15. I can't throw a stone so far.

mwjh se ytni dur pətthər nəhiŋ pheŋka jata.

16. That girl cannot walk two and a half kos.

ws lərki se dhai kos pəydəl nəhiŋ cəla jata.

17. He couldn't stand.

ws se khəɽa nəhiŋ hua jata tha.

18. It was explained to them. (They were warned, etc.)

wn ko səmjha dia gəya tha.

11   قیمت جتنی ٹھہرائی جائے ضرور مان لو۔

12   اگر اسے فارسی پڑھائی جائے تو بہتر۔

13   پاگل زنجیروں سے جکڑا اگیا۔

14   تیری عقل ماری گئ۔

15   مجھ سے اتنی دور پتھر نہیں پھینکا جاتا۔

16   اس لڑکی سے ڈھائی کوس پیدل نہیں چلا جاتا۔

17   اس سے کھڑا نہیں ہوا جاتا تھا۔

18   ان کو سمجھا دیا گیا تھا۔

LESSON 22

MYLNA, MYLANA

See Grammar, pp. 109–10.

1. The horse got only one seer of grain.

ghoɽe ko ser bhər hi dana myla.

2. Well, tell me, did you get permission?

bhəla, bətao to, twmheŋ rwxsət myli?

3. Get leave indeed? I got dismissed.

rwxsət kya? bəlky jəvab myl gəya.

4. Sweepers get less pay than the other servants.

mehtəroŋ ko səb nəwkəroŋ se kəm tənxah mylti həy.

5. We met the ayah in the garden.

aya həmeŋ baɣ meŋ myli.

6. The rajah met a splendid elephant on the metalled road.

pəkki səɽək pər raja ko ek nyhayət xubsurət hathi myla.

7. Perhaps the sahib won't see me after all.

ʃayəd Sahəb mwjh se myleŋ hi nəhiŋ.

8. I will introduce you.

məyŋ myla duŋga.

9. The vizier's two nephews are very like each other.

vəzir ke donoŋ bhətije apəs meŋ bəhwt mylte həyŋ.

10. Sometimes the fakir used to come to see me, sometimes I met him by chance.

kəbhi voh fəqir mwjh se mylne ata tha kəbhi yoŋhi myl jata tha.

١   گھوڑے کو سیر بھر ہی دانہ ملا ۔

٢   بھلا بتاؤ تو تمہیں رخصت ملی ؟

٣   رخصت کیا ؛ بلکہ جواب مل گیا ۔

٤   مہتروں کو سب نوکروں سے کم تنخواہ ملتی ہے ۔

٥   آیا بیں باغ میں ملی ۔

٦   پکی سٹرک پر راجہ کو ایک نہایت خوبصورت ہاتھی ملا ۔

٧   شاید صاحب مجھ سے لیں ہی نہیں ۔

٨   میں ملا دوں گا ۔

٩   وزیر کے دونوں بھتیجے آپس میں بہت ملتے ہیں ۔

١٠   کبھی وہ فقیر مجھ سے ملنے آتا تھا کبھی یوں ہی مل جاتا تھا ۔

11. Our handwritings are very much alike.

həmare xət ek dusre se mylte jwlte həyŋ.

12. I'm afraid the servant may have been dismissed.

mwjhe xəwf həy ky xydmətgar ko jəvab na myl gəya ho.

13. Will these books stay lying here all mixed up?

kya yeh kytabeŋ myli jwli pəṛi rəheŋgi?

14. Compare these three maps to see whether they agree or not.

yn tinoŋ nəqʃoŋ ko ap mylakər dekhie ky mylte həyŋ ya nəhiŋ.

15. He's a very friendly man; you'll see he'll grant an interview to them all (or greet them all).

voh bəhwt mylnsar admi həyŋ ap dekheŋge səb hi se myleŋge.

16. We shall eat together.

həm mylkər khaeŋge.

17. Mud is made by mixing earth and water.

myṭṭi meŋ pani mylakər gara bənaya jata həy.

11 ہمارے خط ایک دوسرے سے ملتے جلتے ہیں.

12 مجھے خوف ہے کہ خدمتگار کو جواب نہ لگیا ہو.

13 کیا یہ کتابیں ملی جلی پڑی رہیں گی ؟

14 ان تینوں نقشوں کو آپ ملا کر دیکھئے
     کہ ملتے ہیں یا نہیں ۔

15 وہ بہت ملنسار آدمی ہیں' آپ دیکھیں
     گے سب ہی سے ملیں گے۔

16 ہم مل کر کھائیں گے۔

17 مٹی میں پانی ملا کر گارا بنایا جاتا ہے۔

LESSON 23

REPETITION

See Grammar, pp. 130–3.

Nos. 3 and 4 illustrate the meaning of pleasant, nice and hot, nice and fresh, dear little children, and a pretty walk. In No. 9 the thought is spread over the various ceremonies constituting the marriage and over the past few weeks.

1. They were all lying apart from each other.	səb log ələg ələg leṭe hue the.
2. In rich men's houses servants get big wages.	maldaroŋ ke haŋ nəwkəroŋ ko bəṛi bəṛi tənxaheŋ mylti həyŋ.
3. Here you are—nice hot tea! Fruit nice and fresh!	pio cae gərm gərm, khao mevə tazə tazə.
4. Oh, just look how prettily these little children walk!	əre dekho zəra yn nənnhe nənnhe bəccoŋ ki kya pyari pyari cal həy.
5. The water of the farther tank is two feet deep.	pərle talab ka pani do do gəz gəhra həy.
6. He works hard, yet he was tired out going on carrying bricks.	mehnəti admi həy, tahəm inteŋ ḍho ḍho kər ajyz a gəya.
7. The girl ran to her mother and clung to her.	ləṛki dəwṛti dəwṛti əpni ma se jake lypəṭ gəi.
8. Brave men escape from many kinds of danger.	dyler admi qysm qysm ke xətroŋ se bəc jata həy.

۱ سب لوگ الگ الگ بیٹھے ہوئے تھے۔

۲ مالداروں کے ہاں نوکروں کو بڑی بڑی تنخواہیں ملتی ہیں۔

۳ پیو چائے گرم گرم' کھاؤ یہ میوہ تازہ تازہ۔

۴ ارے دیکھو ذرا' ان ننھے ننھے بچوں کی کیا پیاری پیاری

    چال ہے۔

۵ پرلے تالاب کا پانی دو دو گز گہرا ہے۔

۶ محنتی آدمی ہے تا ہم اینٹیں ڈھو ڈھو کر عاجز آ گیا۔

۷ لڑکی دوڑتی دوڑتی اپنی ماں سے جا کے لپٹ گئی۔

۸ دلیر آدمی قسم قسم کے خطروں سے نچ جاتا ہے۔

H

9. They've only recently been married and come here to live.

yn ka nəya nəya byah hua həy, əwr əbhi əbhi yəhaŋ rəhne ae həyŋ.

10. What wonderful sights these Englishmen see when they climb those far-off mountains.

yeh əngrez dur dur ke pəhaɽoŋ pər cəɽh cəɽh kər kya kya təmaʃe dekhte həyŋ.

11. In under two years I shall get promotion, and then I shall get two days' leave every month.

do sal ke əndər əndər mwjhe tərəqqi mylegi; phyr məhine meŋ do do dyn chwtti mylegi.

12. I heard a number of sweet songs and was so delighted.

miʈhe miʈhe git swn swn kər mera dyl bay bay ho gəya.

13. His face gradually reddened all over with shame.

rəftə rəftə ʃərm ke mare ws ka cehrə lal ho gəya.

14. Even so you won't get it while you are doing nothing.

phyr bhi bəyʈhe bəyʈhe to nəhiŋ mylega.

٩   اِن کا نیا نیا بیاہ ہوا ہے اور ابھی ابھی یہاں رہنے آئے
ہیں ۔

١٠   یہ انگریز دور دور کے پہاڑوں پر چڑھ چڑھ کر کیا کیا تماشے دیکھتے ہیں ۔

١١   دو سال کے اندر اندر مجھے ترقی ملے گی، پھر مہینے میں دو دو دن چھٹی ملے گی ۔

١٢   بیٹھے بیٹھے گیت سن سن کر میرا دل باغ باغ ہو گیا ۔

١٣   رفتہ رفتہ شرم کے مارے اس کا چہرہ لال ہو گیا ۔

١٤   پھر بھی بیٹھے بیٹھے تو نہیں ملے گا ۔

LESSON 24

PRESENT AND PAST PARTICIPLES

(*a*) Used as attributive adjectives agreeing with some noun (i) expressed, or (ii) understood. See Nos. 1–18.

(*b*) Used as :—

    (i) Predicative and complementary adjectives. See Nos. 19–31.

    (ii) When the participle indicates a state, especially when used adverbially, and above all when it is repeated, it is often put in the oblique masculine singular. See Nos. 32–42.

[*a* (i)].

1. A dead bear was lying on some rotten wood.	ek məra hua rich səɽi hui ləkɽi pər pəɽa tha.
2. There's a spring of flowing water in the deserted town.	wjɽe qəsbe meŋ bəhte pani ka cəʃmə həy.
3. Travellers were seen at a distance.	dur se ate hue mwsafyr dykhai die.
4. One had a laughing face, but the other seemed to be crying.	ek ka to həŋsta hua cehrə tha əwr ek ki roti hui surət.
5. Books written by me.	meri lykhi kytabeŋ.
6. Cloth made of cotton.	kəpas ka bəna kəpɽa.
7. A shirt made at home.	ghər ka syla kwrta.
8. A literate villager.	lykha pəɽha dehati.
9. A vulture with wings cut.	pər kəʈa gydh.
10. Girl companions whose names are written below.	nice lykhi hui səheliaŋ.

١ ایک مرا ہوا ریچھ مٹری ہوئی لکڑی پر پڑا تھا۔

٢ اجڑے قصبہ میں نتے پانی کا چشمہ ہے۔

٣ دور سے آتے ہوئے سافر دکھائی دئے۔

٤ ایک کا ہنستا ہوا چہرہ تھا اور ایک کی روتی ہوئی صورت۔

٥ میری لکھی کتابیں۔

٦ کپاس کا بنا کپڑا۔

٧ گھر کا سلا کرتا۔

٨ لکھا پڑھا دیہاتی۔

٩ مر کٹا گدھا۔

١٠ بچے لکھی ہوئی سہیلیاں۔

11. A sempstress who has   kam sikhi hui dərzən.
    learnt her work.

12. Girls who've got prizes.   ynam pai hui lərkiaŋ.

[a (ii)].

13. A drowning man clutches   ḍubte ko tynke ka səhara
    at a straw.   bəhwt həy.

14. Killing a dead man.   məre ko marna.

15. The fruit of one's deeds.   əpne kie ka phəl.

16. Following his advice.   ws ke kəhe pər cəlna.

17. I can't read my own writ-   məyŋ əpna lykha nəhiŋ
    ing (what I've written).   pəṛh səkta.

18. Don't rouse a sleeping   sote ko nə jəgao.
    man.

[b (i)].

19. She came running.   voh dəwṛti hui ai.

20. The dacoits were caught   ḍaku bhagte hue pəkṛe
    running away.   gəe.

11   کام سیکھی ہوئی ورزن ۔

12   انعام پائی ہوئی لڑکیاں ۔

13   ڈوبتے کو تنکے کا سہارا بہت ہے ۔

14   مرے کو مارنا ۔

15   اپنے کئے کا پھل ۔

16   اس کے کہے پر چلنا ۔

17   میں اپنا لکھا نہیں پڑھ سکتا ۔

18   سوتے کو نہ جگاؤ ۔

19   وہ دوڑتی ہوئی آئی ۔

20   ڈاکو بھاگتے ہوئے پکڑے گئے ۔

21. There's always snow on the summit.

coṭi bərf se ḍhəki rəhti həy.

22. A bed woven with (broad) tape was placed there.

nəvaɽ ka pələng bycha hua tha.

23. Did you see fruit on the trees?

ap ne phəl ləge hue dekhe?

24. You ate burnt bread.

twm ne jəli hui roṭi khai.

25. She was going very fast.

voh dəwɽi dəwɽi ja rəhi thi.

26. She was going very fast.

voh bhagi bhagi ja rəhi thi.

27. I'm almost dead (very tired, etc.).

məyŋ məri jati huŋ.

28. The elephant advanced swinging his trunk.

hathi jhumta jhamta age bəɽha.

29. The deer fled with great bounds.

hyrən cəwkɽi bhərta bhag gəya.

30. My mother speaks hesitatingly.

meri ma əṭəkti hui bolti həy.

31. He doesn't answer even though often called.

bəhwt bwlaya jəvab nəhiŋ deta.

21   چوٹی برف سے ڈھکی رہتی ہے۔

22   نواز کا پلنگ بچھا ہوا تھا۔

23   آپ نے پھل لگے ہونے دیکھے۔

24   تم نے جلی ہوئی روٹی کھائی۔

25   وہ دوڑی دوڑی جا رہی تھی۔

26   وہ بھاگی بھاگی جا رہی تھی۔

27   میں مری جاتی ہوں۔

28   ہاتھی جھوم تا جھام تا آگے بڑھا۔

29   ہرن چوکڑی بھرتا بھاگ گیا۔

30   میری ماں اٹکتی ہوئی بولتی ہے۔

31   بہت بلایا جواب نہیں دیتا۔

[*b* (ii)].

32. Trembling, she began to speak.

kaŋpte kaŋpte [*or* kaŋpti kaŋpti] kəhne ləgi.

33. He was at death's door, but he recovered.

mərte mərte bəca.

34. He became ill while lying there.

pəɽe pəɽe [*or* pəɽa pəɽa] bimar ho gəya.

35. She won't get rich without doing anything.

bəyʈhe bəyʈhe dəwlət-mənd nəhiŋ ho jaegi.

36. She pulled herself together with great difficulty.

səmbhəlte səmbhəlte səm-bhəl hi gəi.

37. The kite (bird) hovered over the rock and fell to the ground.

cəʈan pər məndlate mənd-late [*or* -ti -ti] cil gyr pəɽi.

38. He didn't forget even while falling.

gyrte gyrte bhi voh nə bhula.

39. She cooked till she was tired.

roʈi pəkate pəkate thək gəi [*or* -ti -ti].

40. Even while giving charity he was planning deceit.

zəkat dete dete bhi beimani ki socta tha.

41. They quarrelled all the way home.

ləɽte jhəgəɽte ghər pəhwŋc gəe.

42. I shall stop the work as soon as I arrive.

məyŋ pəhwŋcte hi kam bənd kəra duŋga.

32   کاغذ کا پتہ کتنے گی ئے

33   مرتے مرتے بچا۔

34   پڑے پڑے بیمار ہو گیا ئے

35   بیٹھے بیٹھے دولت مند نہیں ہو جائے گی۔

36   سنبھلتے سنبھلتے سنبھل ہی گئی۔

37   چٹان پر منڈلاتے منڈلاتے چیل گر پڑی ئے۔

38   گرتے گرتے بھی وہ نہ بھولا۔

39   روٹی پکاتے پکاتے تھک گئی ئے

40   زکاۃ دیتے دیتے بھی بے ایمانی کی سوچتا تھا۔

41   لڑتے جھگڑتے گھر پہونچ گئے۔

42   میں پہونچتے ہی کام بند کرادونگا۔

LESSON 25

PRESENT AND PAST PARTICIPLES (continued)

(a) Complementary to nouns and pronouns in oblique cases. See Nos. 1–9.

(b) Used absolutely : changed subjects.

> (i) Participle used absolutely, the noun used with the participle being different from the subject of the sentence. The absolute participle is always oblique masculine singular. Participle affirmative. See Nos. 10–23.
>
> (ii) The absolute use of the participle in the negative. The negative is generally **be**, **bəyəyr**, **byna**, which may be translated literally " without ". See Nos. 24–7.
>
> (iii) The absolute participle may be impersonal, either affirmative or negative. See Nos. 28–35.

(c) Unnatural agreement. See Nos. 36–9.

[a].

1. Someone saw me dancing.	kysi ne mwjhe nacte hue [*or* nacta hua] dekha.
2. Who caught you playing?	kys ne twm ko khelte pəkɽa? [*or* khelte hue]
3. Someone will find him (or her) asleep.	koi wse soe hue paega [*or* soe soe].
4. I found him (or her) dead.	məyŋ ne wse məra paya.
5. The king's been dead a fortnight.	badʃah ko məre do həfte ho gəe.
6. I feel ashamed to make this request.	yeh ərz kərte mwjhe ʃərm ati həy.
7. The Maulvi's been living here for two months.	məwlvi sahəb ko yəhaŋ rəhte do məhine gwzər gəe.
8. While returning, he saw me.	ws ne ləwʈte hue mwjhe dekha.
9. He saw me returning.	ws ne mwjhe ləwʈte hue dekha.

۱ کسی نے مجھے ناچتے ہوئے دیکھا؟

۲ کس نے تم کو کھیلتے پکڑا؟

۳ کوئی اُسے سوئے ہوئے پائے گا؟

۴ میں نے اُسے سرا پایا۔ ۰

۵ بادشاہ کو مرے دو منتے ہوگئے۔

۶ یہ عرض کرتے مجھے شرم آتی ہے۔

۷ مولوی صاحب کو یہاں رہتے دو مہینے گذر گئے۔

۸ اُس نے لوٹتے ہوئے مجھے دیکھا۔

۹ اُس نے مجھے لوٹتے ہوئے دیکھا۔

[*b* (i)].

10. She was coming with bent head and out-stretched arms.

syr jhwkae, hath bəṛhae, a rəhi thi.

11. He was drunk.

ʃərab pie tha.

12. The police caught the thief with the goods on him.

pwlis ne cor ko, mal lie, pəkṛa.

13. The sister was playing with the child in her arms.

bəhyn, bəcce ko god meŋ lie, khel rəhi thi.

14. As long as I am alive, nobody can do you any harm.

mere dəm meŋ dəm hote hue ap ka koi bal bazu bika nəhiŋ kər səkta.

15. As long as you and I are here, what harm can come to him?

ap ke rəhte əwr mere hote ws ka kya bygṛega?

16. He cried till he got the hiccups.

rote rote ws ki hycki bəndh gəi.

17. I laughed so much that I got a stitch in my side.

həŋste həŋste mere peṭ meŋ bəl pəṛ gəe.

18. He went off at dawn (as soon as it was morning, at break of day).

dyn nykəlte (swbəh hote *or* dyn cəṛhe) hi voh cəl dia.

19. At one o'clock.

ek bəje.

10 سر جھکائے ہاتھ بڑھائے آ رہی تھی ۔

11 شراب پئے تھا ۔

12 پولیس نے چور کو بال لئے پکڑا ۔

13 بہن بچّہ کو گود میں لئے کھیل رہی تھی ۔

14 میرے دم میں دم ہوتے ہوئے آپ کا کوئی بال
بیکا نہیں کر سکتا ۔

15 آپ کے رہتے اور میرے ہوتے اس کا کیا بگڑے گا ؟

16 روتے روتے اس کی ہچکی بندھ گئی ۔

17 ہنستے ہنستے میرے پیٹ میں بل پڑ گئے ۔

18 دن نکلتے ہی وہ چل دیا ۔

19 ایک سے ۔

20. As soon as he said that, I shut my ears.

ws ke yeh bat kəhte hi, məyŋ ne kan bənd kər lie.

21. Even though they sang all night, the songs were not finished.

sari rat gate gate bhi git xətm nə hue.

22. On the way they saw a minaret.

cəlte cəlte ek minar nəzr aya.

23. On my arrival the work will be stopped.

mere pəhwŋcte hi kam bənd ho jaega.

[b (ii)].

24. He fell asleep without having written the letter.

bəɣəyr cyṭṭhi lykhe so gəya.

25. Don't go without paying him.

wjrət bəɣəyr die nə jao.

26. He began to bathe without having called him.

ws ko be bwlae nəhane ləga.

27. Without their personal order, this work will not be done.

byna wn ke xwd hwkm die yeh kam nə hoga.

[b (iii)].

28. Gradually.

hote hote.

29. Night passed without sleep.

rat jagte kəṭi.

20 اس کے یہ بات کہتے ہی میں نے کان بند کر لئے ۔

21 ساری رات گاتے گاتے بھی گیت ختم نہ ہوئے ۔

22 چلتے چلتے ایک مینار نظر آیا ۔

23 میرے پہونچتے ہی کام بند ہو جائے گا ۔

24 بغیر چھٹی لکھے سو گیا ۔

25 اجرت بغیر دئے نہ جاؤ ۔

26 اس کو بے بلائے نہانے لگا ۔

27 بنا ان کے خود حکم دئے یہ کام نہ ہو گا ۔

28 ہوتے ہوتے ۔

29 رات جاگتے کٹی ۔

30. The day passed restlessly.   dyn tərəpte bita.

31. She'll not come unless she's called.   be bwlae nə aegi.

32. He fell into it unthinkingly.   be soce səmjhe phəŋs gəya.

33. One tests gold by assaying it, and man by living with him.   sona janie kəse, admi janie bəse.

34. Why tease, when you've not been teased yourself?   byn cheɽe kya cheɽna?

35. He won't leave him alone.   byn cheɽe na choɽega.

   [c].

36. When he was returning.   ləwʈte vəqt.

37. At the time of going.   jati dəfə.

38. While still alive.   jite ji.

39. At sunset.   dyn ḍubte.

30   دن ترٹوٹ بیتا۔

31   بے بلائے نہ آئے گی۔

32   بے سوچے سمجھے یہ ہنس گیا

33   سونا جانئے کسے، آدمی جانئے بسے۔

34   بن چھیڑے کیا چھیڑنا ؟

35   بن چھیڑے نہ چھوڑے گا۔

36   لوٹتے وقت۔

37   جاتی دفعہ۔

38   جیتے جی۔

39   دن ڈوبتے

LESSON 26

CONDITIONAL SENTENCES

See Grammar, pp. 46–8, 51–2.

(a) Fulfilment of condition assumed. See Nos. 1–7.

(b) Fulfilment possible, but not assumed. See Nos. 8–15.

In No. 15 the condition is only implied.

[a].

1. If he did this, he did very wrong.

əgər ws ne yeh hərkət ki to nyhayət bwra kia.

2. She certainly won't go, if you're telling her not to.

əgər ap ws ko məna kərte həyŋ to hərgyz nə jaegi.

3. If the headman keeps away from bribes, I shall always be pleased with him.

əgər ləmbərdar ryʃvət se bəcta rəhega to məyŋ ws se həmeʃə xwʃ rəhuŋga.

4. The corn ripens when the rain falls.

baryʃ hoti həy to gehuŋ pəkte həyŋ.

5. If you were finding mistakes in the translation, who could correct them except you?

əgər ap tərjwme meŋ yəltiaŋ pate the to ap ke bəjae kəwn dwrwst kər səkta tha?

6. If he's insulted him, I shall certainly not recommend him (intercede for him).

əgər ws ne ws ki beyzzəti ki hogi to məyŋ ws ki syfaryʃ hərgyz nə kəruŋga.

١ اگر اس نے یہ حرکت کی تو نہایت برا کیا۔

٢ اگر آپ اس کو منع کرتے ہیں تو ہرگز نہ جائے گی۔

٣ اگر لمبردار رشوت سے بچتا رہے گا تو میں اس سے
  ہمیشہ خوش رہوں گا۔

٤ بارش ہوتی ہے تو گیہوں پکتے ہیں۔

٥ اگر آپ ترجمہ میں غلطیاں پاتے تھے تو آپ کے بجا
  ئے کون درست کر سکتاتھا۔

٦ اگر اس نے اس کی بے عزتی کی ہوگی تو میں اس کی سفا
  رش ہرگز نہ کروں گا۔

7. If he's coming along the road, I shall see him and make my request (shall tell him).

əgər voh səɽək pər a rəhe hoŋge to məyŋ wn se mylke ərz kəruŋga.

[b].

8. If the Government's permission comes, I will start to-morrow.

sərkar se rwxsət ki mənzuri ae, to kəl hi rəvanə huŋ.

9. Yes, if he promises, I can give up my job.

haŋ voh vadə kəreŋ to nəwkəri choɽ duŋ.

10. If one's lamenting his bad luck, he should be comforted.

koi əpni bədqysməti ko rota ho to dylasa dena cahie.

11. If anyone's done something wicked, he will be punished.

əgər kysi ne bədmaʃi ki ho, to səza mylegi.

12. How can a bird escape once it's snared?

pəryndə jal meŋ phəŋs gəya ho to kyoŋkər chuṭ jae?

13. This time, if you spoil the box and chair and other things, don't expect to be paid.

əb ki dəfa əgər sənduq kursi vəɣəyrə ko bygaɽa to wjrət ki wmed nə rəkhna.

14. This is poison, if you eat it, you're a dead man (you'll die).

yeh zəhr həy; khaya əwr məre; [or khaoge to mər jaoge]; [or khaya to mər jaoge].

15. The apples were falling like hailstones.

seb əyse jhəɽte the, jəyse ole pəɽte hoŋ.

۷ اگر وہ سٹرک پر آرہے ہونگے تو میں ان سے ملکے عرض کر
وں گا۔

۸ سرکار سے رخصت کی منظوری آئے تو کل ہی روانہ ہوں۔

۹ باں وہ وعدہ کریں تو نوکری چھوڑدوں۔

۱۰ کوئی اپنی بدقسمتی کو روتا ہو تو دلاسا دینا چاہیئے۔

۱۱ اگر کسی نے بد معاشی کی ہو تو سزا ملیگی۔

۱۲ پرندہ جال میں پھنس گیا ہو تو کیونکر چھوٹ جائے ؟

۱۳ اب کی دفعہ اگر صندوق، کرسی وغیرہ کو لگاڑا تو اجر
ت کی امید نہ رکھنا۔

۱۴ یہ زہر ہے، کھایا اور مرے بیٹھے

۱۵ سیب ایسے جھڑتے تھے جیسے اولے پڑتے ہوں۔

LESSON 27

CONDITIONAL SENTENCES (continued)

(a) Fulfilment improbable or impossible. See Nos. 1–5. In No. 1 the condition is only implied. In No. 6 the protasis (if-clause) is omitted. In No. 8 the apodosis (conclusion) is omitted.

(b) If-clause (protasis) or conclusion (apodosis) omitted. See Nos. 6–10. Note that the protasis is omitted in Nos. 6, 10; and the apodosis is omitted in No. 7.

(c) One or both verbs pluperfect conditional; condition impossible of fulfilment. See Nos. 11–13. Note that the pluperfect in Nos. 11–13 puts the thought emphatically in the past, but it is rarely necessary.

[a].

1. I should have scolded him well if I'd had the power.

mera bəs cəlta to məyŋ wse xub ḍaŋṭṭa.

2. If my father had been there, he wouldn't have dared to be so extravagant.

mere valyd vəhaŋ hote to ws ki kya məjal thi ky əysi fwzul xərci kərta.

3. If the child's mother knew (had known), she would be (would have been) greatly distressed.

bəcce ki maŋ ko xəbər hoti to səxt pərefan hoti.

4. If it had been possible, should I not have gone to see him?

ho səkta to məyŋ jakər nə mylta?

5. If his things had been clean, the maulvi would have got shaved and got his nails pared.

ws ke əwzar saf hote to məwlvi sahəb həjamət bənvate əwr naxwn kəṭvate.

١   میرا بس چلتا تو میں اسے خوب ڈانٹتا۔

٢   میرے والد وہاں ہوتے تو اس کی کیا مجال تھی کہ ایسی
     فضول خرچی کرتا۔

٣   بچّے کی ماں کو خبر ہوتی تو سخت پریشان ہوتی۔

٤   ہو سکتا تو میں جا کر نہ ملتا؟

٥   اس کے اوزار صاف ہوتے تو مولوی صاحب حجامت
     بنواتے اور ناخون کٹواتے۔

[*b*].

6. I shouldn't have spent a farthing on his behalf.

ws ki xatyr məyŋ ek kəwṭi bhi nə xərc kərta.

7. Oh, if only the earth had opened and swallowed him up.

hae, zəmin phəṭ jati əwr wse nygəl jati.

8. If you'd only known that he was dead.

əgər ap ytna jante ky voh fəwt hogəya həy.

9. He didn't tell me, if he had done so, could I have failed to serve him?

wnhoŋ ne yrfad nə kia vərnə kya məjal thi ky məyŋ xydmət nə kərta.

10. No doubt you'd have fought with all your might like a tiger, and he would have run from you like a jackal.

befək twm jan toṛke fer ki tərəh ləṛte əwr voh gidəṛ ki tərəh twm se bhagta.

[*c*].

11. If the house had not been whitewashed, it would have suffered considerable injury.

əgər məkan ki səfedi nə ki gəi hoti to bəṛa nwqsan hota.

12. If this child had not lighted up his dark life, he might have died a long time ago.

əgər ys bəcce ne ws ki əndheri zyndəgi ko rəwfən nə kər dia hota, to fayəd kəb ka mər gəya hota.

13. If he had made this excuse, I shouldn't have been surprised.

əgər ws ne yeh bəhanə kia hota to mwjhe təəjjwb nə hota.

6   اس کی خاطر میں ایک کوڑی بھی نہ خرچ کرتا۔

7   ہائے زمین پھٹ جاتی اور اسے نگل جاتی۔

8   اگر آپ اتنا جانتے کہ وہ فوت ہوگیا ہے۔

9   انہوں نے ارشاد نہ کیا ورنہ کیا مجال تھی کہ میں خدمت
نہ کرتا۔

10   بیشک تم جان توڑ کے شیر کی طرح لڑتے اور وہ کیدڑ
کی طرح تم سے بھاگتا۔

11   اگر مکان کی مینڈی نہ کی گئی ہوتی تو بڑا نقصان ہوتا۔

12   اگر اس بچے نے اس کی اندھیری زندگی کو روشن نہ کر دیا ہوتا
تو شاید کب کا مرگیا ہوتا۔

13   اگر اس نے یہ بہانہ کیا ہوتا تو مجھے تعجب نہ ہوتا۔

LESSON 28

HOW TO EXPRESS " HAVE, POSSESS "

See Grammar, pp. 117–18.

(i) Immovable property : Nos. 1, 2, 3.
(ii) Movable property : Nos. 4, 6, 15, 17.
(iii) Abstract things : Nos. 5, 6, 7, 8, 18.
(iv) Disease, illness : Nos. 9–12.
(v) Parts of the body : Nos. 13, 14.
(vi) Relatives : No. 16.

1. The prince has 100 or 150 acres of land.

ʃəhzade ki səw ḍeṛh səw bighe zəmin həy.

2. The contractor's got 2 houses and 2 wells.

ṭhekedar ki do həveliaŋ əwr do kueŋ həyŋ.

3. The vizier's wife has got lots of very fertile land.

vəzir ki begəm ke pəs bəhwt zərxez zəmin həy.

4. The watchman's got a lantern and a stick.

cəwkidar ke pas lalṭəyn əwr laṭhi həy.

5. My grand-daughter (daughter's daughter) is very fond of wearing a shawl.

meri nəvasi ko cadər oṛhne ka bəhwt ʃəwq həy.

6. My niece hasn't got any jewellery, and she's a great desire to wear it.

meri bhanji ke pas zevər nəhiŋ; wse zevər pəhynne ki bəhwt xahyʃ həy.

7. He's very fond of playing cricket.

ws ko kyrkəṭ khelne ka bəhwt ʃəwq həy.

8. The Brahman's servant has neither ability nor intelligence.

brəhmən ke mwlazym meŋ nə lyaqət həy əwr nə əql.

9. This bull's got a bad cough (has caught a bad cough).

ys bəyl ko səxt khaŋsi həy [or ho gəi həy].

١   شہزادہ کی سو ڈیڑھ سو بیگھہ زمین ہے۔

٢   ٹھیکیدار کی دو حویلیاں اور دو کنویں ہیں۔

٣   وزیر کی بیگم کے پاس بہت زرخیز زمین ہے۔

٤   چوکیدار کے پاس لالٹین اور لاٹھی ہے۔

٥   میری نواسی کو چادر اوڑھنے کا بہت شوق ہے۔

٦   میری بھانجی کے پاس زیور نہیں' اسے زیور پہننے کی بہت

خواہش ہے۔

٧   اس کو کرکٹ کھیلنے کا بہت شوق ہے۔

٨   برہمن کے ملازم میں نہ لیاقت ہے اور نہ عقل۔

٩   اس بیل کو سخت کھانسی ہوگئی ہے ۔

10. I have the hiccups.

mwjhe hyckiaŋ ati həyŋ.

11. The doctor's nephew has fever.

ḍakṭər ke bhətije ko bwxar cəṛha həy.

12. You've got a cold.

twmheŋ zwkam hua həy.

13. Some rams have four horns.

baz menḍhoŋ ke car car siŋg hote həyŋ.

14. A rhinoceros has only one horn.

geŋḍe ka bəs ek hi siŋg hota həy.

15. We have sports' material of every kind.

həmare pas khel kud ka səb saman məwjud həy.

16. My uncle has two sisters and three daughters.

mere cəca ki do bəhneŋ əwr tin ləṛkiaŋ həyŋ.

17. He has two horses, two carriages and a groom.

ws ke pas do ghoṛe, do bəg-giaŋ əwr ek sais həy.

18. How great is God, the Almighty.

Xuda ki kəysi bwzwrgi həy, əjib qwdrət rəkhta həy.

10   مجھے ہچکی آتی ہیں ۔

11   ڈاکٹر کے بھتیجے کو بخار چڑھ رہا ہے ۔

12   تمہیں زکام ہوا ہے ۔

13   لبن مینڈھوں کے چار چار سینگ ہوتے ہیں ۔

14   گینڈے کا بس ایک ہی سینگ ہوتا ہے ۔

15   ہمارے پاس کھیل کود کا سب سامان موجود ہے ۔

16   میرے چچا کی دو بہنیں اور تین لڑکیاں ہیں ۔

17   اس کے پاس دو گھوڑے' دو گیّا ں اور ایک سائیس

ہے ۔

18   خدا کی کیسی بزرگی ہے' عجیب قدرت رکھتا ہے ۔

LESSON 29

VARIOUS DETAILS

See Grammar, pp. 34–6, 122–3.

(a) **səhi.** See Nos. 1–7.

(b) **sa** :—

> (i) like. Note that the **sa** in Nos. 12 and 13 means, so to speak, something like a stream or snake. See Nos. 8–13.
>
> (ii) used as a meaningless speech habit. See Nos. 14–16.

(c) No matter how much, how big, etc. See Nos. 17–21. In Nos. 17, 18, 20, **kyoŋ nə** may be omitted.

1. Show it to me at any rate. — dykhao to səhi.

2. Eat, won't you? (Have a bite.) — khao to səhi.

3. All right, two rupees. — do rwpəe səhi.

4. Oh all right, if not you, then someone else. — twm nə səhi, koi əwr səhi.

5. He went, it's true, but . . . — gəya to səhi.

6. There is always another to take your place. — twm nəhiŋ, əwr səhi, əwr nəhiŋ, əwr səhi.

7. Oh, of course you're right; let's admit that. — twm hi səcce səhi.

8. I've met no one like you, but you have met many like me. — twm sa mwjh ko koi nə myla; mwjh se twm ko bəhwtere.

9. A face like an angel's. — fyryſte ka sa cehrə.

10. A wild beast like a wolf. — ek dəryndə bheṛia sa.

١   دکھاؤ تو سہی ۔

٢   کھاؤ تو سہی ۔

٣   دو روپئے سہی ۔

٤   تم نہ سہی، کوئی اور سہی ۔

٥   گیا تو سہی ۔

٦   تم نہیں اور سہی اور نہیں اور سہی ۔

٧   تم ہی سچے سہی ۔

٨   تم سا بجھکو کوئی نہ ملا' مجھ سے کہو بتہیرے۔

٩   فرشتہ کا سا چہرہ ۔

١٠   ایک درندہ بھیڑیا سا ۔

I

11. A lake, big like the sea.   ek səməndər si jhil.

12. A stream, as it were, was flowing.   ek nala sa bəyh rəha tha.

13. A poisonous snake-like thing crawled between my legs.   ek zəhrila sa samp meri ṭaŋgoŋ ke bic meŋ se reŋgta gwzra.

14. Is so much flour enough for eleven men?   ytne se aṭe se gyarə admi ser hoŋge?

15. A tall camel.   ləmba sa uŋṭ.

16. A blackish bear.   kala sa bhalu.

17. No matter how over-bearing he is, he can't do anything.   kytna hi zəbərdəst kyoŋ nə ho, məgər kwch nə bənega.

18. No matter what kind it is, it won't do.   cahe kysi qysm ka kyoŋ nə ho, kam ka nə hoga.

19. No matter what will happen, he will be disgraced.   xah kwch hi ho, ws ki beyz-zəti hogi.

11   ایک سمندر سی جھیل ۔

12   ایک نالا سا بہہ رہا تھا ۔

13   ایک زہریلا سا سانپ میری ٹانگوں کے بیچ میں سے

      رینگتا گذرا ۔

14   اتنے سے آٹے سے گیارہ آدمی سیر ہونگے ۔

15   لمبا سا اونٹ ۔

16   کالا سا بھالو ۔

17   کتنا ہی زبردست کیوں نہ ہو مگر کچھ نہ بنے گا

18   چاہے کسی قسم کا کیوں نہ ہو کام کا نہ ہوگا ۔

19   خواہ کچھ ہی ہو اس کی بے عزتی ہوگی ۔

20. Even though there are twenty, I shall escape.

bis hi kyoŋ nə hoŋ, məgər məyŋ bəc jauŋga.

21. No matter how ugly he is, I shall continue to associate with him (to meet him).

voh cahe kytna hi bədsurət ho, məyŋ ws se myla rəhuŋga (mylta rəhuŋga).

20 میں ہی کیوں نہ ہوں گمر میں نیچ جاؤں گا۔

21 وہ چاہے کتنا ہی بد صورت ہو میں اس

سے ملار ہوں گا ٹہ

ALTERNATIVE FORMS

Page 200, No. 18 - ﺍﯽ ﻭﮦ ﭼﻞ ﺩﯾﺎ (ﯾﺎ ﺩﻥ ﭼﮍﮬﺘﮯ) ﮐﮯ ﺻﺢ ﮨﻮﺗﮯ

Page 205, No. 32 - ﮐﮯ ﮐﺎ ﻧﺘﯽ ﮐﺎ ﻧﺘﯽ ﮐﻨﮯ ﻟﮕﯽ

Page 205, No. 34 - ﮐﮯ ﭘﮍﺍ ﭘﮍﺍ ﺑﯿﻤﺎﺭ ﮨﻮ ﮔﯿﺎ

Page 205, No. 37 - ﮐﮯ ﭼﭩﺎﻥ ﭘﺮ ﻣﻨﮉﻻﺗﯽ ﻣﻨﮉﻻﺗﯽ ﭼﯿﻞ ﮔﺮ ﭘﮍﯼ

Page 205, No. 39 - ﮐﮯ ﺭﻭﭨﯽ ﭘﮑﺎﺗﯽ ﭘﮑﺎﺗﯽ ﺗﮭﮏ ﮔﺌﯽ

Page 207, No. 1 - ﮐﯽ ﮐﺴﯽ ﻧﮯ ﻣﺠﮭﮯ ﻧﺎﭼﺘﺎ ﮨﻮﺍ ﺩﯾﮑﮭﺎ

Page 207, No. 2 - ﯾﮯ ﮐﺲ ﻧﮯ ﺗﻢ ﮐﻮ ﮐﮭﯿﻠﺘﮯ ﮨﻮﺋﮯ ﭘﮑﮍﺍ

Page 207, No. 3 - ﮐﮯ ﮐﻮﺋﯽ ﺍﺳﮯ ﺳﻮﺗﮯ ﺳﻮﺗﮯ ﭘﺎﺋﮯ ﮔﺎ

Page 208, ' No. 14   ملہ۔ یا ' کھاؤ گے تو مر جاؤ گے ' یا ' کھایا تو مر جاؤ گے '

Page 215, No. 9   ملہ اسی بیل کو سخت کھانسی ہے۔

Page 223, No. 21   ملہ وہ چاہے کتنا ہی بدصورت ہو میں اس سے ملتا ہوں گا

URDU–ENGLISH GLOSSARY

(-i indicates the form of the abstract noun)

əb — now; əb se, in future, from now (looking back).

əbhi (emphatic of əb) — now, yet.

əccha — good; əccha ji, very well (said to an inferior).

ədəb, *m.* — respect; literature.

əda, *f.* — coquetry, etc.; əda kərna, pay (money, etc.).

ədna — small.

əfsos, *m.* — regret, sorrow; *interj.:* alas!

əgər — if.

əgərcy — although.

əksər, *adv.* — generally, often; *adj. pron.:* most people, the majority.

əktubər, *m.* — October.

ələg, *adj.* — separate.

əlavə (ke), *postpos.* — besides.

əlbəttə — certainly, no doubt.

əlmari, *f.* — bookcase, wardrobe, linen-press, cupboard.

əmir — rich

əndər, *adv.* — inside; (ke) *postpos.:* inside.

əndha — blind.

əndhera — dark; *m.,* darkness.

əngia, *f.* — bodice.

əngrez — English man or woman.

əpna — my, your, his, her, its, their; i.e. own; *see* Grammar, p. 33.

əpnana, *trans.* — assimilate, make one's own.

əprəyl, *m.* — April.

əql, *f.*	intelligence.
əre (*f.* əri), *interj.*	O.
ərz, *f.*	submission (verbal).
ərzi, *f.*	petition.
əsami, *f.*	vacant post; *m.* or *f.*, tenant, client.
əsbab, *m.*	furniture, luggage.
əsl, *f.*	source, origin, capital.
əsli	genuine.
əxbar, *m.*	newspaper.
əz	from (Persian), by (of author).
ab o həva, *f.*	air, climate.
abad	inhabited, peopled.
abadi, *f.*	population.
adət, *f.*	habit.
adh, adha	half.
admi, *m.*	man (*homo*, not *vir*).
ahystə	slowly.
aj	to-day; aj-kəl, in these days.
ajyz	humble; -i.
ala	exalted.
alu, *m.*	potato.
alucə, *m.*	plum.
am, *m.*	mango.
amdəni, *f.*	income.
ana	come.
ana, *m.*	anna (coin).
andhi, *f.*	storm.
aŋkh, *f.*	eye; a. ləgna, fall asleep (ki).
ap, (respectful) *pron.*	you (*m.* or *f.*).
apəs meŋ	among our-, your-, themselves.
aram, *m.*	rest.
asan	easy; -i.
avaz, *f.*	voice, sound.
axyr	finally.
azmana, *trans.*	tempt, test.
ybtyda, *f.*	beginning.

ydhər — hither, here.

yhatə, *m.* — enclosed compound, ground round house, small section of country.

yjazət, *f.* — permission.

ylaj, *m.* — medical treatment; ylaj k. (ka), treat.

ylavə, *see* əlavə.

ylm, *m.* — learning, knowledge.

yltyja, *f.* — petition.

ymarət, *f.* — building.

ymdad, *f.* — help.

ymtyhan, *m.* — examination (in school, etc.); ymtyhan lena (ka), to examine; ymtyhan dena, be examined, with ka of subject in which examined.

yn — oblique plural of yeh; ynhoŋ.

ynkar k. — refuse, deny, with ka of thing refused or denied.

ynsan, *m.* — mankind.

ynʃa, *f.* — literary composition.

yntyha, *f.* — end.

ynam, *m.* — reward, prize.

yqrar k. — acknowledge, confess, with ka of thing acknowledged or confessed.

yrʃad, *m.* — command; yrʃad k., to command.

ys — oblique singular of yeh.

yslah, *f.* — correction, amendment (literary).

ystydad, *f.* — ability, capacity.

ystyfa, *m.* — pronounced ystifa, resignation (with dena).

yʃtyhar, *m.* — announcement, advertisement.

ytna — so much, so many.

yttyla, *f.* — information, announcing.

ytvar, *m.* — Sunday.

yvəz, *see* evəz.

yzzət, *f.*   honour, respect; yzzət k. (ki),
                                           to honour, respect.

id, *f.*   religious festival (Muslim).
inṭ, *f.*   brick.
iza, *f.*   pain, trouble inflicted.

wdhər, *adv.*   thither, there.
wjəṛna   become desolate; *trans.:* wjaṛna
                                           = make desolate, lay waste.
wjrət, *f.*   remuneration.
wləṭna, *intrans.*   be turned upside down; *trans.:*
                                           turn upside down; *causal:*
                                           wlṭana.
wıned, wmmid, *f.*   hope, expectation.
wn, wnhoŋ   oblique plural of voh.
wngli, *f.*   finger.
wqab, *m.*   eagle.
wṛhana, wṛhvana, *see* oṛhna.
wṛna, *intrans.*   fly; *trans.:* wṛana, cause to
                                           fly, squander.
ws   oblique singular of voh.
wstad, *m.*   teacher; *feminine:* wstani.
wtərna, *intrans.*   descend, put up (at house, hotel,
                                           etc.), come off (hat, clothes);
                                           trans.: wtarna = take off,
                                           bring down; *causal:* wtər-
                                           vana = cause to be taken off,
                                           brought down.
wtna, *pron., adj.*   so much or many.
wttər, *m.*   north.
wṭhna, *intrans.*   get up, rise; *trans.:* wṭhana;
                                           causal: wṭhvana.

unca, *adj.*   tall, lofty; highly pitched (of
                                           voice or note); -i.
upər, *adv.*   above, upward; ke upər, *post-
                                           pos.,* above.

ehtyat, *f.* — care, carefulness.

eɽi, *f.* — heel.

evəz (ke), *postpos.* — in place of, in return for.

etyraz, *m.* — objection.

əy — O (address).

əynək, *f.* — spectacles (used in singular).

əysa — of this kind; əyse = thus.

ohho, oho, *interj.* — oh !

ola, *m.* — hailstone; ole pəɽe = hail-stones fell.

oɽhna, *trans.* — put on (shawl, etc.); *causal:* wɽhana, wɽhvana.

os, *f.* — dew.

əwr, *conj.* — and; *pron. adj.:* other, more, different, someone else, other people.

əwrət, *f.* — woman.

bə-, — with (Persian).

bəccə, *m.* (*f.* bəcci) — child, young one.

bəcna, *intrans.* — escape from impending danger, be left over; *trans.:* bəcana.

bəcpən, *m.* — childhood.

bəd- (in composition) — evil (*adj.* in Persian).

bədəlna, *trans.* and *intrans.* — change; *causal:* bədlana.

bədən, *m.* — body.

bədəwlət (ki), *postpos.* — thanks to, through (only in good sense).

bədla, *m.* — vengeance, exchange.

bədle (ke), *postpos.* — in place of, instead of, in exchange for; -i.

bədmaʃ, *adj. n.* — bad man, scoundrel; i-.

bədnəsib — unfortunate; -i.

bədqysmət — unfortunate; -i.

bədsurət — ugly; -i.

bəggi, *f.* — two-wheeled carriage.

bəɣəyr (ke) — without, apart from.

bəhəlna, *intrans.* — be amused, entertained; *causal :* bəhlana (generally said of dyl = heart).

bəhəs, bəhs, *f.* — argument.

bəhəsna, *intrans.* — argue.

bəhna, *intrans.* — flow; *trans.:* bəhana.

bəhr, *m.* — sea, etc.

bəhn, bəhən, *f.* — sister

bəhyʃti, *see* bhyʃti.

bəhu, *f.* — daughter-in-law.

bəjae (ke), *postpos.* — in place of.

bəje — o'clock.

bəjna, *intrans.* — sound (of gong, metal, coin, etc.); *trans. :* bəjana, cause to sound, play instrument.

bəkəs, *m.* — box.

bəkna, *intrans.* — talk nonsense; *causal :* bəkana, bəkvana.

bəkra, *m.* — goat, *f.*, bəkri.

bəkrivala, *m.* — goatherd.

bəxubi — well, excellently.

bəl (ke), *postpos.* — on, as in mwnjh or ghwʈnoŋ ke bəl, fall (on one's face), kneel (on one's knees).

bəl, *m.* — twist, kink; usually plural used with pəʈna.

bələnd — high, lofty; -i.

bəla, *f.* — calamity.

bəlky, *conj.* — not so, but on the contrary; e.g. do nəhiŋ bəlky car, not two but four; dəs kya, chəy bhi nəhiŋ, ten? not even six. Not a horse, but a mule, ghoʈa nəhiŋ, bəlky xəccər.

bəmujyb (ke), *postpos.* — according to.

bənana, *see* bənna.

bənavəʈ, *f.* — making, fashion, artificiality.

bənd k., *trans.* — shut; bənd h., be shut.

bəndər, *m.* — monkey.

bəndərgah, *m.f.* — harbour.

bəndə, *m.* — servant, usually servant of God, or self-depreciatory; *f.* bəndi.

bəndhna, *intrans.* — be tied; *trans.:* bandhna, tie; *causal:* bəndhana, bəndhvana, cause to be tied.

bəndobəst, *m.* — arrangement, land settlement.

bənduq, *f.* — gun.

bəngla, *m.* — house (detached, in European style).

bənia, *m.* — shopkeeper.

bənna, *intrans.* — be made; *trans.:* bənana, make; *causal:* bənvana, cause to be made.

bər, *postpos.* — upon.

bərəsna, *intrans.* — rain; *causal:* bərsana.

bərabər, *adj.* — even, level, equal; *adv.:* certainly, continuously.

bəramdə, *m.* — verandah.

bərbad — destroyed; -i.

bərf, *f.* — snow.

bərkət, *f.* — blessing.

bərrə, *m.* — lamb; *f.* madə bərrə.

bərsat, *f.* — the rains, continued rain.

bərtən, *m.* — vessel for cooking, etc.

bərxylaf (ke) — against, in opposition to.

bəṛa — big, great.

bəṛhəi — carpenter.

bəṛhna, *intrans.* — grow, increase, advance; *trans.:* bəṛhana, cause to increase, stretch out (hand, etc.).

bəs — enough, only.

bəs, *m.* — power.

bəsa bəsaya — inhabited.

bəsna, *intrans.* — dwell, be inhabited; bəsana, cause to inhabit or be inhabited.

bətana (rarely bətlana), *trans.* — tell, show.

bətti, *f.* — lamp, wick.

bətna, *intrans.* — be distributed, shared; *trans.:* baṇtna, share, distribute; bətana, bətvana, cause to be shared, etc.

bəyan, *m.* — story, narrative, explanation.

ba — with (Persian).

babət (ki) — concerning.

baba, *m.* — old man, father (also bava).

babu, *m.* — Indian clerk.

bad (ke) — after (of time).

badəl, *m.* — cloud.

badʃah, *m.* — king; -i.

baɣ-baɣ — happy, delighted.

bahər, *adv.* — outside; ke b., *postpos.*, outside.

baja, *m.* — musical instrument; baja-gaja, used jocularly for several instruments, a band.

bandi — maidservant.

baṇtna, *see* bətna.

baŋyaŋ — left (not right).

bapdada, *m.pl.* (*indecl.*) — ancestors.

baqi, *adj.* — remaining, left over; *adv.:* after all, in any case.

bat, *f.* — matter, thing (abstract), word, saying.

bayaŋ, *see* baŋyaŋ.

bazi, *f.* — competitive game, match.

bazu, *m.* — arm.

bays (ke) — on account of

byah, *m.* — marriage.

bycarə, *see* becarə.

bycchu, *m.* — scorpion.

bychana, *trans.* — spread (bedding, carpets, etc.); *intrans.:* bychna.

bygəṛna, *intrans.* — be spoilt, quarrel; *trans.:* bygaṛna.

bygha, *m.* — acre.

bykna, *intrans.* — be sold; *trans.* : becna, sell; *causal* : bykvana, cause to be sold.

bylkwl, *adv.* — altogether; with negative, not at all.

byl, *m.* — small animal's hole.

bylla, *m.* — cat; *f.* bylli.

byna, *postpos.* — without.

bystra, *m.* — bedding.

bij, *m.* — seed.

bimar — sick; -i.

bitna, *intrans.* — pass (of time); *trans.:* bytana.

bivi, *f.* — wife, lady.

Bwdh, *m.* — Buddha.

bwḍḍha — old; same as buṛha.

bwjhna, *intrans.* — be extinguished; *trans.* : bwjhana.

bwxar, *m.* — fever; b. cəṛhna (ko), get fever.

bwlənd, *see* bələnd.

bwlana, *trans.* — call, cause to sound; *causal* : bwlvana; *see* bolna.

bwra, *adj.* — evil; -i.

bwrqa, *m.* — cloak covering whole body worn by Muslim women.

bwṛbwṛana, *intrans.* — mutter, grumble.

bwzwrg — honourable or great by age or position; -i.

buṛha — old; same as bwḍḍha.

buṭ, *m.* — boot, shoe of English pattern.

be, Persian *postpos.* — without.

becarə — mild term of commiseration, as : poor fellow; also bycarə.

becna, *see* bykna.

bed, *f.* — cane, either growing or cut.

begəm, *f.* — lady, wife (used of woman of rank).

behoʃ — unconscious; -i.

behtər — good; in Persian this is comparative, with behtərin, superlative; -i.

beiman — dishonest, untrustworthy; -i.

beʃək — certainly, without doubt.

beṭa, *m.* — son; beṭi, daughter; beṭa is sometimes addressed to daughter.

bevəquf — very foolish. The adjective in address is insulting. The abstract noun is weaker; -i.

bəyl, *m.* — ox, bull.

bəyṭhna — sit; *causal :* byṭhana.

bolna, *intrans.* — speak, sound; *causal :* bwlana, call, *q.v.*; bwlvana.

bona, *trans.* — sow; *causal :* bwana.

botəl, *f.* — bottle.

bəhwt — much, many.

bəhwtera — much, a lot.

bhəi (only in voc.) — my good sir, my good woman; not addressed to superior.

bhəyŋs, *f.* — buffalo; much more common than bhəyŋsa, *m.*, male buffalo.

bhəla — good, worthy; *adv. :* very well then; bhəlamanəs, good or worthy fellow, etc.; *f.*, bhəlimanəs

bhər — used after noun meaning time, distance, amount, as: dyn bhər = a whole day, or as little as a day; ser bhər = a whole ser, or as little as a ser.

bhərna, *trans.* and *intrans.* — fill, be filled; *causal :* bhərana, bhərvana.

bhəɽək, *f.* — flaming up of flame.

bhəɽəkna, *intrans.* — flame up; also metaphorical; *trans. :* bhəɽkana.

bhətija, *m.* — brother's son; *f.* bhətiji.

bhai, *m.* — brother, chum, mate.

bhagna, *intrans.* — run, run away; *trans.:* bhəgana.

bhal, bhalna — used only with dekhna, see, look at; as: dekh bhalkər, looking, looking at.

bhalu, *m.* — bear (animal); no feminine.

bhanja, *m.* — sister's son; *f.* bhanji.

bhao, *m.* — price-rate.

bhari — heavy, important.

bhyjvana, *see* bhejna.

bhyʃti, *m.* — water-carrier; also bəhyʃti.

bhi — also; in negative clauses: even

bhitər, *adv.* — inside; *postpos.* (ke), inside.

bhuk, bhukh, *f.* — hunger; bhukoŋ mərna = die of hunger.

bhuka, bhukha — hungry.

bhul, *f.* — act of forgetting; fault.

bhulna — forget, be forgotten; *causal:* bhwlana.

bhusa, *m.* — straw, chaff, etc.

bhejna, *trans.* — to send; *causal:* bhyjvana, cause to send.

cəca, *m.* — father's younger brother; cəci, *f.* wife of cəca.

cəla ana — come along; cəla jana, go away.

cəlna, *intrans.* — move, accompany (with sath), function; *trans.:* cəlana, cəlvana; cəl dena, go off.

cəmək, *f.* — shine, glitter.

cəməkna, *intrans.* — shine, glitter; *causal:* cəməkana.

cəmca, *m.* — spoon.

cənd — some, a few; do-cənd, double, two-fold.

cəpati, *f.* — flat cake of flour, not containing yeast.

cəṛhna, *intrans.* — ascend, climb; *causal:* cəṛhana, cəṛhvana.

cəʃma, *m.* — spring of water; spectacles.

cət k. — swallow up, gobble up.

cətai, *f.* — grass mat.

cətxəni, *f.* — bolt or catch of door.

ca, cae, *f.* — tea.

cabi, *f.* — key.

cadər, *f.* — shawl; pələŋ ki cədər, bed sheet.

cahe . . . cahe, caho . . . caho — whether . . . or.

cahie — is or are desirable, proper; also ought; *see* Grammar, p. 96, and Sentences, Lessons 12–14.

cahna, *trans.* — wish, desire; in certain constructions, to be about to; see Grammar, p. 96.

caŋd, *m.* — moon.

caŋdi, *f.* — silver.

car — four; (ke) caroŋ tərəf, on all sides.

cyuŋ ti, *f.* — ant.

cyllana, *intrans.* — cry out, shout.

cyraɣ, *m.* — lamp.

cyɽia, *f.* — little bird, sparrow.

cytthi, *f.* — letter, epistle.

cil, *f.* — kite (bird).

cin e jybin (Persian) — a frown.

ciz, *f.* — thing (generally tangible).

cwɣli khana (ki) — slander, speak against.

cwhia, *f.* — mouse.

cwkna — in composition, to finish, to have finished; sometimes sense of " already "; *see* Grammar, p. 69, and Sentences, Lesson 15.

cwp, cwpcap, *adj.* — silent.

cwrana, *trans.* — steal; *causal :* cwrvana.

cuha, *m.* — rat.

cor, *m.* — thief.

cori, *f.* — theft.

coṭ, *f.* — blow, wound.

coṭi, *f.* — peak, summit of hill, etc.

cəwgwna, *adj.* — fourfold.

cəwki, *f.* — wooden stool, police post.

cəwkidar, *m.* — watchman; -i.

cəwkṛi bhərna — gallop drawing four feet together.

cəwtha — fourth; cəwthai, *f.*, a fourth part.

chəpna, *intrans.* — be printed; *trans.:* chapna; *causals:* chəpana, chəpvana.

chati, *f.* — breast.

chydna, chydvana, *see* chedna.

chiŋkna, *intrans.* — sneeze (takes ne with past tenses); *causal:* chynkvana.

chwlana, chwlvana — *causals of* chuna.

chwpna, *intrans.* — hide; *trans.:* chwpana; *causal:* chwpvana.

chwri, *f.* — knife.

chwṛana, chwṛvana, *see* choṛna.

chwṭṭi, *f.* — leave, holiday.

chuna, *trans.* — touch.

chuṭna, *intrans.* — escape, get free; *see* choṛna.

ched, *m.* — hole.

chedna, *trans.* — pierce; *intrans.:* chydna, be pierced; *causal:* chydvana.

cheṛna, *trans.* — tease, stir up; *intrans.:* chyṛna, be teased, stirred up.

choṛna, *trans.* — leave, set free; *causal:* chwṛana, chwṛvana; *see* chuṭna.

choṭa — small.

dəbna, *intrans.* — be pressed, squashed, oppressed; *causals:* dabna, dəbana, dəbvana.

dəftər, *m.* — office, study, register.

dəfa, *f.* — time (as in four times), section of book or legal enactment.

dəya, *f.*	deceit.
dəhi, *m.*	curds, buttermilk.
Dəhli, Dylli, *f.*	Delhi.
dəhna, *adj.*	right (not left).
dəkkən	south.
dər, Persian *postpos.*	in.
dərəxt, *m.*	tree.
dəraz, *adj.*	long.
dəryaft k., *trans.*	inquire about.
dərzi, *m.*	tailor; *f.* dərzən.
dəstanə, *m.*	glove.
dəstur, *m.*	custom.
dəva, *m.*, dəvai, *f.*	medicine.
dəya, *f.*	mercy, pity.
dada, *m.*	father's father; dadi, *f.*, father's mother.
daxyl k., *trans.*	enter someone in school, etc., or something in book; daxyl h., *intrans.*, enter.
dal, *f.*	lentils, etc.
dam, *m.*	price (generally plural).
danə, *m.*	a grain.
dana, *adj.*	wise; feminine the same.
danyʃ, *f.*	wisdom.
dava, *m.*	claim.
dykhna, dikhna, *intrans.*	be visible; dykhana, show; dykhvana, cause to be looked at or shown; *see* dekhna.
dylana, dylvana, *see* dena.	
dysəmbər, *m.*	December.
dijie	respectful imperative of dena.
divanə	mad; *f.* divani.
dwkan, dukan, *f.*	shop.
dwkandar, dukandar, *m.*	shopkeeper.
dwnya, *f.*	world.
dwpəṭṭa, *m.*	shawl.
dwrwst, *adj.*	correct, in order; -i.
dwʃmən, *m.f.*	enemy; -i.

dwa, *f.* — prayer; d. maŋgna, pray; d. dena (with ko), to invoke blessing on.

dudh, *m.* — milk.

dur, *adj.* — far; *f.* distance; bəɽi dur, very far.

durəndeʃ — farseeing, careful about the future; -i.

dusra — second, other.

dehat, *m.s.* — villages, the country.

dehati — belonging to villages; villager.

dekhna, *trans.* — see, look at; *see* dykhna.

dena, *trans.* — give; *causal :* dylana, dylvana; *see* Grammar, p. 61, and Sentences, Lesson 17.

deota, *m.* — god.

der, *f.* — lateness, delay, time.

devi, *f.* — goddess.

donoŋ — both.

dopəhr, *f* — noon.

dost, *m.f.* — friend; -i.

dəwlət, *f.* — wealth.

dəwlətmənd — wealthy; -i.

dəwɽ, *f.* — race, running.

dəwɽna, *intrans.* — run; *causal :* dəwɽana.

dhəbba, *m.* — stain.

dhyan, *m.* — meditation, attention.

dhwlna, dhwlana, dhwlvana, *see* dhona.

dhup, *f.* — sunshine.

dhobi, *m.* — washerman; *f.* dhobən.

dhokha, *m.* — deceit; dhokha dena, deceive; dhokha khana, be deceived.

dhona, *trans.* — wash; *intrans. :* dhwlna, be washed; *causals :* dhwlana, dhwlvana.

ɖər, *m.* — fear.

ɖərna, *intrans.* — fear; *causal :* ɖərana.

ɖak, *f.* — the post for letters.

ḍakṭər, *m.*   doctor; -i.

ḍaku, *m.*   dacoit.

ḍalna, *trans.*   insert, put into; *causal :* ḍəlana.

ḍanṭna, *trans.*   rebuke, threaten.

ḍybia, *f.*   small box.

ḍubna, *intrans.*   sink (in water, etc.); *causals :* ḍwbona, ḍwbana, cause to sink, drown.

ḍeṛh   one-and-a-half.

ḍhəkna, *trans.*   cover; *causal :* ḍhəkana.

ḍhəlna, *intrans.*   sink (of sun), decline (of life).

ḍhənḍhora, *m.*   proclamation by town crier.

ḍhai   two-and-a-half.

ḍhuŋḍna, *trans.*   look for, seek.

ḍher, *m.*   heap.

ḍhona, *trans.*   carry (bricks, earth, etc.); *causal :* ḍhwana.

fəhm, *m.*   understanding.

fəjr, *f.*   early morning.

fəxr, *m.*   pride (may have good sense).

fəqir, *m.*   beggar, holy man (generally Muslim).

fərman, *m.*   command; fərmaŋbərdar, *adj.* obedient; -i.

fərmana, *trans.*   command, say.

fərq, *m.*   difference.

fərʃ, *m.*   carpet, floor, etc.

fərvəri, *m.f.*   February.

fərz, *m.*   duty; *see* Grammar, p. 95, and Sentences, Lessons 12–14.

fəsl, *f.*   harvest.

fətəh, *f.*   victory; fətəh pana, gain victory.

faxtə, *f.*   dove.

Farsi, *f.*   Persian, the Persian language.

faslə, *m.*   distance between two places.

fatyhə, *f.*   the first Surə of the Qwr'an.

fykr, *f.* — anxiety.

fylfəwr, *adv.* — immediately.

fyryʃtə, *m.* — angel.

fwlanə, *adj.* — a certain; *f.* fwlani.

fwrsət, *f.* — leisure.

fwʈ, *m.* — foot (measure of length).

fwzul — useless, worthless.

fwzulxərc — wasting money, spendthrift; -i.

fəwrən, *adv.* — immediately.

fəwt hona, *intrans.* — die.

gədha, *m.* — donkey; *f.* gədhi.

gəhra — deep (also metaphorically); strong (of tea).

gəla, *m.* — throat.

gəli, *f.* — lane in town or village.

gəllə, *m.* — flock; gəlləban, *m.*, shepherd.

gənda, *m.* — dirty; *f.* gəndi.

Gənga, *f.* — the River Ganges.

gərm — warm, hot; -i.

gəŋvana, *trans.* — lose, waste, squander.

gəya, *past partic.* of jana, go.

gəz, *m.* — yard (measure of length).

gae, *f.* — cow; *plural:* gaeŋ, gayoŋ.

gahək, *m.* — purchaser, client.

gali, *f.* — abuse (generally obscene).

gana — sing; *causal:* gəvana.

gaoŋ, *m.* — village.

gara, *m.* — mud and water mixed for building.

gaɽi, *f.* — carriage, train.

gavar, *m.f.*, or *adj.* — illiterate or uncultured person (lit. villager).

gydh, *m.* — vulture.

gyrd, yrd-gyrd (ke), *postpos.* — round.

gyrja, *m.* — church (the building).

gyrna, *intrans.* — fall; *causal:* gyrana, gyrvana.

gidəɽ, *m.* — jackal.

git, *m.* song.

gwana, *see* gana.

gwl k., *trans.* extinguish (lamp, fire, etc.).

gwnah, *m.* sin; gwnah k., to sin.

gwnahgar sinner; -i.

gwɽia, *f.* doll.

gwzərna, *intrans.* pass by, pass (of time), die; *causal :* gwzarna.

gehuŋ, *m.* wheat.

geŋd, *f.* ball (for playing).

geŋɖa, *m.* rhinoceros.

go, go ky, *conj.* although.

god, *f.* lap and arms, as in " on his lap," " in his arms ".

gol, *adj.* round, circular; gol kəmra, drawing-room.

goli, *f.* bullet, medicine pill. It does not mean " ball ".

gora, *adj.* fair (of person's complexion); gora cyʈʈa, very fair; also British soldier or Tommy.

goʃt, *m.* meat.

goya as if.

ghəbrahəʈ, *f.* abstract noun from ghəbrana : confusion, excitement, etc. *See below.*

ghəbrana, *intrans.* be confused, worried, over-excited; also *trans.* (especially when compounded with dena).

ghənʈa, *m.* gong, hour.

ghər, *m.* house.

ghəɽi, *f.* (i) short indefinite period of time, half-an-hour, etc.; (ii) clock, watch; ghəɽi ghəɽi, *adv. :* frequently.

ghəsiʈna, *trans.* drag; *causal :* ghysəʈvana.

ghəʈa, *f.* thick clouds of the rainy season.

ghəʈna, *intrans.* lessen, decrease; *trans.:* ghəʈana.

ghao, *m.*	wound.
ghas, *f.*	grass.
ghysna, *trans.* and *intrans.*	rub, be rubbed against something, be rubbed away.
ghi, *m.*	clarified butter.
ghwsna, *intrans.*	enter (into, meŋ), especially in haste or by force; *causal:* ghwsana.
ghwṭna, *m.*	knee.
ghoṛa, *m.*	horse; ghoṛi, *f.*, mare.
ɣəlti, *f.*	mistake, error.
ɣəm, *m.*	grief; ɣəm khana, be grieved.
ɣərib, *adj.*	poor, wretched; docile (of animal).
ɣəyr, *adj.*	strange, foreign; negative sense with another adjective, e.g. ɣəyr-hazyr, not present, absent.
ɣəzəl, *f.*	love lyric; ɣəzəl-go, writer of love lyrics.
ɣalybən, *adv.*	probably
ɣayb, *adj.*	out of sight; unseen.
ɣyza, *f.*	food.
ɣwlam, *m.*	slave.
ɣwssə, *m.*	anger; ɣwsse hone, ɣwssa ana (ko), be angry.
həgna	to have a motion; takes ne with past tenses.
həjamət, *f.*	shaving, haircut; həjamət bənvana, get shaved, or have a haircut.
həkim, *m.*	doctor.
həlal, *adj.*	ceremoniously lawful (chiefly of food); a Muslim word.
həlka	light (not heavy).
həm	we.
həmara	our.

həmeʃə — always.

həq, *also* həqq, *m.* — truth, God, one's right.

hər, *pron. adj.* — every.

hərj, *m.* — loss, injury.

həram, *adj.* — unlawful; the opposite of həlal, *q.v.*

hərf, *m.* — letter; hərf bə hərf, word by word.

hərgyz — ever, always; but used only with negative in Urdu : never.

hərkət, *f.* — movement, action.

hərkarə, *m.* — messenger, postman.

həʈəp k., *trans.* — gobble up.

həʈtal, *f.* — closing of shops as form of strike, strike in general.

həʈna, *intrans.* — move aside, get out of the way; *causal :* həʈana.

həva, *f.* — wind. *See* ab o həva.

həvale ke, *postpos.* — in or into the care of.

həvass, *m.pl.* — senses (plural of hyss, *m.*).

həveli, *f.* — large house, etc.

həyran — astonished, bewildered; -i.

həzm k. — digest, eat up.

hal, *m.* — condition, state, story, narrative.

haŋkna, *trans.* — drive (animal, etc.); *causal :* həŋkana.

haŋ, *m.* — used like French *chez* : mere haŋ = at my house.

harna, *intrans.* — be defeated; *trans. :* lose (game, bazi); *see* Grammar, p. 57; *causal :* hərana.

həsna, *intrans.* — laugh; *causal :* həsana.

hath, *m.* — hand, forearm; həthkəʈi, *f.* handcuff.

hathi, *m.* — elephant.

hazyr, *adj.* — present (said of or to an inferior).

hazyri, *f.* — attendance (in school, etc.), breakfast.

hazmə, *m.* — digestion.

hyckiaŋ, *f.pl.* — hiccup (ləgna, ko).

hydayət, *f.* — instruction, advice; hydayət dena (ko), hydayət k. (ki), give religious instruction to; hydayət k. (ko), give orders to; *see* Grammar, pp. 81–2.

hyfazət, *f.* — protection; hyfazət k. (ki), protect.

hylna, *intrans.* — shake; *causal :* hylana.

hylna, *intrans.* — become tame, become used to (generally of an animal); *causal :* hylana.

Hyndu, *m.* — Hindu; *f.* Hyndni.

hyqarət, *f.* — contempt; hyqarət k. (ki), despise.

hyrən, *m.* — deer; *f.* hyrni.

hysab, *m.* — account (money, etc.).

hyssə, *m.* — part, share.

huŋ — I am.

hwkm, *m.* — command; hwkm dena (ko), to give order to.

hwzur — your honour, his, her honour.

ho jana, *intrans.* — become.

hona, *intrans.* — be, become.

hoʃ, *m.* — senses.

hoʃyar, *adj.* — alert, intelligent; -i.

jəb — when (*rel.*); jəb se, since; jəb tək, until; jəb kəbhi, whenever; jəbhi, that is why.

jəgəh, *f.* — place; ki jəgəh, in place of.

jəhaŋ — where (*rel.*); jəhaŋ se, whence; jəhaŋ tək, so far as; jəhaŋ kəhiŋ, wherever.

jəkəɽna, *trans.* — fasten with chains, etc.; *causal :* jəkɽana, jəkəɽvana.

jəlal, *m.* — glory (as inspiring awe or fear).

jəldi, *f.* — quickness, haste; *adv.*, quickly.

jəlna, *intrans.*	burn, be consumed; *causals :* jəlana, jəlvana.
jəlsə, *m.*	meeting, assembly.
jəma, *f.*	total of several items; jəma k., collect, add up; jəma h., be collected, added up.
Jəmna, *f.*	the river Jumna.
jənab, *f.*	a great person's presence; usually voc. form of address : Sir !
jəngəl, *m.*	uninhabited or sparsely inhabited place, waste, forest.
jəngli	belonging to the jəngəl, uncouth, unpolished in manner.
jənna, *trans.*	(of woman), give birth to (does not take ne).
jənvəri, *m.f.*	January.
jənub, *m.*	south.
jəṛ, *f.*	root of tree, etc.
jəṭa, *f.*	person's long matted hair.
jəvab, *m.*	answer.
jəvan, *m.*	young man; *adj. :* young (man or woman).
jagna, *intrans.*	wake up, be awake; *causal :* jəgana, jəgvana.
jal, *m.*	net, web.
jan, *f.*	vital principle, life; jan toṛna, try very hard.
jana, *intrans.*	to go; past tense, gəya.
jəṅghia, *f. sing.*	drawers, underclothing.
janyb (ki), *postpos.*	in the direction of.
janna, *trans.*	to know, be of opinion.
janvər, *m.*	animal.
jydhər, *adv.*	whither, where (*rel.*).
jylana, *see* jina.	
jyn, jynhoŋ	oblique plural of jo.
jys	oblique singular of jo.
ji, *m.*	heart, inclination.
jim, *m.*	name of letter of the alphabet.

jina, *intrans.* — live, be alive; ji wṭhna, rise from dead; *trans.* : jylana.

jit, *f.* — victory.

jwda, *adj.* — separate; feminine either jwda or jwdi.

jwlai, *m.f.* — July.

jwlna, *see* mylna.

jwma, *m.* — Friday.

jwmerat, *f.* — Thursday.

jwtna, *intrans.* of jotna.

jun, *m.* — June.

juŋ, *adv.* — as.

juti, *f.* — shoe, pair of shoes.

jeb, *f.* — pocket.

jəysa, *pronom. adj., adj.* — as, like.

jo, *pron., pronom. adj.* — who, which (*rel.*); what (*rel. adj.*); jo koi, whoever; jo kwch, whatever.

jo, *enclitic* — seeing that, since.

joɽa, *m.* — a pair, suit of clothes, pair of shoes.

jotna, *trans.* — yoke (plough, oxen); harness (horses); plough (land); *see* jwtna.

jəwnsa, *pronom. adj.* — whichever.

jhəgeɽna, *intrans.* — quarrel; *causals:* jhəgɽana, jhəgəɽvana.

jhəlna, *trans., see* pənkha.

jhəɽna, *intrans.* — fall (leaves, fruit); fall out (hair).

jhəṭ, *adv.* — at once, immediately.

jhaɽən, *m.* — duster cloth.

jhaɽi, *f.* — bush.

jhaɽu, *f.* — broom for sweeping.

jhyɽki, *f.* — reproach, finding fault; jhyɽki dena, to tell off.

jhil, *f.* — lake, large pond.

jhwkna, *intrans.* — bend, bow; *causals:* jhwkana, jhwkvana.

jhwləsna — generally either jhwləs jana, *intrans.*, be scorched; or jhwləs dena, *trans.*, scorch.

jhumna, *intrans.* — swing; jhumna jhamna, *intrans.*, swing from side to side (e.g. elephant's trunk).

kəb — when? kəbhi, sometimes; kəbhi nəhiŋ, never; kəbhi nə kəbhi, some time or other.

kəbutər, *m.* — pigeon.

kəcca — raw, uncooked, undercooked, unripe, imperfectly made, vacillating, etc. (opposite of pəkka).

kəhaŋ — where?

kəhiŋ, *adv.* — somewhere; kəhiŋ nəhiŋ, nowhere; kəhiŋ nə kəhiŋ, somewhere or other. In comparison, kəhiŋ means " much ", as: kəhiŋ behtər, much better.

kəhlana, *intrans.* — be called.

kəhlvana, *see* kəhna.

kəhna, *trans.* — tell, say; *causals :* kəhlana, kəhlvana.

kəi, *pron. adj.*, also colloquially *pron.* — a good many (always plural).

kəl — to-morrow, yesterday.

kəm, *adj., adv.* — little, too little, less (refers to amount, not size); kəm se kəm, kəm əz kəm, at any rate, at least.

kəminə, *adj.* — mean, base.

kəmra, *m.* — room.

kəmtərin — in signing letters = your servant, yours obediently.

kəpas, *f.* — cotton wool.

kəpṛa, *m.* — cloth, a garment; kəpṛe, *m.pl.*: clothes in general.

kərna, *trans.* — do; much used in composition with nouns or adjectives: jəldi kərna, hasten; maf kərna, forgive; *causals:* kərana, kərvana.

kəroɽ, kəɽoɽ, *m.* — ten million.

kəsna, *trans.* — tighten, assay (of metal); kəsa kəsaya, ready tightened; *causals:* kəsana, kəsvana.

kətərna, *trans.* — snip, cut out, gnaw (of rat, mouse, etc.); *causals:* kətrana, kətərvana.

ka, *postpos., adj.* — of.

kabək, *f.* — pigeon house, dove-cote.

kafi, *adj.* — sufficient.

kafi, *f.* — coffee.

kaɣəz, *m.* — paper.

kahe — oblique of kya.

kala, *adj.* — black; kala syah, very black; kala bhəṭṭ, exceedingly black.

kam, *m.* — work.

kamyab — successful; -i.

kampna, *intrans.* — tremble, shiver.

kan, *m.* — ear.

kaŋṭa, *m.* — thorn, fork (for table).

kapi, *f.* — notebook.

karḍ, *m.* — postcard.

kaʃ, kaʃ ky — would that.

katna, *trans.* — spin; *intrans.:* kətna, be spun; *causals:* kətana, kətvana.

kaṭna, *trans.* — cut; *intrans.:* kəṭna, be cut; *causals:* kəṭana, kəṭvana; kaṭ ḍalna, cut down.

kyn, kynhoŋ — oblique plural of kəwn.

kynarə, *m.* — edge, border.

kyrayə, *m.* — rent, fare.

kyrkəṭ, *m.* — cricket (the game).

kyrpa, *f.* — mercy, pity.

kys — oblique singular of kəwn.

kysi — oblique singular of koi.

kysan, *m.* — farmer.

kyʃti, *f.* — boat.

kytab, *f.* — book.

kytna, *pron. adj.* — how much? or how many?

kia — past tense of kərna.

kicəɽ, *f.* — mud.

kijie, kijiega — ceremonious imperative of kərna = do.

kimia, *f.* — chemistry.

kwch, *pron., pron. adj.* — something, anything; kwch nəhiŋ, nothing; kwch nə kwch, something or other; kwch with plural noun: a few.

kwl, *adj.* — the whole of, all; *adv.:* all in, all included.

kwlhaɽi, *f.* — axe.

kwrsi, *f.* — chair.

kwtta, *m.* — dog; *fem.:* kwtya.

kuaŋ, kuŋaŋ, *m.* — well of water.

kucə, *m.* — lane in town or village.

kud, *f.* — a leap.

kudna, *intrans.* — leap; *causal:* kwdana.

kəysa, *pron. adj.* — of what kind? kəyse, *adv.:* how?

kəy, *pron. adj. (indecl.)* — how many?

ko, *postpos.* — to, for, with respect to, etc.

koi, *pron., pron. adj.* — someone, anyone; koi nəhiŋ, no one; koi nə koi, someone or other; koi sa, any you like; koi, *adv.*, approximately.

kona, *m.* — corner.

kos, *m.* — distance of about one-and-a-half miles.

koʃyʃ, *f.* — effort.

koʈ, *m.* — coat.

koʈhi, *f.* — cottage, etc.

K

koṭhṛi, *f.* small room.

kəwn, *pron.* who? *pron. adj. :* what?

kəwnsa, *pron. adj.* which?

kəwṛi, *f.* little shell.

kya, *pron.* what? with adjective " how ", as : kya xub, how fine.

kyoŋ why?

kyoŋkər how?

kyoŋky because.

khəra pure, sound, genuine.

khəṛa standing.

khana, *trans.* eat; with nouns often means suffer : ɣəm khana = be grieved; ʃərm khana = be ashamed; mar khana = be beaten; juti khana = be beaten with a shoe; cwɣli khana = slander (with ki); *causal :* khylana, give food to be eaten; also to nurse children, bəce khylana; khylvana, cause food to be given.

khaŋsi, *f.* cough.

khylna, *intrans.* bud, blossom; *causal :* khylana.

khylana, *see* khana, khelna, khylna.

khyŋcna, khycna, khycvana, *see* kheŋcna.

khyṛki, *f.* window.

khwlna, khwlana, khwlvana, *see* kholna.

khelna play; *causal :* khylana.

khena, *trans.* row a boat; past, only *feminine* khei; *causal :* khyvana.

kheŋcna, *trans.* pull, also khəyŋcna, khiŋcna — less common; *intrans. :* khyŋcna, be pulled; *causals :* khicvana, khycvana. *See* pənkha.

khet, *m.* field.

khodna, *trans.* dig; *causal :* khwdvana.

kholna, *trans.* — open; *intrans.*: khwlna; *causals*: khwlana, khwlvana.

khəwlna, *intrans.* — boil, come to boil; *causal*: khəwlana.

xəbər, *f.* — news; xəbər k., *trans.*, inform.

xəbərdar — cautious, careful; -i.

xəccər, *f.* — mule.

xəfa, *adj.* — angry; *feminine* the same.

xərab — bad, evil; -i.

xərc, *m.* — expenditure; xərc k., *trans.*, spend.

xərcna, *trans.* — spend.

xəridna, *trans.* — buy; *causal*: xərydvana.

xət, *m.* — epistle, letter.

xətm k., *trans.* — finish; *intrans.*: xətm h.

xətrə, *m.* — danger.

xətt, *m.* — geometrical line, line of latitude or longitude.

xah, *conj.* — whether; xah . . . xah, whether . . . or.

xahyʃ, *f.* — desire, wish.

xalə, *f.* — mother's sister; xalu, husband of xala.

xan — Muhammadan title, often applied to Pathans.

xansamaŋ, *m.* — cook, steward.

xasə — pretty, very fair.

xatyr (ki), *postpos.* — for the sake of.

xun, *m.* — blood, murder.

xydmət, *f.* — service.

xydmətgar, *m.* — servant, generally table servant; -i.

xwd, *pron.* — self, selves; used with subject, not with object.

Xwda, *m.* — God.

xwrak, *f.* — food, dose of medicine.

xwʃ	happy, pleased; -i.
xwʃbu, *f.*	sweet smell, aroma.
ləndna, *intrans.*	be loaded; *trans.* : ladna, load; *causals* : lədana, lədvana.
ləfz, *m.* (pronounced ləfs)	word.
ləgna, *intrans.*	be attached, stick; hence begin; many other meanings, *see* Grammar, p. 70; *causals* : ləgana, ləgvana. *See* Grammar, p. 110, and Sentences, Lesson 16.
ləkir, *f.*	line.
ləkɽi, *f.*	wood, piece of wood.
ləlcana, *intrans.*	long for; *trans.* : excite desire in.
ləmba, *adj.*	long; -*i*.
ləmbərdar, *m.*	head man of village; -*i*.
lənc, *m.*	lunch = ʈyppən.
Ləndən, *m.*	London.
Lənka, *f.*	Ceylon.
ləngɽana, *intrans.*	walk lame; ləngɽa, lame.
ləɽka, *m.*	boy.
ləɽki, *f.*	girl.
ləɽna, *intrans.*	fight; of mosquito, bite; *causal* : ləɽana.
Lahəwr, *m.*	Lahore.
layq	worthy, able, capable; ke layq, *postpos.* : fit for, suitable to.
lal, *adj.*	red.
lalʈəyn, *f.*	lantern.
lana, *trans.*	bring (does not take ne).
lapərva, *adj.*	not caring, free from care, indifferent; -*i*.
laʈhi, *f.*	big stick.
lazym, *adj.*	used of duty, i.e. right, proper. *See* Grammar, p. 95, and Sentences, Lessons 12–14.
lyaqət, *f.*	ability, worthiness.

lykhna, *trans.* write; *causals*: lykhana, lykh-vana.

lypəṭna, *intrans.* cling to, se; *causals*: lypṭana, lypəṭvana.

lie (ke), *postpos.* for the sake of, on account of, for; = ke vaste.

lwṛhəkna, *intrans.* roll round and round; *causals*: lwṛhkana, lwṛhəkvana.

luṭna, *trans.* rob; *intrans.*: lwṭna, be robbed; *causals*: lwṭana, distribute alms (with pəyse, etc.); lwṭvana, cause to be robbed.

leana = lana (does not take ne).

lejana, *trans.* take away (does not take ne).

lekyn, *conj.* but.

lena, *trans.* take; also in composition, *see* Grammar, p. 64; *causal*: lyvana, *see* Grammar, p. 66.

leṭna, *intrans.* lie down; *causals*: lyṭana, lyṭvana.

log, *m.pl.* people.

lomṛi, *f.* fox; no masculine.

ləwṭna, *intrans.* return; *trans.*: ləwṭana, give something back, cause to go back.

məcchli, *f.* fish.

məcna, *intrans.* used with noun meaning noise or disturbance; ʃor məca = there was a noise, there arose a noise; *causals*: məcana, make a noise, etc., məcvana.

mədəd, *f.* help.

mədədgar, *m.f.* helper; -i.

məgər, *conj.* but.

məɣryb, *m.* west.

məhəkna, *intrans.* be perfumed, give forth scent.

məhəllə, *m.* section of town.

məhina, *m.*	month.
məhəl, *m.*	palace.
məhŋga, *adj.*	dear in price, expensive.
məy, *m.f.*	May.
məjal, *f.*	power.
məkəi, *f.*	Indian corn, maize.
məkan, *m.*	house, building.
məkkhən, *m.*	butter.
məlamət, *f.*	reproach, rebuke; *see* Grammar, p. 81.
məlkə, *f.*	queen.
məllah, *m.*	sailor.
məlna, *trans.*	rub.
mən, *m.*	maund (about 78 pounds).
məna k.	forbid.
məndyr, *m.*	Hindu temple.
məngəl, *m.*	Tuesday.
mənzur, *adj.*	agreed to, accepted; mənzur k., accept; agree to; -i.
mərəz, mərz, *m.*	disease.
mərd, *m.*	man (not woman; *vir*, not *homo*).
mərna	die; *causal:* marna, beat, kill.
mərtəbə, *f.*	a time, as : pəhli mərtəba, first time; *masculine :* rank, dignity.
mərz, *see* mərəz.	
mərzi, *f.*	wish, desire.
məsaləh, *m.*	ingredients of mortar, pudding, etc.
məsjyd, *f.*	mosque.
məʃin, *f.*	machine.
məʃryq, *m.*	east.
mətba, *m.*	printing press.
məvəyʃi, *f.*	cattle.
məzbəh, *m.*	altar, place of sacrifice.
məzdur, *m.*	workman, labourer (generally unskilled); -i.

ma, Arabic *postpos.* along with.

ma, maŋ, *f.* mother.

madə, *f.* female; *plural:* madaeŋ.

maf, *see* under mwaf.

mafi, *see* under mwafi.

mafyq (ke), *postpos.* according to, similar to (occasionally pronounced mwafyq).

mal, *m.* property.

mala, *f.* necklace, garland.

maldar, *adj.* rich, possessing property; -i.

malum, *adj.* known; malum hojana, become known; malum hona, appear, seem, be known.

malyk, *m.f.* owner, master, mistress.

malyʃ, *f.* rubbing; malyʃ k., rub; *see* Grammar, p. 80.

mali, *m.* gardener; *feminine:* malən.

mamlə, *m.* affair, etc. (occasionally pronounced mwamlə).

mandə weary.

mane, *m.pl.* meaning, signification.

maŋgna, *trans.* ask for; *causal:* məngana, send for (thing).

manna, *trans.* obey, pay attention to, acknowledge as great; *causal:* mənana; xwʃi mənana = make merry.

manynd (ki), *postpos.* like.

mar, *f.* a beating; *see* khana.

mare (ke), *postpos.* through, on account of (generally of mental states, as: ḍər ke mare = through fear).

marna *causal:* beat, kill; jhuṭ marna, tell lies; juti marna, beat with slipper; mar ḍalna, kill; *intrans.:* mərna, die.

mazi, *m.f.* past tense.

mylənsar, *adj.* friendly, sociable; -i.

mylna, *intrans.* — accrue, meet, be like; *see* Grammar, p. 109; *trans.:* mylana = compare, introduce, mix; *see* Grammar, p. 110, and Sentences, Lesson 22. mylna jwlna, generally in past participles: myla jwla, all mixed together.

mynət, *m.* — a minute.

mynnət, *f.* — entreaty; ki mynnət k., entreat.

myskin — poor; submissive; -i.

mysl (ki), *postpos.* — like.

mysri, *f.* — sugar.

mys-sahəb, mys-sahybə, *f.* — unmarried lady (usually European); plural, generally my-seŋ (omitting sahəb, etc.).

mystri, *m.* — skilled workman.

myṭna, *intrans.* — be blotted out; *causals:* myṭana, myṭvana.

myṭṭi, *f.* — earth, dust, mud.

mim, *m.* — letter of the alphabet.

minar, *m.* — minaret.

mwaf k., *trans.* — forgive (occasionally pronounced məaf or maf).

mwafi, *f.* — forgiveness (occasionally pronounced məafi or mafi).

mwafyq, *see* mafyq.

mwhafyzət, *f.* — protection.

mwhasyrə, *m.* — siege.

mwjh — oblique of məyŋ, I.

mwjra, *m.* — payment on account.

mwlaqat, *f.* — meeting with someone.

mwlazym, *m.* — servant.

mwlk, *m.* — a country.

mwmkyn, *adj.* — possible.

mwnasyb, *adj.* — suitable, proper; *see* Grammar, p. 95, and Sentences, Lessons 12–14.

mwnia, *f.* — amadavat (little bird).

mwŋh, *m.* — face, mouth.

mwqabylə, *m.* — comparison, opposition.

mwrəbba, *m.* — a square.

mwsəlla, *m.* — a prayer-mat.

mwsafyr, *m.f.* — traveller; -i.

mwʃkyl, *f.* — difficulty; *adj.:* difficult.

mwtəəddi, *m.* — transitive or causal of verb.

mwtəəllyq — connected with, related to.

mwtabyq (ke), *postpos.* — according to, conformable to.

mwtaleə, *m.* — reading, study.

mwxalyfət, *f.* — opposition, hostility.

mwamylə, *see* mamlə.

mutna, *intrans.* — make water (takes ne).

mehnət, *f.* — labour, toil (not simply work).

mehnəti, *adj.* — hard-working.

mehrban, *adj.* — kind; -i.

mehtər, *m.* — scavenger; also as Mohammadan title of certain great persons.

memsahəb, memsahybə — married lady (usually European); plural generally memeŋ (omitting sahəb, etc.).

meŋdha, *m.* — ram.

meŋ, *postpos.* — in, into, etc.

mevə, *m.* — fruit.

mez, *f.* — table.

məydan, *m.* — a plain.

məyl, *f.* — dirt.

məyla, *adj.* — dirty.

məyna, *f.* — mynah (kind of starling).

məyŋ, *pronoun* — I.

moci, *m.* — shoemaker.

mohr, *f.* — seal.

mol, *m.* — price; mol lena, *trans.*, buy.

moti, *m.* — pearl.

motər, *m.f.* — motorcar

məwjud, *adj.* — present (said of anyone, high or low); *see* hazyr.

məwlvi, *m.* — learned Mohammadan, especially one learned in religious matters.

məwqa, *m.* — opportunity, place where something happens.

məwza, *m.* — small town, large village.

məwzuŋ, *adj.* — suitable, fitting.

nədi, *f.* — river, stream.

nəfa, *m.* — profit.

nəhana, *intrans.* — bathe; *causals:* nəhlana, nəhlvana.

nəhiŋ — no, not; nəhiŋ to = otherwise.

nəmək, *m.* — salt.

nəmaz, *f.* — prayer, especially recited prayer; nəmaz pəɽhna = recite prayer.

nənga, *adj.* — naked, bare.

nənnha — small (child).

nəqʃə, *m.* — map.

nərsoŋ (rare word) — four days ago, four days from now.

nəsihət, *f.* — advice; *see* Grammar, p. 81; nəsihət ki = gave him advice.

nəʃa, *m.* — intoxication, intoxicant.

nətijə, *m.* — result.

nəvasə, *m.* — daughter's son; nəvasi, *f.*, daughter's daughter.

nəya, *adj.* — new.

nəzər, *f.* — sight; nəzər ana, be visible.

nəzdik (ke), *postpos.* — near; -i.

nəzm, *f.* — poem.

nacna, *intrans.* — dance; *causals:* nəcana, nəcvana.

nala, *m.* — stream.

naməwzuŋ — unsuitable, improper; *see* məwzuŋ.

nana, *m.* — mother's father; nani, mother's mother.

nao, *f.*	boat.
naraz	displeased; -i.
naʃpati, naspati, *f.*	pear.
naxwn, *m.*	nail on finger or toe.
nycoɽna, *trans.*	squeeze out (lemon, etc.); *causal:* nycwɽvana.
nygəlna, *trans.*	swallow; *causal:* nygəlvana.
nygəhban, *m.f.*	protector; -i.
nygrani, *f.*	taking care of, protection.
nyhayət, *adv.*	very, extremely.
nykah, *m.*	marriage; nykah pəɽhna = perform the marriage ceremony.
nykəlna, *intrans.*	go out, come out, turn out; *causals:* nykalna = eject, bring out; nykəlvana: cause to be ejected.
nymbu, *see* nibu.	
nysbət (ki), *postpos.*	concerning, than.
nysf	half.
nyʃan, *m.*	sign, mark, trace.
nyvaɽ, *m.*	broad tape of which beds are woven.
nibu, *m.*	lemon.
nice (ke), *postpos.*	under; *adv.:* below.
niz, *adv.*	also.
nwqsan, *m.*	loss, injury.
nek, *adj.*	good (of persons); -i.
neola, *m.*	mongoose.
nəwkər, *m.*	servant; *feminine:* nəwkərni, nəwkərani.
pəlna, *intrans.*	be reared, be brought, be kept as pet; *causal:* palna.
Pənjab, *m.*	the Panjab.
Pənjabi, *f.*	the Panjabi language; *adj.:* belonging to the Panjab.
pənkha, *m.*	pənkha kheŋcna, pull punkha; pənkha jhəlna, to use a fan.
pər, *conj.*	but.

pər, *m.* — wing, feather.

pəryndə, *m.* — bird.

pəre, *adv.* — to a distance, to the far side.

pəreʃan — anxious, distressed; -i.

pərla, *adj.* — the further (one).

pərsal, *adv.*, etc. — last year.

pərsoŋ — day after to-morrow, day before yesterday.

pərtal, *f.* — audit; pərtal k., to audit.

pərvəryʃ, *f.* — looking after, supporting; ki pərvəryʃ k., to support, etc.

pərva, *f.* — caring about something; ki pərva k., to care about or for.

pəʈha lykha, — literate; *feminine:* pəʈhi lykhi.

pəʈhna, *trans.* — read, recite, study; *causals:* pəʈhana, pəʈhvana.

pəsənd k., *trans.* — choose, like; pəsənd h., be approved.

pəta, *m.* — trace, address.

pətta, *m.* — leaf.

pətthər, *m.* — stone.

pətlun, *f.* — trousers, especially of European style; used in singular.

pana, *trans.* — (i) obtain, find; (ii) [compounded with inflected gerund] manage to (in this case does not take ne); *see* Grammar, pp. 70–1, and Sentences, Lesson 17.

pani, *m.* — water.

pao, *m.* — a quarter.

paoŋ, *m.* — foot.

par, *adv.* — on or to the far side; ke par, *postpos.*, on or to the far side of.

pas, *adv.* — near; ke pas, *postpos.*, near.

pyas, *f.* — thirst; pyas ləgna (ko), become thirsty.

pychla, *adv.* — last, former.

pyghəlna, *intrans.* — melt; *causal:* pyghlana.

pylana, *see* pina.

pynjra, *m.*	cage.
pynsəl, *f.*	pencil.
pyṭna, *intrans.*	be beaten; *causals:* piṭna, pyṭvana.
piche, *adv.*	behind; afterwards (rare); ke piche, *postpos.*, behind, after.
pina, *trans.*	drink; *causals:* pylana, pylvana.
pwkarna, *trans.*	call aloud to.
pwl, *m.*	bridge.
pwlis, *f.*	the police.
pwrva, *f.*	the east wind.
pwṛia, *f.*	paper in which medicinal powder is wrapped, or the powder itself.
puchna, *trans.*	ask (a question); *causal:* pwchvana.
puja, *f.*	worship (especially Hindu); ki puja k., to worship (something).
purəb, *m.*	the east.
peʃgi, *f.*	advance of money.
peṭ, *m.*	stomach.
peṭi, *f.*	(i) wooden box; (ii) belt.
polis, *see* pwlis.	
poŋchna, *trans.*	wipe; *causals:* poŋchana, poŋchvana.
pəwda, *m.*	plant.
pəwn, pəwna, pəwne	three-quarters; *see* Grammar under Numerals.
phəl, *m.*	fruit.
phəl, *m.*	blade of knife, ploughshare, etc.
phəŋsna, *intrans.*	be entangled, be ensnared; *causal:* phəsana.
phəṭna, *intrans.*	split, tear; *causal:* phaṭna, *q.v.*
phaṛna, *trans.*	split, tear; *see* phəṭna.
phəylna, *intrans.*	spread; *causal:* phəylana.

phaṭək, *m.*	gate.
phyrna, *intrans.*	turn, walk about; *causals:* pherna, *q.v.*, phyrana, phyrvana.
physəlna, *intrans.*	slip, slide; *causal:* physlana.
phyṭkar, *f.*	abuse, reproof.
phul, *m.*	flower.
pheŋkna, *trans.*	throw.
pherna, *trans.*	turn; *see* phyrna.
qəbilə, *m.*	tribe.
qəbl (ke), *postpos.*	before (of time).
qəbul k., *trans.*	accept; qəbul h., be accepted.
qədəm, *m.*	footstep, pace.
qələm, *m.*	pen.
qəmiz, *f.*	shirt.
qənd, *f.*	sugar.
qərar pana, *intrans.*	be decided.
qəsbə, *m.*	small town.
qyblə, *m.*	the place in Mecca (Makka) to which Muslims turn in prayer.
qybləgah, *m.*	ceremonious word for " father ".
qysm, *f.*	kind or sort (of thing).
qysmət, *f.*	fate.
qimət, *f.*	price.
qwdrət, *f.*	glory, power (generally of God).
qwfl, *m.*	lock (for key).
qwli, *m.*	coolie.
qwsur, *m.*	fault.
qəyd, *f.*	imprisonment; qəyd k., imprison.
qəydi, *m.*	prisoner.
qəwm, *f.*	race of people; people belonging to one race or religion.
rəddi	worthless.
rəftə, *adv.*	gone; rəftə rəftə, by and by, gradually.

rəfu, *m.* — darning; rəfu k., to darn.

rəgəɽna, *trans.* — rub hard; *causal:* rəgɽana.

rəhm, *m.* — pity, mercy.

rəhna, *intrans.* — remain, dwell; rəh jana, be left behind.

rəhnwma, *m.f.* — leader, guide; -i.

rəkhna, *trans.* — place, keep; rəkh dena, put down on table, etc.; rəkh lena, keep for oneself; *causal:* rəkhvana.

rəpəṭ, *f.* — report.

rəqəm, *f.* — amount of money.

rəssa, *m.* — rope.

rəstə, rastə, *m.* — road.

rəvanə hona, *intrans.* — set out; rəvanə k., despatch.

rəis, *m.* — rich man, man of rank.

rəiszadə, *m.* — [*lit.:* son of rəis] well-to-do person; *feminine:* rəiszadi.

rəiət, *f.* — tenant, subject; *plural:* ryaya.

raja, *m.* — rajah.

rani, *f.* — queen.

rat, *f.* — night; rat ko, by night, at night.

razi, *adj.* — pleased, content, satisfied; *see* naraz.

ryayət, *f.* — favour.

ryʃtə, *m.* — relationship, connection.

ryʃtedar, *m.f.* — relation, relative.

ryʃvət, *f.* — bribe.

rich, *m.* — bear; *feminine:* richni.

rwkn, *m.* — pillar (chiefly metaphorical).

rwxsət, *f.* — leave of absence, permission to go away.

rwlana, rwlvana: *see* rona.

rwpəya, rwpia, *m.* — rupee; *plural:* rwpəe, rwpəoŋ; rwpia or rwpia pəysa also means money in general.

rwmal, *m.* — handkerchief.

rwpia, *see* rwpəya.

rubəru (ke), *postpos.* — face to face with.

rel, *f.*	railway train or carriage.
reŋgna, *intrans.*	creep, crawl.
rona, *intrans.*	weep, mourn for; *causals:* rwlana, rwlvana.
roṭi, *f.*	bread.
roz, *m.*	day; *see* dyn.
səb, *adj., pron.*	all.
səbəb, *m.*	cause, reason.
səbəq, *m.*	lesson.
səbha, *f.*	assembly, company.
səbr, *m.*	patience.
səbz, *adj.*	green.
səbzi, *f.*	vegetables.
səcca, *adj.*	true, genuine (opposite of jhuṭha); *see* əsli.
səfed, *adj.*	white.
səfedi, *f.*	whitewash.
səhər, *f.*	morning.
səhara, *m.*	help, support.
səheli, *f.*	girl's female friend.
səhi, *adv.*	granted, I admit, that's all very well; *see* Grammar, p. 122, and Sentences, Lesson 29.
səhn, *m.*	courtyard.
səjna, *intrans.*	be adorned; *causals:* səjana, səjvana; səja səjaya = be all ready adorned.
səkna, *intrans.*	be able; *see* Grammar, p. 68, and Sentences, Lesson 15.
səxt, *adj.*	severe, hard (both of material things and of character); *adverb:* very (only of unpleasant things); -i.
səməjh, *f.*	understanding.
səməjhna, *trans.* and *intrans.*	understand; *causals:* səmjhana, explain, and hence to comfort, calm; səməjhvana.
səməndər, *m.*	sea.

səmbhəlna, *intrans.* — pull oneself together, be supported; *causal:* səmbhalna, support, take care of, look after.

səmet (ke), *postpos.* — along with.

sənduq, *m.* — box.

səqqa, *m.* — water-carrier.

səra, sərae, *f.* — inn, travellers' resthouse.

sərd, *adj.* — cold.

sərkar, *f.* — the government of a state or country; also: Your honour (masculine if addressed to a man, feminine if to a woman).

səɽək, *f.* — well-made road.

səɽna, *intrans.* — become rotten, rot; *causal:* səɽana.

səsta, *adj.* — cheap.

səva — quarter more than; *see* numerals.

səval, *m.* — question.

səvar, *adj.* — riding (on horse, bicycle, in carriage, train).

səvari, *f.* — (i) the act of riding; (ii) person travelling in vehicle.

səvere, *adv.* — early.

səza, *f.* — punishment.

sa — used as affix or enclitic: (i) like; (ii) as it were; (iii) often used without meaning; *see* Grammar, pp. 34–6, and Sentences, Lesson 29.

sabyt, *adj.* — proved (to be true); sabyt k., prove; sabyt h., be proved.

sadə, *adj.* — simple (generally of human beings).

sadhu, *m.* — Hindu holy man who has renounced the world.

saf, *adj.* — clean; saf swthra = clean and tidy.

safə, *m.* turban.

sahəb, *m.* man in good position, a European; as suffix may refer to a lady, *see* mem and mys; *see also* sahybə; bəɽe sahəb = head of department or large district; the boss.

sahəbzadə, *m.* [*lit.*: son of sahəb] ceremonious word for son; *feminine*: sahəbzadi = daughter.

sahybə Arabic *feminine* of sahyb, used as suffix; both sahybə and sahyb are nearly always sahəb (*q.v.*) in Urdu; *see* mem, mys.

sais, *m.* groom.

sal, *m.* year.

salən, *m.* curry, curried dish, also gravy.

saman, *m.* apparatus, necessaries.

samne (ke), *postpos., adv.* in front (of); amne samne, in front, facing each other.

samp, *m.* snake.

sara, *adj.* all, the whole of.

saɽhe half more than; *see* numerals.

sath (ke), *postpos.* along with.

sathi, *m.* companion.

sayə, *m.* shadow, shade.

syah, *adj.* black; *see* kala.

syahi, *f.* blackness; ink of any colour.

Syalkoţ, *m.* Sialkot.

syfaryʃ, *f.* recommendation, intercession.

sylna, sylana, sylvana, syla, sylaya: *see* sina.

sypahi, *m.* policeman, Indian soldier.

sypwrd (ke), *postpos.* in the care of.

syr, *m.* head.

syra, *m.* head or end of piece of wood, bar, bed, street, etc.

syrf, *adv.* only.

syva (ke), syvae (ke), *postpos.* apart from, except.

sikhna, *trans.* — learn (to do something); *causal :* sykhana, teach, put someone up to something.

sina, *trans.* — sew; *intrans. :* sylna, be sewn; *causals :* sylana, sylvana; syla sylaya = ready sewn.

sinə, *m.* — breast, chest.

swal, *see* səval.

swbəh, *f.* — morning.

swlana, swlvana, *see* sona.

swlgana, *trans.* — kindle, light; *intrans. :* swləgna.

swluk, *m.* — treatment (good or bad), kind treatment.

swnna, *trans.* — hear, listen to; *causals :* swnana = relate; swnvana; swni swnai bat = hearsay.

swst — lazy; -i.

swthra, *adj.* — clean; *see* saf.

sukhna, *intrans.* — become dry; *causal :* swkhana.

surət, *f.* — appearance, form.

se, *postpos.* — than, with, from.

seb, *m.* — apple.

sena, *trans.* — hatch (eggs); *past :* sea, see; *feminine :* sei, seiŋ; *causal :* syvana.

ser, *adj.* — satisfied, having had enough; -i.

səhih, *adj.* — correct.

səykṛa, *m.* — hundred; *see* numerals.

səyr, *f.* — a walk, drive, ride, any journey however short or long which is for pleasure and not business.

so, *adv.* — so, therefore, it follows.

socna, *trans.* — think; no *causal.*

sona, *m.* — gold.

sona, *intrans.* — sleep; *causals :* swlana, swlvana.

skul, *m.* — school.

ʃəfa, ʃyfa, *f.* — cure (used of God, not of the doctor).

ʃəhr, *m.* — city, town.

ʃəhzadə, *m.* — prince; *feminine :* ʃəhzadi, princess; occasionally ʃahzadə, ʃahzadi, are found.

ʃək, ʃəkk, *m.* — doubt.

ʃəkər, *m.* — sugar.

ʃəkl, *f.* — form, appearance, shape.

ʃəxs, *m.* — person.

ʃərab, *f.* — wine, spirits.

ʃərarət, *f.* — wickedness, naughtiness; *see* ʃərir.

ʃərbət, *m.* — sweet, cool drink.

ʃərir, *adj.* — (of boy, girl, animal) mischievous, naughty; (of grown-up person) wicked; *see* ʃərarət.

ʃərm, *f.* — shame, shyness.

ʃərmana, *intrans.* — be ashamed, feel shy.

ʃərt, *f.* — bet; condition (in conditional sentence).

ʃagyrd, *m.* — pupil.

ʃayr, *m.* — poet.

ʃam, *f.* — evening.

ʃama, *f.* — magpie, robin.

ʃayəd, *adv.* — perhaps.

ʃyfa, *f., see* ʃəfa.

ʃykəm, *m.* — belly.

ʃykar, *m.* — prey, hunting; ʃykar k., hunt.

ʃykari, *m.* — hunter.

ʃykayət, *f.* — complaint.

ʃymal, *m.* — north.

ʃiʃə, *m.* — glass.

ʃwүl, *m.* — occupation.

ʃwru, *m.* — beginning; ʃwru k., begin.

ʃer, *m.* — tiger; *feminine :* ʃerni.

ʃer, *m.* — verse.

ʃolə, *m.* — flame.

ʃəwhər, m.	husband.
ʃəwq, m.	desire, liking for something.
təb, adv.	then, hence; used of time when correlation of jəb.
təhqir, f.	contempt, despising, insult; see Grammar, p. 81.
təhsil, f.	acquiring; headquarters of small district, or the district itself.
tək, postpos.	(i) up to; (ii) adverb: even.
təklif, f.	trouble; təklif k., take trouble; təklif dena, give trouble.
tələb, f.	desire, require.
tələb k., trans.	summon.
tələʃ, f.	search; see Grammar, p. 81.
təlvar, f.	sword.
təmənna, f.	desire, hope.
təmam, adj.	all, the whole of.
təmaʃa, m.	a " show ", performance, entertainment.
təmaʃagah, m.	place where təmaʃa takes place.
təmbu, m.	tent.
tənxah, f.	salary, pay.
tərəf, f.	side, direction; ki tərəf, postpos.: towards.
tərəh, f.	manner; as, əcchi tərəh = well.
tərəqqi, f.	progress, increase.
tərəsna, trans.	long for (does not take ne); causal: tərsana.
tərbiət, f.	bringing up, rearing, educating.
tərjwmə, m.	translation; ka tərjwmə k., translate.
tərs, m.	pity, compassion, mercy; tərs khana (pər) = have pity on.
tərtib, f.	arrangement; see Grammar, p. 82.
təɽəpna, intrans.	be agitated, palpitate; causal: təɽpana.

təsvir, *f.*   picture.

təvəjjwh, *f.*   attention to something.

təvəqqw, *f.*   hope, expectation.

təvazw, *m.*   courtesy.

təəjjwb, *m.*   astonishment.

ta, Persian *postpos.*   up to.

tadib, *f.*   rebuke, punishment; *see* Grammar, p. 81.

tahəm   nevertheless.

taky   in order that.

takid, *f.*   insistence, urging; *see* Grammar, p. 81.

tala, *m.*   lock.

talab, *m.*   tank, pond.

talim, *f.*   teaching; *see* Grammar, p. 80.

tamir, *f.*   the act of building; tamir k., to build; *see* Grammar, p. 80.

taqət, *f.*   power.

tara, *m.*   star.

tarif, *f.*   praise, definition; *see* Grammar, p. 80.

taɽna, *trans.*   see, take in; no *causal.*

taviz, *m.*   amulet.

tazə, *adj.*   fresh.

tazim, *f.*   honour, respect, reverence.

tygna, *adj.*   three times as much.

tyhai, *f.*   a third part of anything.

tynka, *m.*   a little bit of straw or grass.

tisra,   third; *see* numerals.

twjh, *pron.*   oblique of tu.

twm   you.

twmhara   your.

twɽana, twɽvana; *see* toɽna.

tufan, *m.*   storm.

tel, *m.*   oil.

tera   thine

tez, *adj.*   swift, sharp (of knife, etc.), pungent in taste.

təyrna, *intrans.*   swim; *causal :* təyrana.

to, təw
: participle of reasoning : then, in that case.

toɽna, *trans.*
: break; *intrans.*: tuʈna; *causals*. twɽana, twɽvana; *see* jan.

təw
: sometimes used for to, *q.v.*

təwbə, *f.*
: repentance; təwbə k., repent.

təwbhi
: nevertheless.

thəkna, *intrans.*
: get tired; *causal :* thəkana.

thəmna, *intrans.*
: stop (of wind, rain, etc.); *causal :* thamna.

thərthərana, *intrans.*
: tremble, shiver.

thukna, *intrans.*
: spit (takes ne with past participle tenses); *trans. :* despise.

thoɽa
: little in amount or time, etc.

ʈəhəlna, *intrans.*
: walk about; *causal :* ʈəhlana.

ʈang, *f.*
: leg.

ʈypən, *m.*
: lunch (from English tiffin).

ʈuʈna, *intrans.*
: break; *see* toɽna.

ʈopi, *f.*
: cap, skull cap; also hat either small or big.

ʈhəhərna, ʈhəyrna, *intrans.*
: stop, pause, be adjudged to be; *causals :* ʈhəhrana, ʈhəyrana.

ʈhənɖa, *adj.*
: cold.

ʈhik, *adj.*
: (of things) correct, accurate; ʈhik ʈhak, in right order, correctly arranged.

ʈheka, *m.*
: contract.

ʈhekedar, *m.*
: contractor; -i.

ʈhəyrna, *see* ʈhəhərna.

ʈhokər, *f.*
: kick; ʈhokər khana = to stumble; ʈhokər marna = to kick.

vəɣəyrə, *adv.*
: and so forth, *et cetera.*

vəhaŋ
: there; emphatic : vəhiŋ.

vəqt, *m.*
: time; ws vəqt = at that time.

vərnə, *adv.*
: otherwise = nəhiŋ to.

vərzyʃ, *f.*
: physical exercise, drill.

vəsile (ke), *postpos.*	by means of, through.
vəzən, *m.*	weight.
vəza, *f.*	manner, state, condition, stylishness.
vəzir, *m.*	minister of state; *feminine:* vəzirni (wife of vəzir).
vadə, *m.*	promise; vadə k., to promise.
vajyb, *adj.*	suitable, right, proper; *see* Grammar, p. 95, and Sentences, Lessons 12–14.
valyd, *m.*	father; valdə, *f.*, mother.
vaqe hona, *intrans.*	happen, occur.
vaqia, *m.*	occurrence.
vaste (ke)	for, for the sake of.
vəysa, *pron.*	of such a kind.
voh, *pron., pron. adj.*	he, she, it, that.
yəhaŋ, *adv.*	here; emphatic : yəhiŋ
yuŋ, *adv.*	thus; yuŋhi, just like this, for no reason at all.
yeh, *pron., pron. adj.*	this, he, she, it.
zəbərdəst, *adj.*	firm, strong, autocratic, tyrannical; -i.
zəban, *f.*	tongue (in mouth), language.
zəbani (ki), *postpos.*	at the mouth of, by the mouth of.
zəccə, *f.*	woman with a newly-born baby.
zəhr, *m.*	poison.
zəhrila, *adj.*	poisonous.
zəkat, *f.*	religious alms.
zəxm, *m.*	wound.
zəxmi, *adj.*	wounded.
zəmin, *f.*	earth, land (not country), ground.
zəmindar, *m.*	landowner; -i.
zənjir, *f.*	chain.
zəra, *adv.*	just (as in " just think "); zəra, zəra sa, *adj.*, insignificant, trifling.

zərie (ke), *postpos.*	by means of.
zərxez, *adj.*	fertile; -i.
zərur, *adv.*	certainly, necessarily; *see* Grammar, p. 95, and Sentences, Lessons 12–14.
zərurət, *f.*	necessity.
zəruri, *adj.*	necessary.
zal, *f.*	letter of the alphabet.
zalym, *adj.*	tyrannical, cruel.
zyadə, *adj., adv.*	more.
zydd, *f.*	obstinacy.
zyddi, *adj.*	obstinate.
zyla, *m.*	administrative district.
zymmedar, *adj.*	responsible; -i.
zymmə, *m.*	charge, responsibility; ke zymme men = in charge of.
zyndə, *adj.*	alive.
zwkam, *m.*	a cold.
zwlm, *m.*	tyranny, oppression.
zevər, *m.*	jewel, ornament.

ENGLISH–URDU GLOSSARY

Further information about some words given here may be found in the Urdu–English Glossary. It should be consulted when there is any uncertainty.

a, an	omit or use ek = one, or koi = some, a certain.
ability	lyaqət, *f.*
able	layq.
about, *see* concerning, approximately.	
abuse, *n.*	gali, *f.*, phyʈkar, *f.*
accept	qəbul k.
accompany	sath cəlna, sath holena.
according to	bəmujyb, mwafyq, mwtabyq.
account of, on	bays, bədəwlət, mare.
account (financial)	hysab, *m.*
accrue	mylna; *see* obtain.
acknowledge	yqrar k.
acre	bygha, *m.*
across	par.
action	hərkət, *f.*
add	jəma k.
address, *n.*	pəta, *m.*
adorn	səjna, səjana; all ready adorned = səja səjaya.
advance, *intrans.*	bəɽhna, or use 'age'.
advance, *n.* (money)	peʃgi, *f.*
advantage, profit	nəfa, *m.*
advertisement	yʃtyhar, *m.*
advice	səlah, *f.*
affair	mwamylə, *m.*
afraid, *see* fear.	
after	piche, bad.

again	phyr, dobarə.
against	bərxylaf.
agitated, be	tərəpna; agitate, tərpana.
agree, to	manna, mənzur k.
air	həva, *f.*
alas !	hae hae !
alert	hoʃyar; alertness, hoʃyari.
alive	zyndə, jita.
all	səb, sara, kwl, təmam, pura.
allow	dena, yjazət dena.
alms	zəkat, *f.*
also	bhi, niz, əwr.
altar of sacrifice	məzbəh, *m.*
although	əgərcy, go, go ky.
altogether	bylkwl.
always	həmeʃə.
am	huŋ.
amadavat	mwnia, *f.*
amazed, *see* bewildered.	
among	meŋ, bic, apəs meŋ.
amulet	taviz, *m.*
ancestors	bapdada, *m.pl.*; bwzwrg.
and	əwr; *see* also.
angel	fyryʃtə, *m.*
anger	ɣwssə, *m.*; *see* displeasure.
angry	ɣwsse, xəfa; *see* displeased.
animal	janvər, *m.*; wild animal = dəryndə.
anna	anə, *m.*
announce	yttyla or yʃtyhar dena.
announcement	yttyla, *f.*, yʃtyhar.
annoy	cheṛna; *see* trouble, irritate.
answer	jəvab, *m.*; to answer = jəvab dena.
ant	cyuŋṭi, *f.*
any	koi, kwch; jo koi.
appearance	surət, *f.*
approved	pəsənd, mənzur; approve, pəsənd k., mənzur k.

approximately	təqribən; koi (*indecl.*) with numeral or quantity.
April	əprəyl, *m.*
argue	bəhəs k.
argument	bəhəs, *f.*
arm	bazu, *m.*; in one's arms or lap = god meŋ.
arrangement	bəndobəst, *m.* (w.k.); tərtib, *f.* (with dena).
arrive	pəwhŋcna.
as	jɔysa, juŋ; as if, goya.
ascend	cəṛhna.
ashamed, be	ʃərmana, ʃərm kərna, nadym hona.
ask (question)	puchna; ask for = maŋgna.
ass	gədha, *m.*; feminine: gədhi.
assay	kəsna (gold, etc.).
assembly	səbha, *f.*
astonished, *see* bewildered.	
attach	ləgana; *intrans.*: ləgna.
attend, *see* attention.	
attendance	hazyri, *f.*
attention	təvəjjwh, *f.*, dhyan, *m.*; kan ləgakər swnna.
audit	pərtal, *f.* (with k.).
August	əgəst, *m.*
aunt	xalə, *i.e.* mother's sister; phwppi, *i.e.* father's sister.
awake, *adj.*	jagta hua; *see* wake.
axe	kwlhaṛi, *f.*
bad	bwra, xərab; of coin, khoṭa.
ball (to play with)	geŋd, *f.*
base, *adj.*	kəminə.
bathe, *intrans.*	nəhana; *trans.*: nəhlvana.
be	hona.
bear (animal)	bhalu, rich.
bear (child)	jənna; *see* lift, carry.

beat	marna, piṭna; be beaten = mar khana, pyṭna.
because	kyoŋky, ys lie ky; because of— *see* account.
become, be	hona, ho jana.
bed	pələng, *m.*
bedding	bystra, *m.*
before	pəhyle, qəbl.
beg	*see* petition.
begin	ſwru k., ləgna.
beginning	ſwru, *m.*, ybtyda, *f.*
behind	piche.
below	nice.
besides	əlavə, syva, bəyəyr.
besiege	mwhasyrə k. (ka).
bet, *n.*	ſərt, *f.*
better, *see* good.	
between	dərmyan, bic, bic meŋ.
bewildered	həyran, pəreſan.
beyond	par, pəre.
big	bəṛa.
bind	bandhna (bəndhna, etc.).
bird	cyṛia, pəryndə.
black	kala, syah.
blackness	syahi (= ink).
blind, *adj.*	əndha.
blood	xun, ləhu.
blot out	myṭana (myṭna, etc.).
blow, *n.*	coṭ, *f.*
boat	kyſti, *f.*, nao, *f.*
bodice	əngia, *f.*
body	bədən, *m.*
boil, *v.*	khəwlna, etc.
bolt, *n.*	cəṭxəni.
book	kytab, *f.*
bookcase	əlmari, *f.*
boot	juti, *f.*, buṭ, *m.*
border	kynarə, *m.*
both	donoŋ.

bottle	botəl, *f.*
bow, *v.*	jhwkna, etc.
box	bəkəs, *m.*, sənduq, *m.*
boy	ləɽka, *m.*
Brahman	brəhmən, *m.*
brave	dyler, bəhadwr.
bravery	dyleri, *f.*, bəhadwri.
bread	roti, *f.*
break	toɽna, ṭuṭna, etc.
breakfast	hazyri, *f.*, naʃtə.
breast	chati, *f.*
bribe, *n.*	ryʃvət, *f.*
brick	inṭ, *f.*
bridge	pwl, *m.*
bring	lana, leana.
broad	cəwɽa.
broom	jhaɽu, *f.*
brother	bhai.
buffalo	bhəyŋs, *f.*
building (the act of)	tamir, *f.*; a building : ymarət; *see* house; məkan, *m.*
bull	bəyl, *m.*
bullet	goli, *f.*
burn	jəlna, jəlana, etc.
bush	jhaɽi, *f.*
but	lekyn, məgər, pər, bəlky.
butter	məkkhən, *m.*, ghi, *m.*
buy	mol lena, xəridna
buyer	gahək.
by	se; a book *by* someone = əz.
cage	pynjra, *m.*
calamity	bəla, *f.*
call, *trans.*	bwlana, pwkarna; be called or named = kəhlana.
camel	unṭ, *m.*; *feminine* : unṭni.
cane	bed; to cane = bed marna.
cap	ṭopi, *f.*
capacity	ystedad, *f.*

car, *see* motor.

care (taking care) ehtyat, *f.*; xəbərdari; in the care of = hevale, sypwrd, zymme; take care, xəbərdar.

careless lapərva.

carelessness lapərvai, *f. or* lapərvahi, *f.*

caretaker cəwkidar, *m.*

carpenter bəɽhəi, *m.*

carriage gəɽi, *f.*, bəggi, *f.*

carry wɽhake lejana, ḍhona.

cat bylla, *m.*; *feminine:* bylli.

cattle məvəyʃi, *f.*

cause bays, *m.*, səbəb, *m.*, vəjəh, *f.*

certain, a certain fwlanə.

certainly beʃək, zərur, əlbəttə; in negative clause, hərgyz.

Ceylon Lənka, *f.*

chain, *n.* zənjir, *f.*; to chain, jəkəɽna.

chair kwrsi, *f.*, cəwki, *f.*

change, *v.* bədəlna.

" chapatty " cəpati, *f.*

charge, in charge of, *see* care.

cheap səsta.

chemistry kimia, *f.*

child bəccə, baba; children, bəcce, balbəcce.

childhood bəcpən, *m.*

choose pəsənd k.

civility ədəbqaidə, *m.*

claim dava, *m.*

clean, *adj.* saf; to clean, saf swthra k.

clerk (Indian) babu.

climb cəɽhna.

cling lypəɽna.

clock ghəɽi, *f.*; *see* o'clock.

cloth kəpɽa, m.; clothes = kəpɽe.

cloud badəl, *m.*, ghəɽa, *f.*

coat koɽ, *m.*

cobbler moci, *m.*

cold, *adj.*   ṭhənḍa; *noun :* ṭhənḍ, *f.*, sərdi, *f.*; a cold, zwkam, *m.*

collect   jəma k.

come   ana, pəwhŋcna; come out, nykəlna; come down, wtərna.

comfort, *n.*   dylasə, *m.*; to comfort, dylasə dena.

command   hwkm, *m.*, yrʃad, *m.*; to command, hwkm dena, yrʃad k.

companion   sathi, *m.*; girl's female companion, səheli, *f.*

comparison   mwqabylə, *m.*, nysbət, *f.*

complaint   ʃykayət, *f.*

complete   təmam, pura.

composition (literary)   ynʃa, *f.*

compound (enclosed ground)   yhatə, *m.*

concerning   babət, mwtəəllyq, nysbət.

condition   hal; (stipulation), ʃərt.

confess   yqrar k.

confused, be   ghəbrana, ghəbra jana; confuse, ghəbra dena

confusion   ghəbrahət.

connected, *see* concerning.

conquer   jitna, hərana.

contempt   hyqarət, *f.*; təhqir.

contract   ṭheka, *m.*, ṭhekedari, *f.*

contractor   ṭhekedar, *m.*

contrary   bərəks; on the contrary, bəlky.

cook, *n.*   xansamaŋ, *m.*; *verb :* pəkana; *intrans. :* pəkna; cooked, pəkka; ready cooked, pəka pəkaya.

cooly   qwli, *m.*

coquetry   əda, *f.*

corn   gehuŋ, m.; Indian corn, məkəi, *f.*

corner   kona, *m.*

correct   səhih, ṭhik, dwrwst.

correction — yslah.

cost, *see* price, rate.

costly — məhŋga, qiməti.

cotton, growing — kəpas, *f.*

cough — khaŋsi, *f.*

country, a — mwlk.

course, of, *see* certainly.

courtesy — ədəb, *m.*

courtyard — səhn, *m.*

cover, *v.* — dhaŋkna.

cow — gae, *f.*

cowry — kəwṛi, *f.*

crawl, creep — reŋgna.

cricket, the game — kyrkəṭ, *m.*

cry — rona, rwlana, etc.; cry out, cyllana.

cupboard, for clothes, crockery, linen, books — əlmari, *f.*

curds — dəhi, *m.*

cure, *n.*, treatment by doctor — ylaj, *m.*; cure by God = ʃəfa, *f.*

curse (mild abuse) — phyṭkar, *f.*

custom, habit of country, etc. — dəstur, *m.*; personal habit = adət, *f.*

cut — kaṭna; cut down, kaṭ ḍalna; snip, kətərna.

dacoit — ḍaku, *m.*

dance, *v.* — nacna.

danger — xətrə, *m.*

dark, darkness — əndhera, *m.* (also adjective).

daughter — beṭi, *f.*; daughter-in-law, bəhu, *f.*

day — dyn, *m.*, roz, *m.*; dyn dəhaṛe, in broad daylight; *see* aj, kəl, pərsoŋ.

deaf — bəhra.

dear (beloved) — pyara; costly, məhŋga.

deceit — dəya, *f.*, dhokha, *m.*

L

December	dysəmbər, *m.*
decide	fəysələ k.; be decided, qərar pana.
decision	fəysələ, *m.*
deed, *see* action.	
deep	gəhra.
deer	hyrən, *m.*
defeat, *n.*	har, *m.*; *verb: see* conquer.
deficient	kəm.
definition	tarif, *f.*
degrees, by	rəftə rəftə.
delay	der, *f.*
Delhi	Dylli, Dəhli, *f.*
deny	ynkar k. (ka); denial = ynkar, *m.*; *see* refuse.
descend	wtərna.
desire	ʃəwq, *m.*, xahyʃ, *f.*, mərzi, *f.*, təmənna, *f.*; *verb:* cahna; ask for, maŋgna.
desolation, *see* destroy, destruction.	
despise	hyqarət k., hyqarət ki nəzr se dekhna, təhqir k. (ki); *see* contempt.
destroy	bərbad k., wjaɽna; be destroyed, bərbad hona, wjəɽna.
destruction	bərbadi, *f.*
die	mərna, fəwt hona.
difference	fərq, *m.*
different	əwr.
difficult	mwʃkyl.
difficulty	mwʃkyl, *f.*
dig	khodna.
digest	həzm k., həzm hona.
digestion	hazmə.
direction, *see* tərəf, ydhər, wdhər, kydhər, jydhər, and words north, south, east, and west; in all directions = caroŋ tərəf.	
dirty	gənda, məyla.
disappear	ɣayb hona.

disciple	mwrid, *m*.
disease	mərz, mərəz, *m*.; bimari, *f*.
disgrace, dishonour	beyzzəti, *f*.; disgraced, dishonoured, beyzzət.
displease	naraz k.; displeased, naraz.
displeasure	narazi, *f*.
distance	faslə, *m*.
distant	dur.
distressed	pərefan, dyqq, həyran.
distribute	bantna; *intrans.:* bətna.
district	zyla, *m*.
divide (= distribute)	təqsim k.; do hysse k., divide into two parts.
doctor	həkim, *m*., ḍakṭər.
dog	kwtta, *m*.; *feminine:* kwtya.
doll	gwṛia, *f*.
donkey	gədha, *m*.; *feminine:* gədhi.
dose, *n*.	xwrak, *f*., dəva, *f*.
double	dwgna, do cənd.
doubt	ʃək, *m*.
dove	faxtə, *f*.
drag	ghəsitna; *see* pull.
draw, *see* pull.	
drawers (for wearing)	jaŋghia, *f*.
drawing-room	gol kəmra, *m*., bəṛa kəmra.
drink	pina; *see* pylana.
dry, *adj*.	sukha; *verb:* swkhana.
duster	jhaṛən, *m*.
duty	fərz, *m*.; lazym, mwnasyb, cahie.
dwell	bəsna, rəhna.
eagle	uqab, *m*.
ear	kan, *m*.
early	səvere.
ease	aram, *m*., asani, *f*.
east	purəb, *m*., məʃryq, *m*.; east wind = pwrva, *f*.
easy	asan.

eat	khana, khylana; *see* gobble.
edge	kynarə, *m.*
educate	tərbiət k. (ki); *see* teach, instruct.
effort	koʃyʃ, *f.*
eject	nykalna.
elephant	hathi, *m.*
emerge	nykəlna.
employee	mwlazym, nəwkər; *see* servant.
empty	xali.
end, *n.*	yntyha, *f.*, syra, *m.*; *verb:* xətm k.
enemy, *see* oppose.	
Englishman	əngrez, *m.*
enough	kafi, bəs.
entangled, be	phəŋsna.
enter	dakhyl hona, ghwsna; əndər ana.
entertainment	təmaʃa, *m.*; place of entertainment, təmaʃagah, *m.*
equal	bərabər.
erase	myʈana.
error, *see* fault.	
escape (from something impending)	bəcna; (from a trouble one is already in) chuʈna.
etcetera	vəɣəyrə.
even	bhi, tək (as in: not even a farthing; level, bərabər).
evening	ʃam, *f.* (about sunset).
every	hər.
evil, *adj.* (person)	bwra, xərab, bədmaʃ, bədxo; *noun:* bwrai, xərabi, bədmaʃi, bədxoi (all feminine).
exalt	bəʈai k.; *see* praise, honour; exalted = ala.
examination	ymtyhan.
examine (in school, etc.)	ymtyhan lena (ka); be examined, ymtyhan dena; look at, dekhna.
except	bəɣəyr, syva, əlavə.

exchange | bədəlna; in exchange, ke bədle, ke evaz.
excited, be | ghəbrana, təṛəpna.
exercise, bodily | vərzyʃ, *f.*
expenditure, expense | khərc; *see* price, rate.
expensive | qiməti, məhŋga.
extinguish | bwjhana; be extinguished, bwjhna.
eye | aŋkh, *f.*

face | mwŋh, *m.*, cehrə, *m.*; face to face, rubəru.
factory | karxanə, *m.*
fairly, good | xasə.
fall | gyrna, jhəṛna, pəṛna.
false | jhuṭa, jhuṭha, khoṭa.
family | xandan, *m.*
far | dur.
fare, *n.* (railway, etc.) | kyrayə, *m.*
farmer | kysan, zəmindar.
farther | age, əwr age, zyadə dur; *see* further.
fashion, *n.* | vəza, *f.*; *see* custom.
fasten, *see* tie. |
fate | qysmət, *f.*; *see* fortune.
father | bap, valyd.
fault | bhul, *f.*, qwsur, *m.*, ɣəlti, *f.*, xəta, *f.*
fear, *n.* | ḍər, khəwf; *verb:* ḍərna, ḍər ana, xəwf k.
February | fərvəri, *m.f.*
feed | khylana; *see* graze.
female | madə, *f.*
fertile | zərxez.
fever | bwxar, *m.*
few | thoṛe; *see* some.
field | khet, *m.*
fight, *v.* | ləṛna, jhəgəṛna; *noun:* ləṛai, *f.*, jhəgṛa, *m.*

fill	bhərna (both *trans.* and *intrans.*).
filthy	gənda.
final	axyri; finally = axyr.
finger	wngli, *f.*
finish	xətm, k.; -cwkna.
firm, overbearing	səxt, zəbərdəst.
firmness, overbearing attitude	səxti, *f.*, zəbərdəsti, *f.*
fire, *n.*	ag, *f.*
first	pəhyla, əvvəl, *m.*
fish	məcchli, *f.*
fitting	mwnasyb; *see* duty.
flame, *n.*	ʃolə, *m.*
flare up (flame)	bhərəkna.
flat	cəwṭa.
flock	gəllə, *m.*
floor	fərʃ, *m.*
flour	aṭa.
flow	bəhna.
flower	phul, *m.*
fly, *n.*	wṛna.
food	khana, *m.*, xwrak, *f.*, yyza, *f.*
fool, foolish	bevəquf, pagəl (*lit.* mad).
foolishness	bevəqufi, *f.*
foot	paoŋ, *m.*; on foot, pəydəl.
for, *prep.*	ko, ke lie, ke vaste; *conjunction :* kyoŋky.
forbid	məna k.
forefathers	bapdada, bwzwrg, əjdad.
foreign	yəyr, bydeʃi.
foresight	dwrəndeʃi, *f.*
forget	bhulna; the *noun* is bhul, *f.*
forgive	mwaf k., bəxʃna, dərgwzər k.
forgiveness	mwafi, *f.*
fork, *n.* (table)	kaŋṭa, *m.*
form	surət, *f.*
formerly	pəhyle.
fortune	nəsib, *m.*, qysmat, *f.*; *see* unfortunate.

forward	age.
fourfold, four times as big, etc.	cəwgwna.
fox	lomṛi, *f.*; no masculine.
free, get	chuṭna; set free, chwṛana, choṛna.
fresh	tazə.
Friday	jwma, *m.*
friend	dost, *m.f.*
friendly	my9lənsar.
friendship	dosti, *f.*
from	se, əz.
front	age, samne; rubəru.
frown	cin e jybin (jybiŋ), cin bər jybiŋ (*Pers.*); ghurna.
fruit	mevə, *m.*, phəl, *m.*
full	bhəra hua; -bhər.
furniture	əsbab, *m.*
further, furthermore, etc.	baqi, niz; *see* farther.
gallop	cəwkṛi bhərna.
game	bazi, *f.*, khel.
Ganges	gənga, *f.*
gardener	mali.
gate	phaṭək, *m.*
gear, apparatus	saman, *m.*
generally	əksər, am təwr pər.
gentleman	sahəb, jənab.
genuine	əsli, xalys.
gift	ynam.
girl	ləṛki, *f.*
give	dena, bəxʃna.
glass	ʃiʃə, *m.*
glory	jəlal, *m.*
go	jana, cəl dena, cəla jana, nykəl jana.
goat	bəkra; *feminine :* bəkri.
goatherd	bəkrivala.
gobble	həṛəp k., kha jana, cəṭkər jana; *see* swallow, eat.

God	Xwda, *m.*; god, deota, *m.*; goddess, devi, *f.*
gold	sona, *m.*
gong	ghənṭa, *m.*
good	əccha, bhəla, nek, behtər, xasə; good fellow, bhəlamanəs; *feminine :* bhəlimanəs.
goodness	neki, *f.*, bhəlai, *f.*
government	sərkar, *f.*
gradually	rəftə rəftə.
grain	danə, *m.*
grandfather	father's father, dada; mother's father, nana.
grandmother	father's mother, dadi; mother's mother, nani.
grandson	daughter's son, nəvasə.
grand-daughter	daughter's daughter, nəvasi.
grass	ghas, *f.*
graze, *intrans.*	cərna; *trans. :* cərana.
great	bəṛa; greatness, bəṛai, *f.*
green	səbz.
grief	yəm, *m.*
grieved, be	yəm khana.
groom	sais, *m.*
grumble	bwṛbwṛana.
guide	rəhnwma; guidance, rəhnwmai, *f.*
gun	bənduq, *f.*
habit	adət, *f.*, xo, *f.*; *see* custom.
hail, *n.*	ola, *m.*
hair	bal, *m.*; matted, jəṭa, *f.*
half	adha, adh, nysf.
hand	hath, *m.*
handkerchief	rumal, *m.*
happen	vaqe hona.
happy	xwʃ, bay bay.
harbour	bəndərgah, *m.*
hat	ṭopi, *f.*; *see* cap.

he	yeh, voh.
head, *n.*	syr, *m.*
heap	dher, *m.*
hear	swnna; hearsay, swni swnai bat.
heart	dyl, *m.*, ji, *m.*
heat	gərmi, *f.*
heavy	bhari.
heel	eɽi, *f.*
help, *n.*	mədəd, *f.*, ymdad, *f.*; *verb :* mədəd k. (ki), mədəd dena (ko).
helper	mədədgar.
here	yəhaŋ, ydhər.
hesitate	ətəkna.
hiccup	hycki, *f.* (ləgna).
hide, *v. intrans.*	chwpna; *trans. :* chwpana.
high	uŋca, bwlənd, ala.
hill	pəhaɽ, *m.*
Hindu	hyndu.
hole (for animal)	byl, *m.*
honour	yzzət, *f.*, tazim, *f.*; your honour, jənab, hwzur, sərkar.
honourable	bwzwrg, etc., yzzətvala.
hope	wmed, *f.*, təvəqqw, *f.*
horn	siŋg, *m.*
horse	ghoɽa; *feminine :* ghoɽi (mare).
hospital	həspətal.
hostile, *see* oppose.	
hot	gərm.
hour	ghənṭa, *m.*
house	ghər, koṭhi, məkan, bəngla, *m.*; həveli, *f.*; at my house, mere haŋ, etc.
how	kys tərəh, kyoŋkər.
humble	ajyz.
humility	ajyzi, *f.*
hunger	bhuk, *f.*; (die) of hunger, bhukoŋ mərna.
hungry	bhuka.

hunter (person)	ʃykari, *m.*
husband	ʃəwhər, *m.*
I	məyŋ.
ill	bimar.
illness	bimari, *f.*, mərz; mərəz, *m.*
immediately	jhəṭ, fəwrən, fylfəwr.
imprison	qəyd k.
in	meŋ; *see* between, middle; inside, bhitər; into, meŋ.
income	amdəni, *f.*
increase, *v. intrans.*	bəṛhna, tərəqqi k.; *trans.:* bəṛhana; *noun:* tərəqqi, bəṛhti, *f.*
India	Hyndostan, *m.*
indifference	lapərvahi, *f.*
indifferent	lapərva; lapərvah.
inferior	kəmtər, kəmdərjə.
inform	khəbər dena, bətana, kəhna, swnana, yttyla dena.
ingredients	məsaləh, *m.*
inhabitant	baʃyndə, *m.;* in the mass, abadi, *f.*
inhabited	abad.
injury	nwqsan, *m.*, coṭ, *f.*
ink	syahi, *f.*
inn	sərae, səra, *f.*
inquire	dəryaft k.
insert	ḍalna.
inside	bhitər, əndər, bic meŋ, meŋ.
instruct	hydayət dena; *see* educate, teach.
instrument, *see* tool, musical.	
intelligence	əql, *f.*, hoʃyari, *f.*, zyhanət.
intelligent	hoʃyar, əqlvala, zəhin.
intercede	syfaryʃ k. (ki).
into	meŋ.
irritate	dyqq k.; *see* annoy, trouble.
it	voh, yeh; often omit.

jackal	gidəɽ, *m.*
January	jənvəri, *m.f.*
jewel	zevar, *m.*
joke	dylləgi, məzaq.
journey	səfər, *m.*, səyr, *f.*
July	jwlai, *m.f.*
jump	kudna.
June	jun, *m.*
jungle	jəngəl, *m.*; *adjective* (wild, etc.), jəngli.
just, *adv.*	zəra.
key	cabi, *f.*
kind, *adj.*	mehrban.
kind, *n.*	qysm, *f.*; what kind of, kəysa; *see also* jəysa, vəysa.
kindle	swlgana, jəlana.
kindness	mehrbani, *f.*, kyrpa, *f.*, dəya, *f.*
ĸing	badʃah, raja. The King of England, etc., is badʃah.
kite (bird)	cil, *f.*
knee	ghwʈna, *m.*
knife	chwri, *f.*
know	janna; *see* knowledge, known.
knowledge	ylm; I do not know anything about it = ys bat ka mwjhe koi ylm nəhiŋ; also, xəbər, *f.*; I do not know = mwjhe xəbər nəhiŋ.
known	malum; I know = mwjhe malum həy.
lady	mem, mys-sahyb, sahybə.
Lahore	lahəwr, *m.*
lake	jhil, *f.*
lamb	bərrə, *m.f.*
lame, *adj.*	ləngɽa; walk lame = ləngɽana.
lamp	bətti, *f.*; cyraɣ, *m.*

land (as property)   zəmin, *f.*

lane (in town, etc.)   gəli, *f.*

language   zəban, *f.*

lantern   laltəyn, *m.*

lap   god, *f.*; *see* arms.

last   axyri; last year = parsal; last (week, month, year), gwzra, pychla.

late   der, *f.* (*lit. :* lateness).

lawful (food, etc.)   həlal.

laziness   swsti, *f.*

lazy   swst.

leaf   pətta, *m.*, pətti, *f.*

leap   chəlaŋg marna, or chəlaŋg ləgana.

least   səb se chota, kəm, etc.; at least, kəm se kəm, kəm əz kəm.

learn   sikhna.

leave, *v. trans.*   chorna; *noun :* chwtti, *f.*; rwxsət, *f.*

left (not right)   bayaŋ; left over = baqi.

leg   taŋg, *f.*

leisure   fwrsət, *f.*

length   ləmbai, *f.*

lessen, *intrans.*   ghətna, kəm hona; *trans. :* ghətana, kəm k.

lesson   səbəq, *m.*

letter (epistle)   cytthi, *f.*, xət, *m.*; of alphabet, hərf, *m.*

lie, *n.*   jhut, *m.*; tell lie, jhut bolna; lie down, letna.

life, vital principle   jan, *f.*

lift, *v.*   wthana.

light, *n.*   rəwʃni, f.; *adjective :* (colour and weight) həlka; *verb :* jəlana, swlgana; *see* kindle.

like, *adj.*   manynd, -sa; *verb : see* desire, choose.

line, *n.* — ləkir, *f.*; of poetry, mysra, *m.*

listen — swnna.

little (size) — choṭa; (amount) thoṛa, zəra, or zəra sa; too little, kəm, thoṛa.

live — jina; *see* alive, dwell.

load, *v.* — ladna; *intrans. :* lədna.

lock, *n.* — tala, *m.*, qwfl, *m.*; *verb :* tala or qwfl ləgana.

lofty — uŋca, bwlənd; *see* high.

London — ləndən, *m.*

long, *adj.* — ləmba, dəraz; so long as = jəb tək.

long for — ləlcana, tərəsna; *see* desire.

look, look at — dekhna, dekhnabhalna; look for, *see* search; look after, səmbhalna.

lose — khona, gəŋvana; be lost, kho jana; *see* defeat.

loss — hərj, *m.*, nwqsan, *m.*

luggage — əsbab, *m.*

lyric — ɣəzəl, *f.*

mad — divanə, pagəl.

maize — məkəi, *f.*

majority — əksəriət.

make, *v.* — bənana; be made, bənna; make, *n.*, bənavət, *f.*; ready-made, bəna bənaya.

man — mərd, admi, ʃəxs.

mango — am, *m.*

manner, *see* kind.

mansion — həveli; *see* house.

many — bəhwt, bəhwtere, kəi; how many? kytne, kəi; so many, ytne, wtne; as many, jytne.

map — nəqʃə, *m.*

mare — ghoṛi, *f.*

mark — nyʃan, *m.*

marriage	byah, *m.*, nykah, *m.*
master	malyk, *m.*
mat	cǝṭai, *f.*; prayer-mat, mwsǝlla, *m.*
May	mǝy, *m.f.*
meaning	mane, *m.pl.*, also mǝtlǝb.
means	zeriǝ, *m.*, vǝsilǝ, *m.*; by means of, ke zǝrie, ke vǝsile se.
meat	goſt, *m.*
medicine	dǝva, dǝvai, *f.*; *see* dose, treat.
meditation	dhyan, *m.*
meet	mylna (with se for interview, and ko for accidental meeting).
meeting, interview	mwlaqat, *f.*; assembly = jǝlsǝ, *m.*, sǝbha, *f.*
melt, *intrans.*	pyghǝlna; *trans. :* pyghlana.
mercy	dǝya, *f.*; kǝrǝm, *m.*
middle	dǝrmian, bic; *see* between.
mile	mil, *m.*, kos, *m.* (kos is approximately a mile and a half).
milk	dudh, *m.*
minaret	minar, *m.*
minute, *n.*	mynǝṭ, *m.*
mistake, *see* fault, forget.	
moderately good	xasǝ.
mongoose	neola, *m.*
monkey	bǝndǝr, *m.*
month, *m.*	mǝhina, *m.*
more	zyadǝ, ǝwr, ǝwr bhi.
morning	fǝjr, *f.*; swbǝh, *f.*
mosque	mǝsjyd, *f.*
most people	ǝksǝr log; ǝksǝr is also an adverb meaning generally.
mother	maṇ, valydǝ.
motion	hǝrkǝt, *f.*; *see* move.
motor	moṭǝr, *f.*
mountain	pǝhaṛ, *m*
mountainous	pǝhaṛi.

mouse	cuhia, *f.*
mouth	mwŋh, *m.*; by word of mouth, mwŋh zəbani; through hearsay from, ws ki zəbani.
move	hylna; *trans.*: hylana; (said of the bowels, have a motion), həgna; move aside, həṭna; *trans.*: həṭana.
much	bəhwt, bəhwtera; how much = kytna; so much = ytna, wtna; as much = jytna.
mud	gara, *m.*, kicəṛ, *f.*, myṭṭi, *f.*
murder	xun, *m.*
musical instrument	baja, *m.*; of various kinds, baje gaje.
my	mera.
nail (hand or toe)	naxwn, *m.*
naked	nənga.
narrative, *see* story.	
nation	qəwm, *f.*
near	nəzdik, pas.
necessary	zəruri.
necessity	zərurət, *f.*; *see* Grammar, p. 95.
necklace	mala, *f.*
need	ehtyaj, *f.*, zərurat, *f.*
nephew	brother's son = bhətija; sister's son = bhəŋja.
net	jal, *m.*
never	kəbhi nəhiŋ; hərgyz with negative.
niece	brother's daughter = bhətiji; sister's daughter = bhəŋji.
night	rat, *f.*; also ʃəb.
no	nəhiŋ.
noon	dopəhr, *f.*
north	wttər, *m.*, ʃymal, *m.*
not	nəhiŋ.
notebook	kapi, *f.*

November	nəvəmbər, *m.*
now	əb, əbhi.
nowadays	yn dynoŋ meŋ, ajkəl.
O, *interj.*	o, ohho; əre (*feminine :* əri).
oath	qəsm, *f.*; take oath = qəsm khana.
obedience	fərmaŋbərdari, *f.*
obedient	fərmaŋbərdar.
obey	hwkm manna, bat manna, fərmaŋbərdari k.
object, *v. trans.*	etyraz k.
objection	etyraz, *m.*
obtain	pana; mylna with ko = accrue to, come to.
occurrence	vaqia, *m.*
o'clock	bəje.
October	əktubər, *m.*
of	ka, ke, ki.
office	dəftər, *m.*
often	bəhwt dəfa, əksər; *see* repeatedly, habit.
oil	tel, *m.*
old	bwḍḍha, buṛha, baba, bwzwrg.
only	syrf, bəs, hi.
open, *v. intrans.*	khwlna; *trans.:* kholna, khwlvana; *adjective:* khwla hua.
openly	dyn dəhaṛe.
opportunity	məwqa, *m.*
oppose	mwxalyfət k.; mwxalyf hona, dwʃməni k.; enemy: dwʃmən, mwxalyf.
opposition	mwxalyfət, *f.*, dwʃməni, *f.*
oppress	dəbana, zəbərdəsti k.
order (arrangement)	bəndobəst, tərtib, *f.*, etc.; *see* command.
order, *v. trans.* (arrange)	bəndobəst k.; tərtib dena; *see* command.
original, *n.*	əsl, *f.*; *adjective:* əsli.

ornament · zewər

other · dusra, əwr; *pron. adj.:* yəyr.

otherwise · nəhiŋ to, vərnə.

ought · cahie, lazym, mwnasyb, vajyb, fərz; *see* duty.

our · həmara.

over, *prep.* · ke upər; *adverb:* upər; *see* upon.

overbearing · zəbərdəst; —ness, zəbərdəsti, *f.*

out, outside, *adv.* · bahər; *postpos.:* ke bahər.

own · əpna; *see* Grammar, p. 33; make one's own, əpnana.

owner · malyk, *m.f.*

ox · bəyl, *m.*

pain · iza, *f.*

pair · joɽa, *m.*

Panjab · Pənjab, *m.*

paper · kayəz, *m.*

part, *n.* · hyssə, *m.*; *verb:* *see* divide, distribute.

pass (time and general use) · gwzərna; *trans.:* gwzarna; (time alone) bytna, bitna; *trans.:* bytana.

past tense · mazi, *f.*

patience · səbr, *m.*

pay, *n.* · tənxah, *f.*

payment on account · mwjra, *m.*

peak · coɽi, *f.*

pear · naʃpati, *f.*

pearl · moti, *m.*

pen · qələm, *m.*

pencil · pynsəl, *f.*

people · log, *m.pl.*; *see* nation.

perfume · xwʃbu, *f.*; məhək, *f.*

perhaps · ʃayəd.

permission · yjazət, *f.*

perplexed · həyran, pəreʃan; *see* agitated, bewildered.

Persian	farsi.
petition	ərzi, *f.*, dərxast, *f.*
pice	pəysa, *m.*
picture	təsvir, *f.*
pierce	chedna; be pierced = chydna; cause to be pierced, chydana, chydvana.
pigeon	kəbutər, *m.*; pigeon-house = kabək, *f.*
pity	*see* mercy; what a pity ! əfsos !
place, *v.*	rəkhna; *noun :* jəgəh, *f.*; in place of = ke bədle, ke evəz, ke bəjae, ki jəgəh.
plain, *n.*	məydan, *m.*
plant, *n.*	pəwda, *m.*
play, *v.*	khelna; *noun :* khel, *m.*, bazi, *f.*
pleased	razi, xwʃ; to please = razi k.; xwʃ k.; *see* happy.
plough, *n.*	həl.
plough, *v.*	jotna; *intrans. :* jwtna; *see* harness, yoke.
plum	alucə, *m.*
pocket	jeb, *f.*
poem	ʃer, *m.*
poison	zəhr, *m.*
poisonous	zəhrila.
police, the	pwlis, *f.*; police post : cəwki, *f.*
polite, *see* civil.	
politeness	ədəb, *m.*
pond	talab, *m.*
poor	myskin, yərib; poor fellow = becarə.
populate	abad k.
population	abadi, *f.*
possible	mwmkyn; or use səkna.
post (letters, etc.)	ḍak, *f.*
postman	hərkarə, *m.*
potato	alu, *m.*

pound (weight)	ser, *m.* (= 2 lbs.).
poverty	ɣwrbət, ɣəribi, *f.*, myskini, *f.*
powder (for medicine, etc.)	pwɽia, *f.*
power	bəs, *m.*; məjal, *f.*; (of God) qwdrət, *f.*
praise	tarif, *f.*, bəɽai, *f.*; *see* honour.
pray	dwa, *f.*, nəmaz, *f.*; prayer-mat, mwsəlla, *m.*
present, *adj.*	hazyr, məwjud.
press (linen)	əlmari, *f.*
press, *v. trans.*	dəbana; *intrans.:* dəbna; *see* print.
price	dam, *m.*, qimət, *f.*, mol, *m.*
prince	ʃahzadə.
princess	ʃahzadi.
print, *v. trans.*	chapna; *intrans.:* chəpna.
printing press	mətba, *m.*
prisoner	qəydi.
probably	ɣalybən.
profit	nəfa, *m.*
progress	tərəqqi, *f.*
promise	vadə, *m.*
proper	*see* duty, ought, suitable.
property	mal, *m.*
protection	hyfazət, *f.*, nygəhbani, *f.*, mwhafyzət, *f.*, pərvəryʃ, *f.*; provide for, nygrani k.
protect	use the above words with k.
prove	sabyt k.
pull, *v. trans.*	kheŋcna (also khincna, khəyncna), ghəsiṭna.
pull oneself together	səmbhəlna.
pungent (in taste or word)	tez.
punish	səza dena.
punishment	səza, *f.*
pupil	ʃagyrd.
purchase, *see* buy.	
purchaser	gahək.

pursue   dərpəy hona (ke), picha k.

put   rəkhna; put in = ḍalna; put on (clothes) = pəhynna, oṛhna.

quarrel, *v.*   jhəgəṛna, ləṛna; *noun :* jhəgṛa, *m.*; ləṛai (latter also battle, war).

quarter   pao, cəwthai, *f.*; *see* numerals.

queen   rani, məlykə.

question   swal, səval, *m.*; ask question, puchna, swal k.

quiet, *adj.*   cwp, cwp cap; to quiet, *v. trans. :* cwp kərana.

race (running)   dəwṛ, *f.*; nation, etc., qəwm, *f.*

rain, *intrans.*   bərəsna, pani pəṛna, baryʃ hona; *noun :* baryʃ, *f.*; the rains = bərsat, *f.*

ram (animal)   meṇḍha, *m.*

rat   cuha, *m.*

rate (price, etc.)   bhao, *m.*

rather, *adv.*   kwch; but rather (*conj.*), bəlky.

raw, not properly cooked   kəcca; *see* unripe.

read   pəṛhna; study, mwtaleə k.

real   əsli, əsl.

reality, in   əsl meṇ.

rear, *v. trans.*   palna, pərvəryʃ k. (ki).

reason   vəjəh, vəjeh, *f.*; səbəb, *m.*, bays, *m.*; for this reason = ys səbəb se, ys vəjəh se; for no reason, anyhow, yuṇhi.

rebuke, *n.*   jhyṛki, *f.*, məlamət, *f.*, təmbih, *f.*, tadib, *f.*; *verb trans. :* ḍaṇṭna; or one of the above words with suitable verb.

receive, *see* accept.

recognise   pəhcanna.

recommend   syfaryʃ k. (ki).

red   lal, swrx.

refuse   ynkar k.; *see* deny.

relate, *v. trans.*   swnana.

relationship   ryʃtedari, ryʃtə, *m.*

relative, *n.*, relation, *n.*   ryʃtedar.

remain, *intrans.*   rəhna

remaining (left over)   baqi.

remuneration   wjrət, *f.*; *see* pay.

rent   kyrayə, *m.*

repeatedly   ghəɽi ghəɽi; *see* habit, often.

repent   pəchtana, təwbə k.

repentance   təwbə, *f.*

report   rəpəʈ, *f.*

reproach, *see* rebuke.

reproof, reprove; *see* rebuke.

request, *n.*   ərz, *f.*, dərxast, *f.*, yltyja, *f.*; *verb :* these nouns with k.; *see* petition.

resign   ystyfa (*m.*) dena (pronounced ystifa).

respect, *n.*   ədəb, *m.*; *v. trans. :* ədəb k. (ka); *see* honour.

responsible   zymmedar.

responsibility   zymme (ke); zymmedari, *f.*

rest, *n.*   aram, *m.*, qərar, *m.*; *verb :* aram k., qərar pana (find rest); rest, *adj., pron. :* baqi.

restless, *see* agitate.

result   nətijə, *m.*

return   ləwʈna, pələʈna; *trans. :* ləwʈana, pələʈana.

reward   ynam, *m.*

rhinoceros   geŋɖa, *m.*

rich   dəwlətmənd, əmir, maldar.

riches   dəwlət, *f.*

ride   səvar hona.

riding, *n.*   səvari, *f.*

right (not left)   dəhna; (not wrong) ʈhik, dwrwst, səhih; *noun :* həqq. *m.*

ripe — pəkka.

river — dərya, *m.*, nədi, *f.*

road — rəstə, *m.*, rastə, *m.*, səɽək, *f.*; *see* way.

rob — luʈna.

robin — ʃama, *f.*

roll — lwɽhəkna.

room — koʈhri, *f.*, kəmra, *m.*

root — jəɽ, *f.*

rope — rəssa, *m.*

rot, *intrans.* — səɽna.

round, *adj.* — gol; *postpos.:* ke gyrd; all round, caroŋ tərəf, ke cəw-gyrd.

rouse — jəgana, cheʈna.

rub, *v. trans.* — ghysna, rəgəɽna, məlna, malyʃ k.; be rubbed, ghysna, ghys jana, rəgəɽ khana.

run — dəwɽna; run away, bhagna.

rupee — rwpəya, *m.*

sadhu — sadhu, *m.*

sailor — məllah.

sake (for the sake of) — ke lie, ke vaste, ki xatyr.

salary — tənxah, *f.*

salt — nəmək, *m.*

save — bəcana; be saved, bəcna.

say — kəhna.

scavenger — mehtər, *m.*

scent — xwʃbu, *f.*

school — skul, *m.*

sea — səməndər, səmwndər, *m.*

seal — mohr, *f.*; *v. trans.:* mohr ləgana.

scorch — jhwləsna (*trans.* and *intr.*).

scorpion — bycchu, *m.*

search — dʰuŋdʰna, təlaʃ k.

seat, *v. trans.* — byʈhana.

see — dekhna.

seed	bij, *m.*
seize	pəkəɽna.
sell	becna; *causal:* bykvana; be sold, bykna.
send	bhejna.
senses	hoʃ, *m.* (alertness, intelligent).
separate, *adj.*	ələg, jwda; *v. trans.:* ələg k., jwda k.
sepoy	sypahi, *m.*
September	sytəmbər, *m.*
servant	nəwkər, mwlazym; servant of God, Xwda ka bəndə (*feminine:* bəndi, bandi); your servant, bəndə; in signing letter, kəmtərin; table servant, khydmətgar.
service	nəwkəri, *f.*, xydmətgari, *f.*; *see* servant.
severe	səxt, zəbərdəst.
sew	sina; ready sewn = syla sylaya.
shade	sayə, *m.*, chaoŋ, *f.*
shame	ʃərm, *f.*; *see* ashamed.
shape	surət, *f.* (form, appearance).
share, *n.*	hyssə; *see* divide.
sharp (edge or words)	tez.
sharpness	tezi, *f.*
shave	həjamət k.
shawl	cadər, *f.*, dwpəṭṭa, *m.*
sheep	bheṭ, *f.*
sheet	cadər, *f.*
sherbet	ʃərbət, *m.*
shine, *v.*	cəməkna; *noun:* cəmək, *f.*
shirt	qəmiz, *f.*
shoe	juti, *f.*, juta, *m.*, buṭ, *m.*
shoemaker	moci, *m.*
shop	dwkan, *f.*
shopkeeper	dwkandar, bənia.
shout	cyllana, pwkarna.
show	dykhana.

shut — bənd; *v. trans.*: bənd k.; be shut, bənd hona.

shy — ʃərmila, *m.*, ʃərmili, *f.*

sick — bimar.

sickness — bimari, *f.*

side — tərəf, *f.*; on all sides, caroŋ tərəf.

sign — nyʃan, *m.*

silver — cəŋdi, *f.*

simple — sadə.

sing — gana.

sink — ḍubna; of sun, moon, stars, ḍubna; of day, ḍhəlna.

sir ! — ji, sahəb, jənab.

sister — bəhn, *f.*

sit — bəyʈhna (i.e. assume sitting posture).

slander — hətək, *f.*; *verb*: hətək k.

slave — ɣwlam, *m.*

slavery — ɣwlami.

sleep — sona; go to sleep, so jana.

slip — physəlna.

slowly — ahystə.

small — choʈa, nənnha.

snake — samp, *m.*

snip — kətərna.

snow, *m.* — bərf, *f.*; *verb*: bərf pəɽna.

so, *adv.*, thus — *see* thus; *adj. pron.*: vəysa, əysa.

some — baz, kwch, koi, cənd, kəi.

sometimes — kəbhi, kəbhi kəbhi.

somewhere — kəhiŋ.

son — beʈa.

song — git, *m.*

sound, *n.* — avaz, *f.*; *verb*: bəjna; *trans.*: bəjana.

south — dəkən, *m.*, jənub, *m.*

sow — bona.

sparrow — cyɽia, *f.*; *see* bird.

speak	bolna.
spend	xərc k.
spendthrift	fwzulxərc.
spices	məsaləh, *m.*
spit	thukna (takes ne).
spite (in spite of)	bavwjude ky (*conj.*); ke bavwjud, *postpos.*
spirits (intoxicating)	ʃərab, *f.*
split, *intrans.*	phəṭna; *trans.* : phaṛna.
spoil	bygaṛna; *see* destroy; be spoiled = bygəṛna.
spoon	cəmca, *m.*
spring, *see* leap, jump.	
square	mwrəbba, *m.*
squeeze (fruit)	nycoṛna.
squirrel, *f.*	gyləhri.
stain	dhəbba.
standing	khəṛa; to stand, khəṛa hona or hojana.
star	sytarə, *m.*
starling	məyna, *f.*
start, set out	rəvanə hona; *trans.* : rəvanə k.
stead, instead of	ke bəjae; *see* place.
steal	cori k.
step	qədəm, *m.*
steward	xansaman, *m.* (usually used for cook).
stick, *intrans.*	ləgna; *trans.* : ləgana; *noun* : ləkṛi, *f.*, laṭhi, *f.*
stitch, *see* sew.	
stomach	peṭ, *m.*
stone	pətthər, *m.*
stoop	jhwkna.
stop, *intrans.*	əṭəkna, ṭhəhərna, ṭhəyrna; *trans.* : rokna, əṭkana, ṭhəhrana.
storm	andhi, *f.*, tufan, *m.*
story, narrative	dastan, *f.*, bəyan, *m.*
straw	bhusa, *m.*; a straw = tynka, *m.*

stream	nala; *see* river.
strike, *n.*	həɽtal, *f.*
strike, *v. trans.*	marna.
stumble	ʈhokər khana.
stumbling-block	ʈhokər, *f.*
style	vəza, tərəh, *f.* (of dress, etc.).
stylish	tərəhdar, vəzadar.
subject	rəiət, *f.* (tenant, subject of king).
success	kamyabi, *f.*
successful	kamyab.
such, *adj. pron.*	əysa, vəysa; *see* so.
sugar	mysri, *f.*
suitable	məwzuŋ; *see* right, duty.
summit	coʈi, *f.*
summon	tələb k.
Sunday	ytvar, *m.*
sunshine	dhup, *f.*
support, *n.*	səhara, *m.*; *v. trans.*: səmbhalna, səhara dena (ko); *see* rear.
swallow, *v. trans.*	nygəlna.
sweep	jhaɽu dena.
sweeper, *see* scavenger.	
sweet	miʈha.
swift	tez.
swiftness	tezi, *f.*
swim	təyrna.
sword	təlvar, *f.*
table	mez, *f.*
tailor	dərzi, *m.*
take	lena; take in, understand (by seeing), taɽ jana; take off (clothes), wtarna.
tall	uŋca, ləmba.
tank	talab, *m.*
tape (broad, for weaving beds)	nyvaɽ, *m.*

tea	ca, cae, *f.*
teach	sykhana; *see* educate, instruct.
teacher	wstad, *m.*
tear, *trans.*	phaṛna; *intrans.* : phəṭna.
tease	cheṛna; *see* annoy, irritate, trouble.
tell	kəhna, swnana, bətana.
temple	məndyr, *m.*; *see* mosque.
tenant	əsami, *f.m.*; rəiət, *f.*
than	se, ki nysbət, ke mwqabyle meŋ.
thanks to (by means of)	ki bədəwlət.
that, *pron. adj.*	voh; *conj.* : ki; in order that, taky.
the	voh or yeh; often omit.
theft	cori, *f.*
then (of time)	ws vəqt; of reasoning, to, təb, təb to.
there	vəhaŋ, wdhər, ws tərəf.
thief	cor, *m.*
thing (object)	ciz, *f.*; (matter) bat, *f.*, mwamylə, *m.*
think	socna.
third	tisra, *m.*; a third part, tyhai, *f.*
thirst	pyas, *f.*
thirsty	pyasa.
this	yeh.
thorn	kaŋṭa, *m.*
though, *see* although.	
throw	pheŋkna.
Thursday	jwmerat, *f.*
thus	yuŋ, ys tərəh.
tie, *v. trans.*	bandhna, kəsna.
tiffin	ṭypən, *m.*
tighten	kəsna; *see* tie.
tiger	ʃer, *m.*
tigress	ʃerni, *f.*
till, until	təb tək, jəb tək ky, with negative.

time (general)   vəqt, *m.*; as in four times, dəfa, *f.*, mərtəbə, *f.*

tire, *trans.*   thəkana.

tired   thəka hua, thəka mandə; be tired, thəkna, ajyz ana.

to   ko, ki tərəf.

to-morrow   kəl, *m.*; day after to-morrow, pərsoŋ.

tongue   zəban, *f.* (both part of body and language).

tool   əwzar, *m.*

top, *see* summit.

touch   chuna.

town   məwza, *m.*, qəsbə, *m.*

trace, *n.*   pəta, *m.*

train, *n.*   gaṛi, *f.*, rel-gaṛi, *f.*

translation   tərjwmə, *m.*; translate, tərjwmə k.

treat   swluk k.; (medically), ylaj k.

treatment   swluk, *m.*, ylaj, *m.*

treble   tygna; *see* numerals.

tree   dərəxt, *m.*

tremble   kampna, thərthərana.

trip (pleasure trip)   səyr, *f.*; *see* stumble.

trouble   təklif, *f.*; *v. trans.:* təklif dena; take trouble = təklif kərna; *see* annoy, irritate, tease.

trousers   paejamə, *m. sing.*

true   səcca, səcc.

Tuesday   məngəl, *m.*

turban   safə, *m.*

turn, *intrans.*   phyrna, pələṭna, ləwṭna; *trans.:* pherna, phyrana, ləwṭana.

twice   do dəfa, dogwna, dwgna, do mərtəbə, do cənd.

ugly   bədsurət.

ugliness   bədsurəti, *f.*

unadulterated	xalys.
uncle	father's brother, cəca; mother's brother, mamuŋ.
under	ke nice.
understand	səməjhna; *see* intelligence, intelligent.
unfortunate	bədnəsib, bədqysmət.
unlawful	məna, həram (Islam).
unripe	kəcca.
unseen	ɣayb.
unsuitable	naməwzuŋ.
until, *see* till.	
up	upər.
upside down	təle upər.
urge	takid k.
veil	bwrqa, *m.* (from head to foot, *see* shawl).
vengeance	bədla, *m.*
verandah	bəramdə, *m.*
very	bəhwt, bəɽa, nyhayət; (for unpleasant things), səxt.
vessel (cooking)	bərtən, *m.*
victory	fətəh, *f.*, jit, *f.*; *see* conquer.
village	gaoŋ, *m.*
villager	gavar.
visible, be	nəzr ana; dykhna, dikhna.
vizier	vəzir.
voice	avaz, *f.*
vulture	gydh, *m.*
wages	məzduri, *f.*; *see* pay.
wait	ʈhəhərna, ʈhəyrna.
wake, *intrans.*	jagna; *trans.*: jəgana.
walk, take a walk	səyr k.; on foot, pəydəl.
wanted	cahie; *see* wish, desire.
warm	gərm.
wash	dhona.

washerman	dhobi.
waste (worthless)	rəddi; *v. trans.*: squander, gəŋvana, wɽana; lay waste, wjaɽna; be laid waste, wjəɽna; *see* destroy.
wasteful	fwzulxərc.
wastefulness	fwzulxərci, *f.*
water	pani, *m.*
watercarrier	bhyʃti, *m.*
wave, *v.* (as elephant's trunk)	jhumna.
wealth	dəwlət.
wealthy, *see* rich.	
wear (clothes)	pəhynna; *see* put on.
Wednesday	bwddh, *m.*
weep	rona.
well, *n.*	kuaŋ, *m.*
well, *adv.*	bəxubi; əcchi tərəh se; *interj.*: xəyr!
wheat	gehuŋ, *m., gen. plur.*
where	kəhaŋ? kydhər? *relative*: jəhaŋ, jydhər; wherever, jəhaŋ kəhiŋ.
whether	ky, cahe, caho . . . caho, xah . . . xah.
which, *inter.*	kəwnsa; whichever, jəwnsa, koi sa; *relative*: jo.
white	səfed.
whitewash	səfedi, *f.*
who, *inter.*	kəwn? *relative*: jo; whoever, jo koi.
whole	təmam; -bhər; *see* all.
why?	kyoŋ, kahe ko; *see* reason; that's why = jəbhi.
wicked	bədmaʃ, ʃərir; *see* bad, evil.
wickedness	bədmaʃi, *f.*, ʃərarət, *f.*
wide	cəwɽa.
width	cəwɽai, *f.*
wife	bivi.

wind	həva, *f.*
window	khyʈki, *f.*
wine	ʃərab, *f.*
wing	pər, *m.*
wipe, *v. trans.*	poɳchna.
wise	dana; *see* intelligent.
wisdom,	danai, *f.*; *see* intelligence.
wish, *n.*	xahyʃ, *f.*, ʃəwq, təmənna, *f.*, mərzi, *f.*; *verb*: cahna.
with	se; ba-; along with, ke sath, səmet, ma.
without, be	bəɣəyr, byna.
wolf	bheʈia, *m.*
woman	əwrət, *f.*
wood (not forest)	ləkʈi, *f.*; *see* jungle.
word	bat, *f.*, hərf, *m.*, ləfz, *m.*
work, *n.*	kam; labour, toil, mehnət, *f.*: *verb*: these nouns with k.; hard-working, mehnəti.
workman	məzdur, mystri.
world	dwnya, *f.*
worry	dyqq k., cheʈna; *see* annoy, trouble, irritate; be worried, ghəbrana.
worship, *n.*	puja, *f.*; *verb*: mənana, puja k. (ki).
worthy	layq.
would that !	kaʃ, kaʃ ky.
wound	zəxm, *m.*, coʈ, *f.*, ghao, *m.*
wounded	zəxmi.
wrestle	kwʃti ləʈna; wrestling, kwʃti, *f.*
wrestler	pəhlvan, *m.*
write	lykhna.
yard	gəz, *m.* (= 3 ft.); courtyard, səhn, *m.*
year	sal, *m.*, bərəs, *m.*
yes	haɳ.
yesterday	kəl, *m.*

yet	əbhi (with negative).
yoke, *v. trans.*	jotna; be yoked, jwtna.
you	ap, twm.
young man	jəvan; also adjective for young man or woman.
your	ap ka, twmhara, tera.